detachment is spiritual space
between me and another person

from

SURVIVAL

to

RECOVERY

Al-Anon books and their ISBN listings:

Al-Anon Faces Alcoholism
0-910034-55-9

Alateen: Hope for Children of Alcoholics
0-910034-20-6

The Dilemma of the Alcoholic Marriage
0-910034-18-4

Al-Anon Family Groups
0-910034-54-0

One Day at a Time in Al-Anon
0-910034-21-4
0-910034-63-X Large Print

Lois Remembers
0-910034-23-0

Al-Anon's Twelve Steps & Twelve Traditions
0-910034-24-9

Forum Favorites Vols. 1,2,3 & 4
0-910034-51-6

Alateen: A Day at a Time
0-910034-53-2

As We Understood . . .
0-910034-56-7

. . . In All Our Affairs: Making Crises Work for You
0-910034-73-7

Courage To Change: One Day at a Time in Al-Anon II
0-910034-79-6
0-910034-84-2 Large Print

from SURVIVAL *to* RECOVERY

GROWING UP IN AN ALCOHOLIC HOME

AL-ANON

FAMILY

GROUPS®

for families & friends of alcoholics

For information and catalog of literature write World Service Office
for Al-Anon and Alateen:

Al-Anon Family Group Headquarters, Inc.
P.O. Box 862 Midtown Station
New York, New York 10018-0862
212-302-7240   Fax 212-869-3757

Library of Congress Catalog Card No. 94-72327
ISBN-0-910034-97-4

Publisher's Cataloging in Publication
From survival to recovery: growing up in an alcoholic home / Al-Anon
Family Groups.
p. cm.
Includes index.
ISBN-0-910034-97-4

1. Children of alcoholics. 2. Adult children of alcoholics. 3.
Alcoholics—Family relationships. 4. Alcoholism—Psychological
aspects. 5. Alcoholics—Rehabilitation—United States. 6.
Alcoholism—Treatment. 7.Al-Anon Family Group Headquarters, inc.
8. Alcoholics Anonymous. I. Al-Anon Family Group Headquarters,
inc.
HV5132.F76 1994   362.2'923
                         QBI94-1324

Approved by
World Service Conference
Al-Anon Family Groups

1-100M-94-12.00   B-21   PRINTED IN U.S.A.

PREAMBLE

The Al-Anon Family Groups are a fellowship of relatives and friends of alcoholics who share their experience, strength, and hope, in order to solve their common problems. We believe alcoholism is a family illness and that changed attitudes can aid recovery.

Al-Anon is not allied with any sect, denomination, political entity, organization, or institution; does not engage in any controversy, neither endorses nor opposes any cause. There are no dues for membership. Al-Anon is self-supporting through its own voluntary contributions.

Al-Anon has but one purpose: to help families of alcoholics. We do this by practicing the Twelve Steps, by welcoming and giving comfort to families of alcoholics, and by giving understanding and encouragement to the alcoholic.

The Suggested Preamble to the Twelve Steps

CONTENTS

PREFACE

Many of us in Al-Anon grew up in families affected by alcoholism. However, we do not always recognize the part this disease played in shaping us into the individuals we are today. Not suspecting that the experiences we had as children affect us as adults, is it any wonder we are bewildered when we find that our lives today are unmanageable?

Through the honest sharings of Al-Anon members, who as children experienced the alcoholism of others, we come to see ourselves more clearly. Despite the often severe hurt and abuse they endured, each individual held tightly to the hope so essential to recovery.

We all have family history that includes embarrassing, even devastating events. Fortunately, the experience, strength, and hope of our fellowship expressed on these pages can help each of us to explore our own roots and lead us to new heights of recovery.

A SPECIAL WORD TO ANYONE CONFRONTED WITH VIOLENCE[1]

Al-Anon's gentle process unfolds gradually, over time. But those of us facing violent, potentially life-threatening situations may have to make immediate choices to ensure safety for ourselves and our children. This may mean arranging for a safe house with a neighbor or friend, calling for police protection, or leaving money and an extra set of car keys where they can be collected at any time in case of emergency. *It is not necessary to decide how to resolve the situation once and for all*—only how to get out of harm's way until this process of awareness, acceptance, and action can free us to make choices for ourselves that we can live with.

Anyone who has been physically or sexually abused or even threatened may be terrified of taking any action at all. It can require every ounce of courage and faith to act decisively. But no one has to accept violence. No matter what seems to trigger the attack, we all deserve to be safe.

---

1. . . . *In All Our Affairs: Making Crises Work for You,* ©Al-Anon Family Group Headquarters, Inc., 1990.

Tapping Other Resources

Al-Anon's purpose is to help families and friends of alcoholics. We come together to find help and support in dealing with the effects of alcoholism. In time we discover that the principles of our program can be practiced in all our affairs. But there are times when, in order to work through especially challenging circumstances, we may need more specialized help and support, such as therapy or legal counsel. Many of us have benefitted from taking care of these needs in addition to coming to Al-Anon.

part One

OUR MANY FACES

DO WE BELONG IN AL-ANON?

"I feel like I should be in this program and I want to belong, but when I look at my family, the only person I can honestly say is probably an alcoholic is my mother, and she didn't have much effect on me because she left me the day I was born." The young man speaking at an Al-Anon meeting innocently revealed his longing to belong somewhere and his need to find someone—anyone—who could really care. We greeted him with knowing smiles, encouraging words, and a ripple of warm laughter. He most certainly belonged! His isolation and confusion about the significance of his terrible loss at the very start of life are among the common characteristics all of us share who have grown up in families affected by alcoholism.

Anyone who has experienced the devastating effects of another's alcoholism is welcome in Al-Anon. Even if we feel we were only mildly affected, we belong. Here we come to know that laughing together in spite of the darkness and pain we experienced is one of Al-Anon's greatest healing balms. We laugh with each other not only because we think we're funny—as often we are—but because we recognize the many aspects of ourselves in each other.

We can see in others our own attitudes, actions, and feelings. We can feel their pain and recognize their denial of reality because we too have suffered and hidden from the truth. Yet we have learned that in order to heal and claim the joy that can be ours, we need to see the world as it really is.

Learning to do so can be frightening, but in Al-Anon we have the understanding and love of others like us who are traveling the same road, and together we find the courage to change the things we can.

In an alcoholic family, the needs and demands of the alcoholic frequently dominate all other needs. Preoccupied with the alcoholic, the other family members may be too exhausted, irritated, or overwhelmed to provide for the children's needs as well. Some children try to help their families cope by being quiet, good, and asking for nothing. While mastering the art of disappearing into a remote part of the house, going to a friend's home, or becoming invisible in the midst of a crowd, those of us who "got lost" also lost a sense of self and the belief that our own needs had any validity. Some of us became human chameleons who changed our personalities to fit whatever social or personal environment we encountered.

Growing up with the chaos and unpredictability created by alcoholism caused many of us to mask our confusion, anger, and shame by trying to be perfect. To prove to ourselves and the world that there was nothing wrong with us or our families, we scrambled hard in school to get straight A's, or worked feverishly at home to keep everything neat and tidy. We became star athletes, artists, corporation leaders, humanitarians, and outstanding citizens. Inside, however, we feel driven, terrified of failure, unable to relax or play, and lonely. Toward less responsible people who seem to make our efforts at perfection harder, we often feel self-righteous and angry. Convinced that something terrible will happen if we lose control, we run ourselves ragged trying to take charge of everything and never know how much is enough. Until we begin to recover, many of us are trapped in a compulsive need to give more, love more, and do more.

Watching those we love and depend on act erratic and irrational, destroying themselves and threatening others, is devastating. As children, we needed a cohesive family that loved us. But alcoholism prevented our parents from being models of love and sometimes made them models of fear. To diffuse the battles that often raged around us, or to divert our parents from their attacks on one another or other members of the family, some of us learned to entertain. We tried to blunt family crises with jokes, stories, musical performances, or even comedy revues. We became quite talented and popular with our classmates. Society rewarded us with laughter, applause, and attention, but in time we found that even when we desperately wanted to shed it, the mask would not come off. We felt driven to perform or talk compulsively even when we were exhausted or needed comfort ourselves. Intimacy was difficult for us to achieve, because tender or passionate moments prompted us to joke or wisecrack.

Some of us who grew up in alcoholic homes were faced with unbelievable violence and sexual assault when we were very young. Though it would seem logical that we would seek to escape such a horrible environment, as children we were dependent and utterly powerless, and as adults we found we had few positive relationship skills. Instead we got caught in a compulsion to repeat the very circumstances we loathed. We blamed, judged, and hated with the same intensity our parents had demonstrated. Instead of escaping, we became victims again and again and created a new generation of victims in our own children. Sometimes alcoholism seemed to skip a generation but was manifested instead in workaholism, compulsive control, eating, and mental or physical illness. Grandparents' disease reached through the generations to ruin lives of the yet unborn among us.

Growing up with adults who displayed extremes of emotion or no emotion at all left us afraid of our own feelings, confused, and very angry. Without any healthy demonstration of how to handle potent emotions, some of us acted them out in destructive ways. Relatives who are consumed with the disease of alcoholism put themselves and their need for alcohol first, ahead of the needs of everyone else in the family including their own children. We, the children, often craved attention to such a degree that any attention was better than none. Even negative behavior at least called attention to us and robbed the drinker of the spotlight for a moment. We were temporarily relieved of the nagging suspicion that we were not worthy of anyone's care or even notice. Attention for our negative behavior cost us a fearsome price in plummeting self-esteem and soaring guilt, but in our young minds, it seemed better than facing the abandonment and horror of realizing that the adults we depended upon were actually absent or abusive.

Alcoholism is a cunning, powerful, baffling disease not only for the alcoholic but for all the people who associate with the alcoholic. It is a progressive, multi-generational, physical, emotional, and spiritual disease with wide-ranging, often tragic effects. We who have had to cope with the problems created by an alcoholic have tried to force solutions only to find ourselves defeated again and again. We became exhausted, angry, frustrated, and unreasonable without even knowing it.

Those of us who grew up in families affected by alcoholism were particularly vulnerable to its effects because the disease touched us early in our lives, in our impressionable formative years. As dependent children, we had no possibility of escape and we naively believed that our families reflected the entire world—a world that seemed dangerous and unpredictable. We learned not to talk, not to trust, and not to feel. Family alcoholism also made us vulnerable to abusers outside our families when we sought love and solace anywhere we could find them.

Each member of an alcoholic family tries to adjust to the problem in his or her own way. Our adjustments depend on our situation in the family (whether spouse, sibling, distant relative, or child) and on our individual temperaments. We have in common the tendency to keep changing *ourselves* to try to fix something that is not in our power to fix—someone else's alcoholism.

Trapped in the uncertain, confusing, lonesome, and sometimes terror-filled world of another's alcoholism, many of us devised extraordinary means of adapting. We denied the existence of anything unusual, or we rearranged our memories to minimize their impact on us. "It wasn't that bad," we said, or we believed it had all ended when we left home. We created alternate realities and tried to live in an imaginary world. We put the past away so deeply we couldn't remember childhood at all, or we remembered but separated our feelings from our consciousness so well that we could speak without apparent emotion of events filled with abandonment and cruelty. We judged our families harshly and tried to rise above them, or we knew nothing but alcoholism for so long that we were like the fish who didn't realize its environment was wet. What else could it be? Some of us became alcoholics or married alcoholics, while others aggressively avoided alcoholics and distanced ourselves from our families trying to escape the disease. One thing was clear, nearly all of us tried to remold ourselves in some way to fit into or fix the situation, and in the process we lost touch with our own true feelings.

Behaviors we adopted to cope with alcoholism in our families became so habitual we thought they were part of our identity. Yet no matter how hard we had tried, how well we managed, or how successful we were on the outside, self-esteem, comfortable intimacy with those we loved, and peace of mind eluded us. We were not at home in our own skins. Before coming to Al-Anon, we did not recognize that our lives still reflected our old responses to someone else's drinking, and we didn't know how to make healthier choices. When we came through the doors of Al-Anon, some of us were in intense pain, others practically numb. We all found welcome here.

Today we no longer live alone in a crazy universe. We have learned about the disease and are recovering from its effects. As we attended meetings and listened to others courageously share their truths, we were surprised at first to hear pieces of "our stories" coming out of the mouths of apparent strangers. We recognized similar situations and felt comforted and less lonely when we realized that our experiences were not unique. We experienced long-buried emotions akin to those of the speakers and began to understand each other as few others could because we too had been there. Understanding another person brought us the courage to extend awareness to ourselves. Sometimes slowly and gently and sometimes with piercing recognition, we began to see how we were trapped in our old roles.

In many ways we who have grown up with alcoholism are all miracles of survival. We have survived violence in our homes and threats to our very existence. We have survived incest and sexual abuse of ourselves and our loved ones. We have survived prisons, broken homes, and social humiliation. Some of us have survived the murder or suicide of our dearest relatives. Others of us have survived the much more subtle but still devastating experience of emotionally unavailable parents who simply disappeared quietly into the bottle night after night.

We survived, but we found we were not free. For many of us, joy was a faraway dream. Constantly driving ourselves at top speed, feelings of always being on the outside and never belonging, struggles with sex and intimacy, depression, and even thoughts of or attempts at suicide were too often our realities. Surviving a childhood marked by alcoholism left us with invisible wounds that would not heal, but in Al-Anon we found a Twelve Step program of spiritual help and human caring that has brought us the priceless gift of serenity and has shown us a path toward emotional maturity that was lacking in our families.

Surrounded by other recovering people, we are learning how to heal our broken hearts and create healthy, productive, joyful lives. We hope you will try our program, for it has led many of us to serenity, fellowship, and relief from loneliness and pain. Today we are still growing one day at a time, and we would like to share our stories with you.

I'M HIDING

What is it like?

Read

What is it like to grow up in an alcoholic home? If you asked me a few years ago, I would have had to say, "I have no idea." My childhood was so painful that the only way I could survive was to block out the pain; I also blocked out the good. It was as if I had no life. When my family talked about events, I felt stupid because I couldn't remember them, and it frightened me that I couldn't remember. I couldn't feel, either. I was numb.

What is it like? It's unremitting fear—fear of rejection, fear of the unknown, fear of being known—a constant, nagging fear that never goes away.

It's lonely. It's wanting so desperately to be a part, yet pushing people so far away I couldn't possibly be connected. It's isolating myself and then being the outsider looking in and never fitting in. I'm often ashamed. I'm afraid to lose the only people who say they love me. I'm afraid they won't come back, and then I'm afraid they will. It's confusing. People say they love me and then they hurt me. In my gut, I know something is wrong, but I'm told I overreact or I'm too sensitive. So I learn not to trust my instincts.

It's being needy. It's being convinced I am unloved and unlovable. It's needing to hear over and over, "You're wonderful!" yet never believing it. So I always need to hear it again, and it's still not enough. It's feeling that *I* am not enough. It's having to do for others so that I can earn their love, yet feeling that what I give is never enough.

It's about trust. It's being told I didn't see what I just saw, and believing other people instead of believing my own eyes. It's never being able to trust anyone—not even myself— because my whole life is based on pretense and denial of reality. And I don't even know what I feel about it.

One day, when my life had become totally unmanageable, I walked into an Al-Anon meeting, hurting. I was a victim. Someone had said I should go, and I was an obedient victim, so I did what I was told. It was the one time this strategy worked for me. I walked in alone and afraid. The people I met said they too were "lonely and frustrated" and it would be possible to find "contentment and even happiness." At the break they hugged and laughed. I thought, what a bunch of phonies! They'll never keep up this charade. They're just like me, laughing on the outside and crying on the inside. Then came the clincher! Someone said I would "come to love them the same way they already loved me." Impossible! I was so unlovable. No one loved me, and even if someone did, what would the price be?

Nevertheless, I bought the book *One Day At A Time in Al-Anon (ODAT)* that night. I read just one page a day because someone told me to. I didn't use the index. I couldn't. I could never figure out what I was feeling, so I couldn't look it up. I didn't have a clue what a feeling was.

Somehow I found a wonderful, loving sponsor. I don't know how I did it because I didn't trust anyone. I suspect that my Higher Power had something to do with it. Warm and compassionate, my sponsor always said, "Love you lots!" I never had to say it back. I didn't say it just to see if she would still say it to me, and she did. Every once in a while, I would throw in a "Yeah, me too," because I was afraid she would stop, but she didn't. For the first time in my life, I felt lovable just because I was me.

From the time I came to Al-Anon my life has changed. I don't know how it happened. I guess it came "little by little, one day at a time." I don't isolate myself as much. I'm not as fearful or lonely. I've learned to trust myself and others. I feel loved and lovable. I've even learned to laugh at myself.

Do those old feelings come back? Sure they do. But now I recognize them. I can actually look them up in the *ODAT* for I can identify what I feel today. I can pick up the phone and know that someone else has felt the same way. I no longer need to suppress all feelings because so many are painful.

The most important thing I have learned is compassion, not only for others but for myself. So when people don't understand why someone hides away in isolation, I do. When I hear, "Why don't they just leave?" I know they can't. When I hear, "I said I love them—isn't that enough?" I know it's

not. When they say, "Why don't they *do* something?" I know
they don't know what to do or how to do it. Not yet.

But I'm here to offer them love, compassion, and a hug. I'm
anxious to share the understanding, peace, and love of the
program because the blessing of life was given to me and I
want to pass it on. Love you lots!

Loneliness hurts.

When my girlfriend entered an alcohol treatment program,
I had been in a relationship with her for three years but had
no idea she was an alcoholic. I knew she drank every day, but
it was only beer. I had someone I could take care of and that
was all that mattered. Visiting her two or three times a day, I
grilled program administrators and anyone I could find on
what I should do to help her. They kept saying, "Have you
ever been to an Al-Anon meeting?" I was there to help her,
not myself, so I brushed it off until one horrible day when she
asked me to stop coming.

Alone with myself and increasingly afraid she would be
cured and wouldn't need me any more, my anxiety began to
mount. I tried everything I knew to numb the feelings. I ate,
drank, watched hours of TV, and went on spending jags.
Nothing worked. With all my home remedies exhausted, I
finally heard the question posed by the hospital staff, "Have
you ever been to an Al-Anon meeting?"

Thoroughly defeated, I went to an Al-Anon meeting. I sat on
the floor behind the last row of chairs, next to the door in case
I needed to escape. Though I am very shy, the pain growing
inside me threatened to burst if I didn't speak, but I knew if I
talked I would cry, and I couldn't bear that. I grabbed a pen-
cil and paper, wrote down what I needed to say, and asked a

stranger to read it for me. When she spoke my words, I began to cry anyway, and I cried through the rest of the meeting. Members loved me unconditionally and told me I was in the right place. Today I know that those tears began my recovery.

I noticed that the people at the meetings I attended who seemed most like me identified themselves as adult children of alcoholics, so I began attending Al-Anon meetings that focused on adult children, though at the time I couldn't imagine who in my family was an alcoholic. There I began to regain a sense of personal identity I hadn't realized was lost.

One morning, early in recovery, I stood in my bathroom staring at a perfect stranger in the mirror. Large blue eyes stared back at me from an expressionless face. Looking into my own eyes, I plunged into a bottomless river of sadness. I wanted to escape the sadness, but it was too late; I had begun to notice myself. Shocked, I recoiled and hurried off to work.

In the car, I noticed I maneuvered through traffic like a soldier at war. At work, I saw that I functioned more like a machine than a man. Oh, I knew when to laugh and when to be serious and when to elicit co-workers' confidences. But I shared none. Like a calculated chameleon, I hid well from any real human contact—and I was desperately lonely.

At home, the mirror showed me a man who had hidden from himself and the world so effectively that he was a complete mystery even to himself. To solve the mystery, I had only the impetus of the great sadness, the loving support of new friends in the program, and the Twelve Steps of Al-Anon.

To find the man, I needed to reclaim the child, but I had no memories of my childhood. To defend myself against the intolerable pain of growing up in an alcoholic family I had buried all emotions and forgotten everything that happened as soon as it was over. Now I couldn't remember and my family wouldn't. For the barest outline of my life, I had to dig hard. Apparently, after I was born, I came to live with my grandmother straight from the hospital because my alcoholic mother, who already had a violent husband and two boys, refused to take me home.

When memories did emerge, they were all of loneliness. As a toddler, I played alone in the backyard for hours, staying out of my grandmother's way as much as possible. Perhaps I sensed I was a bother to her and I was trying to protect my home. After all if I wasn't good enough to be kept by my parents, I had better be really careful or she might also decide to get rid of me! My grandmother seemed angry most of the time, and she often called me incorrigible. I didn't know what it meant, but I knew it was bad. If I felt anything, I usually felt terrible, so I tried not to feel at all.

By the time I reached fifth grade, I was so miserable that I decided to kill myself. I took some seeds I thought were poisonous to school, where I planned to eat them and die. I chewed them up in class and put my head down on my desk, expecting never to wake up again. Fortunately, I was mistaken: the seeds had no ill effect at all. I believe God sometimes does for us what we cannot do for ourselves and saves us from our own angry folly.

Needy and lonely, my young life was one long plea for attention. A counselor once paid attention to me so I confided in her. She told me the problems I was having were not my fault but my grandmother's. Elated, I couldn't wait to get home and tell my grandmother. Enraged, she marched straight to school; I never saw that counselor again, and I learned never to talk about my family.

The older I got, the less I thought of myself. Not being sure of myself was deadly on the playground. Local bullies made me their favorite target. Finally I made a friend who was funny and popular. As long as I hung around with him, I didn't have to worry about being alone or attacked. He made many jokes at my expense, and some of them hurt a lot, but I was willing to pay *any* price to be included. In high school when I managed to attract a girl, my jolly, popular, and ruthless best friend always stole her. I finally found a girl who treated me kindly, and I fell hopelessly in love. For six months I floated around on the clouds until I found out she was only dating me to get close to him. Whatever scraps of confidence and trust I had vanished that day.

Convinced that being myself would never get me the love and attention I craved, I became a desperate people pleaser and did anything I could to be whatever everyone else wanted. For a while, it seemed I had discovered the secret of success—if I took care of someone else, she paid attention to me. But attention to me, with my empty reservoir, was like the first drink to the alcoholic. The more I got, the more I wanted. Even when I succeeded in getting attention, it wasn't satisfying because it created a double bind. I needed it, but I also mistrusted those people who gave it. Paradoxically, while I took care of everyone who would let me, I tried to be completely self-sufficient. I was the "motor home man" (completely self-contained). Ever vigilant of my "friends," I waited for them to let me down. They usually obliged, and then I redoubled my efforts at self-sufficiency. The repeating cycle of caretaking and emotional starvation led to the desperate tears of my first night in Al-Anon.

In Al-Anon I found a safe place to experience grief from all the losses of my childhood. Each time I grieve, I feel a little lighter and a little more free. As the lost feelings of sadness and grief surface, other feelings bubble up as well and I discover a range of emotions including humor and happiness. The Steps show me how to release the past and not fear the future. Al-Anon members give me unconditional love and healthy attention. With their help, I am growing into a different man from the one who once sat on the floor of a room and asked a stranger to speak the words he could not choke out.

If you look at me only from the outside, you might not think that much has changed. I still work at the same job, attend the same school, and sometimes drive like a soldier in a war zone. But inside of me a metamorphosis is taking place. With each day that passes I come closer to becoming a happy, joyous, free child of God. Inside, my attitude is changing, and attitude makes all the difference in the world.

I was at the end of my rope holding the scissors.

I am a survivor of an alcoholic family. As far back as I can remember I thought life was a drag, and I blamed it on being born female. I was blessed with an active imagination, so I lived in a fantasy world (as a boy, of course). Memories of my childhood were painful. I remember lying in bed late at night, crying and listening to the fighting. Even though I was safe and warm in my bed, I was sure something awful would happen. Cold chills ran down my spine. I prayed a lot.

I loved Mom and Dad, and I wanted everyone to be happy. Meme (my wonderful grandmother) loved me and I knew it, but I was never sure about the others. We moved a lot and I wanted to stay with Meme. She was my only security.

When Dad drank a little, I really liked him. He wrestled and played with us children. I especially loved the times he'd teach us songs, but Mom acted so strange that I thought she didn't want us ever to have any fun. I believed that if she would just stop crying, yelling, and complaining, Daddy wouldn't drink so much. I didn't want him to stop drinking, because when he did he was jumpy and Mom yelled at us if we got in his way.

I never knew what to expect. I learned to keep quiet, out of sight, not to bother anyone, and to do anything I was told. When dishes flew, my brothers and sisters cried, and I fled deep inside myself to a fantasy world. I could sit on a kitchen chair right in the middle of things and disappear by closing my eyes. Suddenly one day without explanation, Dad disappeared. Deserted and desolate, I prayed to God to send my Daddy home, but no one came. I believed that if he loved me, he'd stop drinking and come home. When I saw friends walking with their fathers, I hid and cried.

I blamed myself. I had overheard my Mom telling a friend that things really weren't that bad before I was born. She said Dad was able to cope with four children, but seven was just too much responsibility for him to handle. I was the fifth of seven children, and in my child's mind I thought I had tipped the scales against us. It was all my fault, and I began to wish I had never been born and to think that everyone would be happy if it weren't for me. I decided that if God existed, He'd made a mistake, and I quit praying.

To support seven children, Mom had to work very hard, and she was too tired to pay much attention to me. Secretly I feared that one day she'd leave too so, trying to keep her, I became mother's helper, the "good girl," the "only one she could trust." I tried to be happy, but I didn't know how so I pretended. I even resorted to laughing when others did and saying whatever I thought people wanted me to say.

When I was nine, I got a little job cleaning a shoemaker's shop on Saturdays. I really liked the owner. He told me I was smart and pretty. He paid a lot of attention to me and said I was special to him. I craved love so much and was so young, I didn't understand that what this man was saying—and the way he touched me—was sick. I only knew he liked me, so I went back again and again, even though at some level I knew it was bad. He threatened me with the loss of his love if I told anyone. For three years, I told no one and tried not to think about it. Guilt and lies started then. I had two big dark secrets: I had made my Daddy go away, and I was no longer a "good girl." God must hate me for sure.

In a convent school, I had a terrible sixth grade year that confirmed my worst fears. My teacher told us that God could see everything we did, hear every lie we told, and make us die any time He wanted. If we were bad, we'd go straight to hell and burn in a big hot fire forever. I knew I was bad, and I was terrified.

One day my teacher hung a little "spirit" (made from a marble wrapped in a tissue) by a long piece of thread over every desk. She told us the little "spirit" was our soul and the thread was our lifeline to heaven. God could cut us down when we were bad or whenever He wanted to. All morning I looked up at "my soul" swinging above my head. I was so scared, I couldn't pay attention. In my mind I desperately begged for Dad to come back and rescue me. Of course he didn't, and I started to cry. I closed my eyes and tried to disappear. I thought I heard my name, but I couldn't answer. A loud "thunk" forced me to open my eyes and there on my desk was my "spirit," my little soul. My teacher stood over me with a pair of scissors in her hand. Eyes flashing, she screamed at me that I was a very bad little girl and God had just sent me to hell, where I would burn forever. I remember clearly experiencing some sort of separation taking place inside me. There was the inside that no one would ever know and the outside that didn't matter anyway. I believe that was the day I lost my will to live.

Shortly after that, quite by accident, I discovered alcohol. Meme gave me a big mouthful of sherry to hold in my mouth to stop a toothache. I still remember the warm sensation of the wine sliding down my throat and the glow it created in my belly. After two more mouthfuls, I said to Meme, "Oh! This is why Daddy drinks." That night, I not only talked with Mom and her friend, I even sang a song. Mom beamed at me and said, "My little wallflower has just come off the wall." I was happy and felt safe for the first time in my life.

This is not the time to say what the next twenty-three years held in store for me, except that I became an alcoholic and an addict. I did go straight to hell, and I never grew up. The unbearable separation of self caused me to lose everything. I nearly lost my life. After many suicide attempts, I finally found Alcoholics Anonymous.

In the first year of sobriety I found Al-Anon, and I've been on the road upward out of hell ever since. Today I understand the disease of alcoholism and the effects it had on me and my whole family. There are many sick people in the world, and among them are my sixth grade teacher, my abuser, my dad, and I.

Today I am not doomed or condemned by God, as I understand Him. God did not make a mistake when He made me. It wasn't a mistake that He made me a girl. I'm not bad. Sometimes I am sick, but I am loved by many people, including my mom and dad. Five years ago Dad stopped drinking and started attending Alcoholics Anonymous. He came back to us. Mom never left us. Today she attends Al-Anon and she and Dad are happy. Today we are rebuilding our family, and when we sing together, Mom doesn't act strange.

I am no longer alone; I have lots of friends. A very special friend with great patience and understanding helped me find myself. He took me to Al-Anon, stuck by me through all the temper tantrums, crying spells, and sharing of the terrible burdens in my heart. He helped me understand my dad, and he believed in me before I could. With his love and the love in Al-Anon, I have come to understand that everyone in my family was screaming so loud to be loved and accepted that we drowned each other out. The separation within me is slowly healing. I have traced the terrors of my past, faced them, and let them go.

When I came to these Twelve Step Fellowships, I was at the end of my rope and holding the scissors. I cannot express in words my gratitude for having been given back my life, my God (I had sorely missed God), and a plan for living (the Steps and Traditions) that I can follow for the rest of my life. Best of all, I am glad to be alive and I am happy to be a woman.

I'VE GOT TO BE PERFECT

I didn't escape.

I am the only child of an alcoholic father and a martyred, guilt-inducing mother. By the time I found Al-Anon, I almost believed it was my fate to fight my way out of bed every morning and live with the dull ache of chronic depression. In more than five years of therapy with four different therapists to whom I always mentioned my father's drinking, no one had ever suggested Al-Anon to me. I had prayed without result for forty years and had finally given up on God. Without a popular self-help book that confronted me at every newsstand, I might never have recovered.

I am not an alcoholic; I avoid alcoholics like the plague, and I didn't marry an alcoholic. I thought I had escaped after college and was determined never to marry a man like my father. I didn't. I married a man like my mother instead! Twice! I was a successful college teacher, the mother of two beautiful children, trying everything I knew to be a good wife to my second husband, and I was utterly miserable. Neither of my husbands drank, hit me, beat the children, or chased other women. There must be something terribly wrong with me, I concluded, to be miserable under such reasonable circumstances. My family and each successive husband agreed. They always said, "The trouble with you is . . ."

My father is a periodic drinker. Every six months to a year, while I was growing up, he got drunk for three to six weeks. The rest of the time, he never touched alcohol. Drinking turns my father from a mild, humorous, if irrational man into a violent, ugly-talking, sexually abusive, raving maniac. The change is so dramatic that anyone would recognize he had a problem. What I didn't know, and my mother still refuses to see, is that his alcoholism affects us all even when he is sober.

When drunk, my father accused my mother of frigidity and used ugly sexual language no child should hear. He'd put me on his lap, cry, and hug me too tight. He'd give me wet kisses, and if I flinched, he'd berate me for not loving him enough. He smelled terrible and drooled; if I recoiled he'd snap into anger and threaten to tear me limb from limb. When mother hid his guns, he'd bully her into telling him where they were, take them out, clean them, or load them, and wave them around, threatening to blow us to pieces. He never shot anyone, but there was murder in his eyes. My mother insists that he rarely hit me, that I exaggerate and have "such an imagination," but I remember a life intermittently filled with terror and revulsion. As a child, I believed him when he said he could kill us, and I woke each morning when he was drinking afraid I would find my mother slashed to bloody pieces on our living room floor. As an adult, I still often wake at four a.m., shaking with fear. I believed him when he told me I didn't love him enough. I have spent my life trying to love enough. Only since I found Al-Anon have I begun to conceive that I might *be* lovable.

When we couldn't take his violence any more, Mother and I would sneak around, pack some clothes, and hide out with a neighbor or friend until, vomiting and cursing, Dad would sober up. We would come home, and all three of us would pretend that nothing had happened. Though my mother never mentioned the drinking, she didn't really recover from each bout of abuse. Drunk or sober, she didn't trust him. She criticized him every time she got the chance, picking and picking at every little fault, and then I felt sorry for him.

I loved when he got sober because he would buy me gifts and be an easy touch for a while before he returned to not paying much attention to me. Clearly my mother's child, I clung to her fiercely even as I felt contempt for her cowardice in staying with him. Though she had a job and ran the family, she obviously felt she couldn't survive emotionally without a man. She told me about her desperately lonely childhood, and I felt responsible for being the "only joy in my mother's life." Today I struggle with self-contempt because I too have a deep, dependent need for male love and affirmation. I judge myself mercilessly whenever I am needy, and asking for help is the hardest thing for me to do. Recently I realized that whenever I cried or needed help as a child, I either heard, "The trouble with you is . . ." or "Quit crying or I'll give you something to cry about!" As a wife and adult child of my parents, the refrain, "The trouble with you is . . ." continued whenever I admitted need. No wonder it's so hard for me to ask.

Though I play all the roles in the family, mostly I try to be perfect. I am competent, dependable, honest, successful, and

friendly, yet I feel insecure, and no matter how well I do or
how much I love, I feel it is never enough. I fear both being
abandoned and being consumed; therefore my relationships,
especially intimate ones, are like a minefield.

My parents heaped guilt on me, but I held onto it fiercely
because at least if it was my fault I could fix it. To believe that
the people I loved and depended on abused me terribly and
that I couldn't control them made me feel so vulnerable it was
worse than guilt. Today I still can't control them, but I can set
boundaries for myself, determine what I need, and learn how
to protect my own interests.

As a child, when I told the truth as I saw it, my mother so
often insisted I had "such an imagination," that even today I
feel I can't trust myself to see reality. After two years in recovery, memories of incest began to surface. My first response to
this information was not gratitude to the program but anger. I
felt betrayed that I had worked the program so hard, only to
face this new horror from my past. I was so appalled I kept
trying to deny every bodily sensation and mental picture, saying to myself, "Oh, surely not!" Crawling with revulsion, I
despaired that now I was really hopelessly damaged and no
man would ever want me.

It appears that I was molested and raped by my father
sometime before I was five. The two people who could vali-
date my experience insist I am making this up and claim that
my childhood wasn't that bad. In Al-Anon I am learning to
trust myself in the face of my parents' denial.

The greatest tool I have is that I am once again connected
to my Higher Power. It took a long time to make that connection because I felt (still do on the bad days) that a God who
would let a child be raped and live in continuous fear either
didn't exist or was vicious. I didn't have difficulty with Step
One; I knew I was powerless and my life hurt. Step Two was

the real challenge. I knew I had to face God in order to work Step Two, but fortunately all I was asked to do was to "keep coming back." For over a year I simply attended meetings, listened to others, shared what felt safe to share, and said the Serenity Prayer over and over. I began turning my life over five minutes at a time and watching God very carefully to see what happened. Listening helped me realize that other members had grudges to settle with God and gave me permission to rant and rave until at last I managed to find a Power, a feminine Power, greater than myself that I could trust. When I said, "Our Mother, Who art in heaven," and no one glared or threw me out of the meeting, I decided it was safe to stay. It would have helped to have the Steps rewritten to eliminate "He," but I decided that *as we understood* meant "She" for me.

Recovery has been a bumpy, roller coaster ride. Being strong but frightened, I do not change easily, especially if it requires asking for help. Sometimes my Goddess must knock very hard at my door to get my attention. After a year in Al-Anon, my first "world collapse" occurred. I had a new, more difficult job, my husband left me, and my son suddenly had a seizure. He was due to have a brain scan to see if it was a tumor, and in a truly desperate moment I did an uncharacteristic thing. I actually got up in a meeting and asked people to call me and to help me. And they did! One of those callers is today my new husband.

The next Christmas, another series of crises challenged me. My mother had a cerebral hemorrhage, my best new program friend and my boyfriend abandoned me, my aunt who lived with my parents was dying of cancer, and my teenage daughter ran away from home. That Christmas, I offered my Goddess a whole year of my life. I figured She couldn't mess it up any worse than I had! Since that time—"the essential u-turn"—my life has gotten slowly but steadily better.

Today I am capable of gratitude. I'm especially grateful for all the tools Al-Anon has provided. They all work at one time or another. The Twelve Step path leads to maturity, enlightenment, and peace of mind. With the help of Al-Anon, I have been able to let people love me until I could love myself, believe in me until I could dare to believe in myself, and accept my feelings of rage, pain, hurt, and humiliation until at last, slowly, I began to accept all of my feelings. As I accept the unacceptable feelings, the depression that has been my companion for more than forty years lifts. I even feel joy and tenderness. Unfamiliar joy sometimes frightens me, but I know I can call an Al-Anon friend who understands about being afraid of happiness, and we can laugh together. That alone is worth the price of admission (no dues or fees), and besides, if I don't like it, a long-time member assures me they will refund my misery. Since I don't want my misery back, I'll keep coming back until I am fully mature. Until then, see you at a meeting!

Loafing is fun.

As the years go by in my recovery, I realize more and more that control is a major issue for me. When I started attending Al-Anon, I didn't think it was an issue at all, let alone a major one. In fact, I had a tremendous need to control everything and everyone around me in order to feel safe. When they complained about my advice, I thought my parents and brothers were overreacting and just didn't understand me. Pointing out their mistakes, telling them what to do, say, think, or feel didn't seem unreasonable to me, since I was sure I was correct and they needed a lot of monitoring and help.

I saw how out of line my excessive assumption of responsibility was only when my own exhaustion forced me to be "irresponsible" for a day. It was my mother's birthday and I had promised to provide a favorite food for our family gathering. Over-committed as usual, I ran late. I had been dragging myself through inertia for days. I had an important job outside the family, I rationalized.

Arriving at the party late and without the dish, I sat down exhausted, feeling terribly disappointed in myself and certain everyone else would be upset that I had let the family down. The party was sure to be a disaster, and it would be my fault, but I simply could not move. For the first time in my life, I sat and watched the world go by. Amazingly, the meal was served, birthday cake appeared, complete with candles and songs, and the celebration proceeded happily. No one confronted me for my failures. It was a little disconcerting not to be needed, but having the burden lifted from my shoulders allowed me to relax and sit up straight at the same time. At last I could let go.

That was the beginning of my recovery of real trust. I could turn something over to my Higher Power, and even to members of my family. I am a very responsible person and will probably never be truly irresponsible, but learning to occasionally loaf and let others fill my plate for a change is a delightful and unexpected blessing.

Little white lies confuse.

What was it like growing up with alcoholism? Confusing! Embarrassing. Mixed up. Frightening. It was so difficult to find the part of life that was mine that I had trouble doing things for myself and instead ended up doing lots of things for other people.

I still don't really know what happened. My parents both did their best to hide the disease from themselves as well as the world, and I tried not to notice. Unconsciously, I automatically ignored situations I found puzzling or uncomfortable.

I poured my energy into my life at school, where I excelled. I went to a boys' prep school where the primary goal was to gain admission to one of a few select colleges. My parents expected me to be admitted to the college of their choice. Eager to please, in the school's protective confinement, I distinguished myself as a model student and I succeeded.

I'd like to report that I was happy in this role, but I don't think I was. I was fairly isolated and lonely. I had one friend, and we spent three years at the school playing chess. I participated in the accelerated program to finish ahead of schedule. Today I wish wistfully that I had followed the four-year program, taking more time for football, basketball, or just plain playing.

My obsession with school activities and achievement was probably an attempt to compensate for a home life where nothing was simple, where problems were always complicated and burdensome, and where no one was ever pleased. Even during periods of sobriety, my parents feuded. They battled over things like whether the lawn should be professionally mowed or if Dad's haphazard attempts should be acceptable. I tried to solve or mediate, but only succeeded in making both of them angry with me. Their conflicts never actually focused on the real problem—Dad's drinking and irresponsibility. I felt confused and uneasy, and when he drank, confusion gave way to a deep fear, which I desperately tried to suppress.

In our family, ordinary human exchanges became slippery. Subtle lies and continuing denial made honesty, trust, and intimacy elusive at best. Recently I was struck by a good example of this.

My brother laughingly remarked that his daughter had come back from a visit with her grandmother and asked him,

"Dad, why does Gramma lie?" Our mother had walked her granddaughter a fairly long distance back to her apartment, while repeatedly reassuring her that it was only a few blocks away.

I said, "She doesn't really lie. She just doesn't always tell the truth." As I uttered those words, however, I immediately recognized the part I played in creating confusion, just I had been confused as a child by my parents. I wish I had been there and could have said, "I don't know why Gramma lies. Perhaps it's one of the effects of her having lived with Grandpa's alcoholism." I was impressed with my niece's candor and dismayed to realize that my own attempt to make light of an uncomfortable question was itself less than forthright.

White lies in our family were a form of denial that became habitual until every interchange was potentially dishonest. In my family Dad was sick with alcoholism, but when he drank we pretended not to notice. Later, when he sobered up, we pretended he was well but treated him with kid gloves, since now we actually viewed him as sick. We were very mixed up. As I see it today, lying was wishful thinking given a voice. Perhaps we believed that if we insisted we were "one big, happy family," we would become one.

A good example of how we substituted wishes for reality came from my father. One year he was taken with a cartoon character whose slogan was, "Jes' fine, sez Bug." Dad took it up as his phrase of the hour, and no problem was too complex or daunting for the response, "Jes' fine, sez Bug." Thinking of it today, I suppose that absurd expression could have been our family motto. Everything, even a thorny problem, was "Jes' fine, sez Bug!"

In many ways, my childhood looked just fine. There was money, status, and community respectability. Still, I missed the encouragement, consistency, emotional support, and love that not only affirms but nurtures with rigorous honesty and fills the soul with trust. Without self-trust, trust of others and thus deep intimacy is impossible. A large part of my recovery in Al-Anon has been the difficult business of giving myself permission to grieve the loss of these intangibles and learning to allow members to restore them to my life. I still have a tendency to minimize my experiences. Surely they don't compare with those of other members, I tell myself. But their memory still bites. It gnaws at those tender places, and I know that all is not "Jes' fine, sez Bug."

LET ME ENTERTAIN YOU

I wore two faces.

I grew up with a terrible fear of holidays. They always turned into a big battle. Each parent tried to outdo the other with accusations. Regularly, my mother would threaten to "call New York," and my father would pull the phone cord out of the wall and wrap it around her neck until I screamed and begged him to stop. I had no idea what was in New York, but I certainly knew how murderous it made my father.

Family outings were also disastrous. They always included a cooler full of booze. Off to the park we would go, and sometime during the day my parents would turn into other people, fall down, or pass out. I felt greatly embarrassed. Once my mother, quite drunk, tried to swim and almost drowned. People had to pull her out of the water. Where was my dad? Passed out somewhere. Where was I? Probably hiding, trying to fade into the bushes so I didn't have to admit I knew them.

As I got older, I learned to joke to survive the pain of

watching my parents destroy each other. I became the class clown. Like the two-faced drama mask of comedy and tragedy, I had a laughing face for the world, and a tragic face turned inside. The inside one sat in class, wondering if I would find a screaming match or dead silence at home.

I spent many hours alone or baby-sitting to escape. I prayed nightly to be a better daughter, or to get better grades, so God would stop the fighting. I didn't know then that I was powerless over alcohol. I thought God must be very angry with me to punish me with so much misery. It has taken years of Al-Anon to believe that God really does love me just the way I am.

As a teenager, I continued to clown, to try to make everyone happy, and to work very hard at being good and responsible. Yet my mother called me stupid, a tramp, and uglier terms. To her dying day, she never said she loved me. My father tried to love me, but he was so wrapped up with his own alcoholism and enabling my mother with hers that he simply couldn't.

To escape, I married one of the few people I dated in high school. Both from alcoholic homes, we took up the fight where our parents had left off. Two immature children, we fought over who got to be the child in the family. With no idea how to communicate or grow up emotionally, we clawed at each other for five miserable years, until my clown face became sad all the time and there was no one to relieve either of us.

During that period my father died, and I began to have strange memories. I felt like I didn't fit, as if I had been in the wrong family, perhaps even was adopted. The feelings were so persistent that I started to ask questions, and one day I sent for my birth certificate. What a shock! The last name on the certificate was different from mine. I remembered my mother always threatening to "call New York," and I finally did.

Amazingly, I found a phone number in the name of the man on the certificate. I called the number and asked the total stranger who answered if she had ever heard of anyone by my name. She said, "Yes. That's my baby sister. Why do you want to know?" I started to cry and tell her who I was, but I couldn't finish, so I handed the phone to my husband who told her about me. There was a cry of mixed joy and pain at the other end of the phone, then a crack, and silence. She had fainted from the shock. My brother-in-law picked up the phone, and he and my husband started putting the pieces together.

I thought I was an only child, but actually I have three sisters. The father who raised me was not my father, although both fathers were in fact alcoholics. The last time my sisters saw our mother, she was driving out of town with her boss from a club where she worked, with me—a three-year-old—standing between them. I was a late-in-life baby, much younger than the other three, but much beloved by my sisters, who had become my caretakers. My disappearance had been a tremendous loss to them.

I am now reunited with my sisters, and the bond of sisterhood is there, although the closeness of growing up together isn't. I also met my biological father two months before he died.

Today I am the only one in our family who has peace and serenity in her life. We have all struggled with the effects of the disease of alcoholism in our own ways, but thanks to Al-Anon, I seem to have more clarity and ease. I love them dearly, and I am particularly grateful to the program that has helped me to uncover and accept the past. Today I know I didn't cause anyone's alcoholism, I can't cure it, and I can't control it. I can accept that I make mistakes and that the program will help me correct them. I don't have to be perfect or always on stage, and I can laugh and cry. Having found recovery in Al-Anon, I can acknowledge all three parents and live happily one day at a time. It is a blessing I share eagerly with newcomers when I tell them they too can grow in fellowship if only they keep coming back.

I didn't "get it."

I didn't see any alcohol while growing up. Dad sometimes got a case of beer during hay time. That was it. Even though I had joined Al-Anon because of marriage to an alcoholic, I had a hard time relating to the adult children in the program. They seemed to whine a lot, and I always identified with the spouses more than them, never realizing that I too was an adult child. Even as an adult in Al-Anon, I never saw the bottle or the drinking, but my children did! They were playing in the hayloft and found all these little bottles. I was crushed. I felt deceived. Worse, I felt stupid! Later the children were washing the truck and found a bottle under the seat. What did we do? Six of us adults knew, and we hushed it all up. I began what I now realize is a knee-jerk reaction toward unacceptable awareness. I started telling farming stories and talking about my own childhood to divert them from the bottles as best I could. Adult children do not talk about "those things."

I knew Dad and Mom weren't really available, but it was always blamed on work. Dad was always working. Mom was always working and doing all the child care too. Dad worked through our measles, mumps, ruptured appendix, birth of new baby, and school plays. Mom worked as a hairdresser and did everything else. She worked and resented. We didn't have celebrations. On my thirteenth birthday, I jumped out of bed and went downstairs excited. I thought someone would surely say, "Welcome! Teenager!" Instead I heard, "Do you know what you did to me thirteen years ago?" As I remember these bits and pieces, I begin to understand the old, hidden pain that the adult children in our fellowship were revealing to me. I don't call them "whiners" any more because I can feel compassion for them and for myself. I can understand why I made up stories to salve my own pain.

All this has come from working the Steps and serving the fellowship. Since I began the program of Al-Anon, and especially since I worked my Fourth and Fifth Steps, most of my life is named, claimed, and accepted. I no longer resent my parents, because I choose to be happy every single day. If I make mistakes, it doesn't ruin my day. I make amends by changing my behavior rather than just apologize and go on.

The keys to my happiness are sponsoring and service. I try to be a model to newcomers and encourage them to participate in service too. I may share a funny or sad story from my own life if I think it will help someone, but I don't feel driven to come up with a tale every time someone admits their pain. Because I accept the truth of my own childhood pain, I don't have to cover up someone else's quickly with a quip in order to avoid my own feelings. Without service, I might have dodged those adult children who had so much to teach me. Serving keeps Al-Anon and my own recovery alive, so I am really helping myself whenever I serve.

Service deepened my recovery.

I had been in Al-Anon for twelve years when adult child focus meetings started in my home town. Until that time I truly believed I had never been affected by alcoholism before I met and married my husband. Because adult child meetings were new and were often seeking Al-Anon speakers and other help, I decided to serve them and attended a few meetings. I read some of the literature, and had an incredible awakening.

I discovered that my maternal grandfather was an alcoholic and that my mother had been severely affected by his active alcoholism. Choosing an alcoholic husband for myself was simply a learned behavior!

After twelve years finding whole layers of me that still needed recovery upset me. For a while I flitted in and out of adult child meetings because the pain of looking back at my childhood created a double-edged sword. Every time I looked back and saw what had happened to me, I could see what I in turn had done to my own children. I had learned the behavior, certainly, but it was one thing to feel rage and hurt toward my own mother and quite another to experience those same feelings coming from my children.

I finally realized that the only way to recover was to work the program, and I committed to adding another meeting to my busy schedule. I made up my mind to attend the group as a newcomer to listen and learn, because I had already learned about my dangerous tendency to be a know-it-all. When I am being self-righteous, I am not teachable. As a child I had often acted quite insufferably right, always trying to direct whatever went on. I had no idea how compulsive my actions were until I tried to eliminate them through my recovery in Al-Anon. One of the gifts of having to work the adult child issue from both sides as daughter and mother is the deep compassion I have finally developed for my mother. I know that if she had known better, she would have done better, for I would have certainly changed if I had known better. Recognizing how I talked constantly to attract attention and fill up space whenever I felt fear also helped me become tolerant of my children when they demanded attention through misbehavior or by lecturing each other like bossy little know-it-alls.

In the process, I, like other adult children, had to feel my hurt and anger at the abuse my mother inflicted on me. I also had to begin to set boundaries. I could no longer allow her to put me between herself and my father by complaining to me about him. I could not tolerate her concept of a punishing God. There were subjects we could no longer discuss. My mother rejected my boundaries angrily.

Fortunately, God can fill my heart with love even when Mother is shaking like an earthquake because I changed the rules. After a while, I could go back slowly and love her, because the members of Al-Anon and my Higher Power had filled my cup to overflowing. Though she fought at first, she began to accept the love I offered. I knew I had to do the loving, since I was the one with the resources for recovery.

Shortly after this happened, she started to go blind. She has now lost almost all of her sight. I am grateful that I can care for her without becoming her caretaker, and I am amazed at the softening of my mother as she accepts—and even blossoms from—the love she once believed she simply had to do without. A bonus for me is the realization that I too can give up my martyrdom. I don't have to do without dressing well and looking good to be a good person. I don't have to chatter compulsively to call attention to myself. I can let the outside of me reflect the new self-esteem inside of me, thanks to the Twelve Steps and the understanding I now have that loving does not mean a life of endless sacrifice. Loving means extending acceptance and compassion to ourselves and to those we love, for only then can we love others *as* ourselves.

Wealth and social standing are no protection.

I don't think any one thing has affected me more in my life than the alcoholism that dominated my childhood. Both of my parents were daily drinkers and we lived an upper-class life in San Francisco and all over the world. I am the middle child of four children, all of whom but one are today alcoholic.

Because of alcohol, and the daily cocktail hour, there was no structure at home. We never ate breakfast because the thought of food in the morning nauseated my mother. Dinner was never served before ten because we had to wait for parents to finish their cocktails. Often we didn't eat at all and the long wait was for nothing.

In our family, resentment and religion were strangely intertwined. My mother hated Catholics, but my father was Catholic, and I began school in a Catholic convent at age three. Eating fish on Friday became a cause for huge battles, which often resulted in our getting neither fish nor meat.

When I was six, Mother decided to take the three older children to Europe. She placed the two oldest children in boarding school in Switzerland, but took me from the convent school, which I loved because of its structure and dependability, to travel the continent with her. I believe that my tendency to swing between extremes of wanting to be entirely invisible and wanting someone, anyone, to notice me began during that period. I became very conscious of Mother's drinking, for she often fell down or passed out in public. Once she passed out in an airport. People carrying their suitcases glanced down as they hurried past. I tried to pick her up but she was too heavy. Not one person stopped to help and I sat down on the floor of the long hall and cried. The sense of desolation and not mattering to anyone in the world still haunts me sometimes today. On the other hand, because of the embarrassment I felt so often, I tend to clam up. I feel as if I'm dancing on a thin wire screaming, "Look at me, please!" but if anyone does, I respond with a surly, "What do you think you're looking at?" With such contradictory messages, it's no wonder people don't know how to take me. At least today, I am learning compassion for myself and beginning to understand why I so often feel confused.

On this first of many trips to Europe, my mother met a Catholic monk, and our life changed forever. She became enamored of him, and eventually he left the church. She divorced my father and married him. He never drank, and he had no idea about alcoholism. He kept saying she wasn't drunk, just tired. I know today that he wasn't lying; he was actually in complete denial. When he finally figured it out, I was relieved, but by that time, after twenty-four years of trying to tell him and having him deny it, I had stopped trusting in people and my own perceptions.

Confusion and extremes of behavior on all sides of my family have affected me greatly; I am very uncomfortable with inconsistent people and sudden changes. I didn't even realize how confused it all was until my father died and another man reappeared, who my mother had told me was dead. He had lived with us until I was five, and I had loved him very much. By the time he again showed up in my life he was an alcoholic recovering in AA, and he told me that *he* was my biological father. Shortly after that he committed suicide.

When I was thirteen, I tried to get help. I went to the central office of Alcoholics Anonymous in San Francisco. There I met a woman who was about my mother's age and who said she was a recovering alcoholic. For one moment I felt the greatest hope I had ever known, then I felt the greatest despair because I knew my mother would never join AA. I didn't try again until I was thirty-one. I consulted a psychologist about Mother. He didn't know much about the disease, but he did learn about Al-Anon and directed me there. At long last my emotions and reactions began to make some sense. Today the great fog of confusion is slowly dissipating; I no longer feel compelled to demand attention or hide from it.

I am healing, but alcoholism continues to ravage my family. My frail, seventy-year-old mother still drinks and is often pathetic. When I am faced with the continuing pain of watching her, I say the Serenity Prayer over and over. It helps me accept the fact that I cannot force my family to turn away from the destruction and death of alcoholism, but I can change my own life. The hardest thing I have to do is lovingly detach from alcoholic family members. It feels as if I am abandoning them, as I felt desolate and abandoned in that airport long ago. I am learning, however, that people deserve the dignity of making their own decisions, even when they seem wrong to those of us who love them. It is one way to acknowledge their humanity. Without the program, I couldn't do it, and even with Al-Anon, I can only do it one day at a time.

POOR ME

I'll never be like my mother!

I am the fifteenth child in a family of eighteen children. As long as I can remember, my father had a problem with alcohol. There was a lot of physical and mental abuse, as well as incest, in our house. Many nights we locked ourselves up in a small room, fearing for our lives. Daddy always carried a gun or knife, and he used them to threaten Mama. On several occasions, he tried to kill her. The one I remember most clearly is the time he tried to kill her with an ax. By that time, I had grown to hate her. I blamed her for keeping us in a bad situation, and I prayed to God to let me be like anyone but her.

Terrified from youth, I hated and feared everyone I knew.

By the time my father died when I was seven, I had retreated into a world of silence where it was almost impossible to reach me. When I started school, everyone thought I was retarded.

I didn't understand death, but I was glad he wouldn't be coming home. I thought things would get better, but instead they got worse. My brothers, who had been in the background, took over. Instead of one Dad, there were seven brothers, and my older brother started sexually molesting me. He told me I was bad and I deserved what he had to do for punishment. He also told me he would kill me if I told anyone. A few months ago I found out he did the same thing to some of my sisters.

One night, when I was eleven, my mother took us to church and walked out, telling us she was going to the bathroom. We didn't see her again until years later when she came home to die.

My first marriage at age thirteen was to a much older man who already had a drinking problem. I was living with my sister at the time, and she arranged the marriage. After the ceremony I heard my brother-in-law making crude remarks about what was going to happen to me that night. Knowing what my brother had done to me, I couldn't go through with it again. I begged my sister to let me live with her, but she refused to even consider it, so I ran out of the house, knowing I could never return.

On my own, I found an empty house, where, exhausted, I made myself a bed in the bathtub with some curtains I found on the floor. For the next two weeks, I spent days stealing what I could to eat and slipping back into the house at night. One morning, the lady who owned the house found me sleeping there and took me home with her. I told her I didn't have any family and for some reason she believed me. I stayed with her for the next couple of years, and my marriage was annulled.

At sixteen I had decided it would be best for me to leave my home state, and I married a soldier who promised to take me away with him when he finished his duty tour. Already a full-blown alcoholic, my husband was unfaithful and beat me; nevertheless, I started having babies every year until I had had five. Though the beatings regularly landed me in the hospital, I lied so well that I don't think anyone knew what was wrong. Finally I filed for divorce and moved with my children back home.

I knew before I married him that my next husband drank, but I didn't know I had become mentally sick myself. The violence started very early in our marriage, and this time I fought back. I was so frustrated that sometimes when my husband came home so drunk he could hardly walk, I would attack him with whatever was handy, almost as soon as he came in the door. Once I picked up a shoe and hit him until my strength gave out. That was the first time it occurred to me that I might be sick, but I brushed it aside by telling myself it was his fault. If he hadn't done the things he did, I wouldn't have had to do the things I did. I had learned to rationalize and justify everything I did—even my suicide attempts—as his fault.

When my husband was stopped for the fourth time, driving drunk, the judge gave him a choice of jail or a treatment program. Of course he chose the treatment program because it was shorter. He called me from the center to tell me he had found something that might work for him and asked me to talk with his counselor. All I remember of that meeting is that I thought she was saying that *I* was the crazy one! Even though I was spending my days locked in my bedroom and letting the kids fend for themselves, I swore at her and told her she didn't know what she was talking about.

I decided to test his newfound sobriety on my birthday, so I announced I wanted to celebrate. When my husband agreed, I picked the nearest bar. He didn't say much as we sat there, but he didn't drink, and soon I became very uncomfortable. We left and went to a meeting, where he got a little medallion for his months of sobriety. "Some birthday present!" I thought bitterly to myself.

It scared me to death to realize he was serious about Alcoholics Anonymous. I had never in my life been around sober people, and I didn't know how to handle it. I tried Al-Anon but decided it wasn't for me. I tried AA meetings, but I felt so jealous of his new friends that it was extremely painful. I tried to get him drunk, but he caught on to my game. I felt sure that I was going insane.

A year after my husband joined AA, my only son ran away. I thought I might find him with my daughter whom I had not seen for several years because she wanted no part of me. She had two children whom I had never seen because she didn't want me to influence them. My lovely daughter came to the door and ranted and raved at me. With tears streaming down her face, she told me how much she hated me for what I had done to her life. Looking into her eyes that day, I saw all the things I had felt for my own mother many years before. All my justifications and rationalizations collapsed. I had become what I hated most—*my mother!*

Coming face to face with what I had done to my children was ugly but healing. I hadn't cried for years—I had lost the ability. That day I could not stop crying. My husband invited me to come with him to a meeting. I entered Al-Anon crying, and I found people who asked for nothing, not even an explanation. That night I said the three most important words I have ever said, "God help me."

Since the night I asked for help, my life has slowly gotten better. I had never asked anyone for help, but in Al-Anon I got a sponsor and followed her suggestions. Gradually our lives started to change as my husband and I learned to communicate and help each other. Slowly the children are starting to come around again.

Al-Anon does not keep me from all difficulties, but it does give me the strength to deal with them. When our daughter tried to take her life, I became afraid and bitter again, but with help and guidance from my sponsor and with the love of the people in the program, I got through it. When my beloved younger daughter abused drugs and alcohol, I found the strength in Al-Anon to let her go. Today she is clean and sober, has finished school, and is about to get married. Today I have a caring relationship with my husband I didn't think was possible. I hope never to forget the source of my strength, and I will feel blessed indeed if I can give back even a small portion of what God has given me through the Al-Anon program.

I blamed everyone especially myself.

I was born on Christmas day, the oldest in what would become a family of six children. For the first six years of my life, I was an only child and I felt loved—but only if I did the "right" things. I was timid, shy, and very eager to please.

My mother is an adult child of an alcoholic, but to this day she minimizes Grandfather's drinking. Grandfather was a talented carpenter, and he often came to our farm to help with the upkeep of the buildings. Frequently he would get "sick" and wet his pants. I had never heard of anyone getting sick quite like that, but it was my crabby, irritable grandmother that I really resented. After all, everyone said my grandfather was sick and couldn't help himself.

My mother didn't drink, but I think she was a workaholic. She always had a million things that had to be done, and she often sent me to visit my other grandparents. I didn't mind; I loved it. My carefree childhood ended when I was six and the two most tragic events of my young life occurred—my first brother was born and my father took a job that kept him constantly on the road. I was put in charge of my baby brother and eventually all the others as well. By the time I was fourteen, I felt like a mother of five, and I resented it, but I wanted to please everyone too, so I said nothing.

Mother worked compulsively except when Father came home and they went to town. A heavy social drinker, my father didn't get sick like my grandfather, but arguments between my parents sounded eerily familiar. One night I woke up and saw him chasing her around the house. The next morning she had a black eye, and he seemed very remorseful. I blamed my mother for the problem.

I grew up and married an alcoholic and began assuming responsibility for our problems while resenting my burdens. It seems that all my life I have felt ashamed when anything went wrong and have always blamed the mother for family problems caused by the alcoholic. I must have learned this strange assignment of responsibility in my family, for years later when my spouse entered treatment, my mother said to me, "It's a shame you couldn't cure your husband's drinking. I cured your dad's, you know." In the meantime, I suffered a series of health problems that led to several hospitalizations, but no physical causes were ever determined. Neither I nor the doctors connected my problems with stress due to another's alcoholism. Today, after years in Al-Anon, my physical problems are almost all gone.

I entered Al-Anon because of another crisis, one that shattered our family. Our daughter's grades had been dropping rapidly and I had asked the school counselor to do an alcohol evaluation of her. She confided to the counselor that her father had been molesting her during the wee hours of the morning on days when he drank. My husband was arrested, and he voluntarily entered treatment for his alcohol problems. Our daughter became very isolated, refusing even to attend school. Alone with this horrible revelation, I felt confused, lonely, and filled with murderous rage.

In recovery, my husband heard about a three day "Live-in" and suggested I go. What did I have to lose? I was exhausted and could use three days of rest. I had a big surprise in store for me. Instead of rest, they expected me to look at myself, discover my rights, and realize I had needs. For the first two days, I hid in total denial. I didn't have a problem. I blamed my husband for everything. If he got his act together and my daughter straightened up, I would be fine.

My denial broke when they asked me to write a letter to myself. How could I? I had no idea who I was writing to. The floodgates opened and I cried for hours. Rivers of repressed anger, disappointment, and hurt streamed down my cheeks. When I finally got in touch with the real me, I discovered I was no longer alone. There were people I could relate to and Al-Anon meetings to attend.

The First Step was the toughest and most rewarding. I was powerless over alcohol, and everything was not all my fault. The funny thing about blame is that the more we point the finger at others, the more we secretly believe we must really be guilty. I had been blaming myself and holding my breath since childhood. As I began to release responsibility that was not mine and learned to let go and let God, not only did my emotions heal, but my body began to heal as well.

Detachment was tremendously difficult and equally rewarding. Al-Anon members supported me in loving my husband while refusing to accept his unacceptable behavior. The consequences of his behavior were his to experience. Because of the sexual abuse, he had to live away from home for twenty-eight months. During that time, he learned for the first time in his life how to take care of himself, and I learned to let him.

With the use of the Twelve Steps and the slogans, our lives began to change. Today we are living reunited, and both of us are healthier. We enjoy life. We attend weekly meetings and have found a closeness to our Creator. I am tremendously grateful to my Higher Power and am discovering I have God-given talents to use.

Our daughter still suffers, and I hurt when I cannot reach through her isolation. My Al-Anon sponsor helps me to understand her pain and anger without further abusing myself. We know she will probably need therapy as well as recovery and our unconditional love. There are events in life that can never be undone. With the help Al-Anon affords, I hope to be able to accept all of my daughter's feelings when she is ready to share them, and not wound her further by trying to deny her pain in order to protect myself. I couldn't do this without the love and support the fellowship affords. I am also grateful that there are meetings to help our children heal and that if she becomes willing, she can attend Al-Anon adult child focus meetings to heal the wounds of a trauma neither of us would have wished upon her but which my husband did create, and from which I did not manage to protect her. It is very comforting to me to know that no matter where or when she may recognize the need, Al-Anon will be available for our daughter as it is for me.

IT MUST BE MY FAULT

Buried terrors surfaced, bringing healing.

My younger sister, an alcoholic, suffered terrible grief over the death of her only son. He was a victim of a young man's careless driving after an all-night bachelor party. Though she lives eighteen hundred miles away, she burst into my home over the telephone night after night. For three months, I listened to three A.M. calls informing me of her impending suicide. I became scared and began to fear for my own sanity. Thank God, I finally walked through the doors of Al-Anon and got help.

Not too long after joining the program, I began to suspect I might also be an alcoholic. My self diagnosis has proven correct. I moved over to Alcoholics Anonymous, where I began a journey back into my long-forgotten past. It was a rocky journey. I just couldn't seem to grasp the AA program and recover.

Frustrated and desperate, I begged whatever God there is to heal me and my family. I promised myself and my Higher Power that I would faithfully work both the Al-Anon and Alcoholics Anonymous programs if only He would help—and I meant it. In time my Higher Power opened a door into my past that I had locked and bolted when I was very young. I remembered awakening abruptly from sleep as a tiny child to find myself flying up out of my body. My father, who seemed to be in a trance and a state of rage, was raping me.

Innocent child that I was, I told my mother that my daddy hurt me. Both my parents are alcoholics and still living. Though it seems hard to believe possible, my mother is even more violent than my father. Her response to my disclosure of what my daddy did to me was to beat me. She shook me fiercely, screaming with rage, "Don't you ever say that again!" I was terrified and felt utterly alone in a hostile world. I might die. She yanked me around and battered me. Suddenly she turned and picked up a knife and stuck it in my baby sister's shoulder. All I remember is terrible fear, seeing blood, and feeling it was all my fault. Again she switched personalities. She went to her purse and pulled out a nickel and handed it to me saying, "Go to the store like a good girl and buy your-self a chocolate." I ran out frightened and totally confused.

As awful as it was, that horrible memory was the beginning of my recovery. Since then I have had other memories of incest and violence, including the night Dad molested my lit-tle sister as I pretended to sleep, and the guilt and terror I felt the next morning when my mother beat her and called her a whore.

To keep my sanity through these brutal memories and excruciating feelings, I have needed therapy, two Twelve Step programs, and a great deal of help from my Higher Power. I have kept my promise to God and have faithfully attended meetings and worked the Steps of both Al-Anon and AA. God, in return, has given me a voice where once I was voice-less and has provided loving people to hold me as I cry. God is doing for me what I can't do for myself—slowly relieving me of the hatred and bitterness I feel toward my parents.

Even with God's help, many dedicated and loving Al-Anon friends, and an increasing shower of spiritual experiences, the path is sometimes rocky. My parents deny everything and punish me for telling the truth with scorn, ridicule, and by distancing themselves from me. Though I cannot make them love me, I have found the strength to stop further emotional abuse.

I am still nervous and I cry a lot, but I am beginning to want to live, and slowly my heart is mending. Before I came to Al-Anon, I had been labeled at various times catatonic, psychotic, crazy, and worthless. By working the Steps, I am unearthing my past and learning to accept the truth of it. It's no wonder I found life before recovery such a burden that I thought often of suicide. Thanks to Al-Anon, I have my roots, and I am working on my wings.

I was the "queen of contempt."

A good book, good friends, and fear of losing my job brought me to Al-Anon. The crisis that became a blessing began when my fiancé arrived late for a date and proceeded to vomit and pass out on my bathroom floor. Disgusted with him, I turned to a friend and neighbor who happened to be a social worker specializing in children from alcoholic homes. She invited me to join her and her friend for dinner. (We left the wretch passed out on the floor and I didn't mind a bit!) After dinner they guided me to a book about marriage and alcoholism. I read it eagerly, but I wasn't ready to go to Al-Anon. After all, *I* didn't have a problem; *he* did.

The next day, tense and miserable with my private life, I got into a dispute at work and ran out of the place crying. When my supervisor called me at home and gently asked me why I had walked off the job, I fell apart and sobbed out the whole story. He suggested I try Al-Anon. My neighbor had mentioned Al-Anon, the minister I ran to from the job disaster told me about Al-Anon, but I didn't go to Al-Anon until my boss suggested it and I feared I'd lose my job if I didn't.

I don't know what I expected to find at Al-Anon, but I didn't expect so many people. Seeing them, I decided I wasn't going to talk, but I did. The kindness, acceptance, and support from a room full of strangers amazed me. A few people stopped by after the meeting to tell me I couldn't get the alcoholic to stop drinking. I was delighted. At last it wasn't my responsibility. I replied, "He can drink himself to death for all I care." I was so tired of constantly being upset, I couldn't even hear the utter contempt in my voice.

Little did I know I was starting a journey that would take me to places I never imagined. As a big-hearted gesture to my fiancé, whose mother was an alcoholic, I decided to read a chapter from the book my neighbor had given me about what happens to the children of alcoholic families. I thought by reading it I might get a better understanding of my fiancé. It was spooky! The chapter wasn't about him; it was about me. Those pages so clearly revealed my life that it felt as if someone had hidden a camera in our house.

I had thought my father couldn't be an alcoholic because he always held a job. Mother certainly nagged him; she was always saying, "Stop making the drinks so strong. Not everybody likes drinks the way you do." Then I remembered how I used to call my father a happy drunk. Every night he'd have his highballs sitting in front of the TV and fall asleep. That was it. He didn't get violent or angry, but he was unavailable and uninvolved. His body was there, but he wasn't really there—just like the men I chose. What a jolt!

When I joined Al-Anon, I made myself really unpopular in my family. I thought it was hallelujah time. Now we knew what was wrong and could fix it. So I told them what they needed to fix, and they told me what a horrible person I was for even suggesting that Dad was an alcoholic. At least I had learned enough in meetings to continue my program in spite of (perhaps to spite?) them.

About three months into recovery, I went through my most painful and embarrassing Al-Anon realization. Part of my misery was caused by *me*. I had thought all of it would disappear if only my family and fiancé would get themselves

straightened out. It was wrenching to admit that my own martyrdom had the makings of a film spectacular. Slowly I would
climb the grand staircase to my pity throne, singing out my
suffering, my dress trailing a fifty-foot train of grief, while
enjoying every minute of it. And I wondered why people
sometimes found me hard to be around. That moment of awful
awareness was a turning point in my recovery. From then on I
put the focus on me and what I could do to heal myself.

I didn't marry my fiancé. He joined AA for a while but kept
leaving it, and I kept leaving him. I never understood how
much contempt I had for him until a couple of years after we
split for good. I had learned contempt from my mother, who
sneered at my father, "I had only *one* drink; I don't *need* any
more than that!" but I practiced it well myself. I let my fiancé
know how many meetings I attended, and I counted his. I
rejected his sexual advances. I confused detachment with
lording my "better" program over him. The queen of contempt
was busy ascending her martyr's throne. I'd said it at the first
meeting: I didn't care if he drank himself to death. I didn't
care if he died. My God, I was cruel.

I am ashamed of my behavior, but I don't know where he is
so I can't make amends. Every once in a while, I say a prayer
for him and ask my Higher Power to forgive me. I try to accept
myself and understand that my anger and contempt are as
much a part of the disease as is his drinking.

Of course, I didn't always know I had anger. This disease
is very crafty. I have had to eat many a word I have said.
Fortunately, loving members just sprinkle them with a little
sugar to help the medicine go down. Once I announced to my
group, "I can identify with every emotion here except anger.
I don't feel anger. Anger is one feeling I don't have." Maybe
not, but I was taking anti-depressants and fighting frequent

thoughts of suicide. It is no exaggeration that I might be dead today without Al-Anon. My anger was stuffed so deep inside that I hadn't a clue, until one day in a meeting tears suddenly filled my eyes, and I furiously demanded of the group, "How could God have let that happen to me? I was just a baby!"

Recently I moved and in the process I got a picture of myself as I had been before. As I unpacked I threw on some old records I hadn't heard in years. The lyrics were furious. The music I had loved was the music of rage. Today, as my anger melts, it seems like a curio in my past.

The love of my Higher Power came slowly too. I told that same group, "I can accept every part of this program except the spiritual part. I don't believe in it. As far as I'm concerned, you can keep your spirituality." They smiled and said to keep coming back and the spirituality would come to me. I answered, it would have to come, because I certainly wasn't going to look for it. It came.

Self-pity masked shame and guilt.

My mother abused alcohol. I believe my parents stayed together for the children's sake, but they were both so focused on their own problems that they were emotionally unavailable to us in spite of their good intentions. We all denied Mom's alcoholism and rejected my sister when she tried to tell us about hidden bottles under the kitchen sink.

When Mom got drunk, she sometimes confided in me all her unhappiness at being married to Dad. I resented being placed between them and especially hated it because that was the only time she confided in me.

My brother and sister were basically the good children. I

felt that I was the bad one. I lied, hit others, stole, cried, complained, and whined a lot. From a very early age, I obsessed
about sex. I realize now that all my friends came from troubled and alcoholic homes, and my male friends were addicts
and alcoholics. We attracted each other like magnets.

I desperately longed for love and attention, and I thought
sex was the way to get it. I got involved with an older boy, who,
I thought, would reject and abandon me if I didn't give him
what he wanted. I didn't know anything about choices then.
At sixteen, pregnant and unwed, I was secretly packed off by
my scandalized family to a home for unwed mothers.
Ashamed and guilty, I felt I had to give up my beautiful baby
boy for adoption. Through the whole ordeal, no one asked me
about my feelings; therefore, I stuffed them deep inside to
protect myself from further pain.

When I returned home, it seemed that family problems
were now entirely focused on me. My family watched what I
did, who I saw, and worried that I'd end up pregnant again.
To escape, I married an alcoholic who was also an adult
child of an alcoholic. The last few years of our eight-year
marriage were filled with crisis, chaos, and violence on both
our parts.

Feeling very sorry for myself gave me plenty of justification
for my own irrational behavior. I spent money recklessly,
engaged in numerous affairs, lived in fantasy, abused pills
prescribed for depression, and attempted suicide. I was emotionally immature and hid behind any handy mask I could
find. I thought if anyone knew who I really was, they wouldn't
like me, let alone love me.

Several years after my divorce, I married my present husband. I actually believed him when he told me he drank
because he was lonely, and I thought I could wipe out his

loneliness with lots of love, devotion, and control. I didn't cure his loneliness, but he did manage to get himself into an alcoholism treatment center. Thank God they encouraged me to go to Al-Anon.

I made a commitment to the recommended six meetings and was hooked. No doubt about it; my life was totally unmanageable. I wanted what all those smiling, cheerful people had, and I was willing to go to any length to get it. In those meetings, I discovered I was powerless over people, places, and things, but I was not hopeless. I finally found hope.

I began to understand what an unhealthy way of life I had chosen. I realized how I had become sick through the family disease of alcoholism. I discovered how I had used and abused sex to avoid closeness, love, and emotional intimacy, to prove my attractiveness, and to control others. In fact, I was the one controlled by shame, loneliness, fear, and denial of feelings.

Today I have learned to love and respect myself and others. I can love unconditionally, and I no longer equate love with pain. I am able to experience an intimate, trusting relationship with my husband, a recovering member of Alcoholics Anonymous. I am grateful for his patience, love, tolerance, and understanding. Thanks to doors opened by Al-Anon, he is my best friend.

I am very thankful for Al-Anon because it has opened up my life to wellness. I feel that sponsorship is an extra special Al-Anon benefit. With a sponsor we learn how to love. We learn that acceptance, understanding, giving, and receiving must be a two-way street. Though many of us lost the ability to trust or even to relate during our alcohol-drenched childhoods, we can regain these vital skills by relating to a sponsor. We cannot do it alone because the betrayals and losses occurred with people and we need people to help us heal. I am eternally grateful for the great healing of my relationships that Al-Anon has assisted, and I stay involved in service work because I want to give to others what has so generously been given to me.

Suggestions for Recognizing and Breaking Denial

We who grew up with alcoholism have lived in a world of denial for so long that distinguishing normal stress from the effects of the disease can seem quite impossible. We wonder if we have problems that are different from those other people have. Doesn't everyone feel insecure or experience crisis? Denial is largely an unconscious process in which knowledge of the impact of what is really going on is gradually suppressed until consciousness of it is lost entirely. Denial and confusion become intertwined, and family denial increases the confusion. We may mistake healthy self-esteem for selfishness or wonder if life in our families was "really that bad" (since everyone else insists it wasn't).

Some of us found our way into Al-Anon when the alcoholic in our life joined AA. Some of us stood alone, the only one who suspected anything was wrong, while other family members became incensed that we even contemplated going to Al-Anon. We came because therapists sent us or we read a book and decided to try it. How do we know if we belong if we're not sure? Al-Anon is a fellowship of people who feel uncomfortable about another person's drinking. We are people living with sober alcoholics, people living with active drinking in their homes, friends of people who seem to have problems with drinking, and people who have severed all relationships with alcoholics or drinkers of any sort. We are a varied lot.

Recovery can begin when we recognize that someone else's drinking has affected us. How can we tell? We have found that the answers to the following questions [2] helped us decide if we grew up with or live with alcoholism, and they may help you.

1. Do you constantly seek approval and affirmation?

2. Do you fail to recognize or believe your accomplishments?

3. Do you fear criticism?

4. Do you overextend yourself?

5. Have you had problems with your own compulsive behavior?

6. Do you have a need for perfection?

7. Are you uneasy when your life is going smoothly, continually anticipating problems?

8. Do you feel more alive in the midst of a crisis?

9. Do you still feel responsible for others, as you did for the problem drinker in your life?

10. Do you care for others easily, yet find it difficult to care for yourself?

11. Do you isolate yourself from other people?

12. Do you respond with anxiety or hostility to authority figures and angry people?

13. Do you feel that individuals and society in general are taking advantage of you?

---

2. "Did you grow up with a problem drinker?"©Al-Anon Family Group Headquarters, Inc., 1984.

14. Do you have trouble with intimate relationships?

15. Do you confuse pity with love, as you did with the problem drinker?

16. Do you attract and seek people who tend to be compulsive?

17. Do you cling to relationships because you are afraid of being alone?

18. Do you often mistrust your own feelings and the feelings expressed by others?

19. Do you find it difficult to express your emotions?

20. Are you attracted to people who have lots of problems you can fix?

If you answered "yes" to some or all of the above questions, Al-Anon may also help you. We have found that the disease of alcoholism disrupted our youth and continues to affect our adult lives in both subtle and blatant ways. Because of the disease, our parents were unable to give us what we needed as children in order to fully mature. Our lack of emotional grounding sometimes takes the disguise of excessive responsibility. We can appear extremely mature and serious, while in reality we lack confidence and feel driven.

The fear that accompanies the disease of alcoholism creates difficulty in talking about our problems, trusting ourselves or others, and feeling our authentic emotions. Not talking, not trusting, or not feeling helped us survive as children, but those things keep us stuck as adults in patterns that do not work. As long as we are caught in childhood patterns of relating that were learned in alcoholic homes, we will achieve the same unhappy results.

Repeating behaviors while expecting different consequences is one form of insanity we learn to stop in Al-Anon.
Before a behavior can be stopped, it must be recognized, and
this requires breaking the denial that we have rigged around
those unhappy years to keep our secrets hidden from ourselves. Denial is broken when we quit hoping for a better past,
accept the reality of that past, and set about creating a different present. In Al-Anon we learn alternate approaches to
our old problems. As we attempt to change, we are encouraged to grow at our own pace and use the suggestions that
work for us—thus self-responsibility and individualism,
important aspects of maturing, are developed.

Grieving our losses is painful and sad, but we find comfort
in the fellowship. Discovering buried anger and fear can
frighten us, but we find en*courage*ment. Detaching can feel as
if we are abandoning or being abandoned, but we have new
support. As we attend Al-Anon meetings we make new
friends and find kindness and unconditional love. Working
the Twelve Steps opens us to spirituality and teaches us to
love instead of enable. Breaking denial is worth the price. In
Al-Anon we learn to empower our true selves and discover
that we are no longer alone.

Understanding alcoholism as a disease allows us to take it
out of the realm of blame and shame, freeing us to see our
own mistakes. Eventually, as we discover what a marvelous
pattern for living the Twelve Steps afford, we develop gratitude for the spiritual gifts of recovery.

When some of us heard we would become grateful for alcoholism, we were sure the members of our group were indeed
crazy. Today we are aware that although we might not actually be grateful for alcoholism, we are indeed thankful for having discovered the world of healing and wholeness that

Al-Anon offers. We do not claim that working an Al-Anon program has eliminated challenges and problems, but we have found effective new ways to handle them. And living serenely in the midst of life's challenges is a spiritual gift we would like to share.

I'm responsible.

Ten years ago I found myself at an Al-Anon meeting. I remember feeling scared, lonely, confused, hurt, angry, stifled, hopeless, helpless, and miserable! Still, I didn't know why I was at this meeting. What could these people do for me? I had no consciousness at the time that the alcoholism of my childhood home was still affecting my life. I had gone merely to humor a co-worker.

In the months preceding my first meeting, I knew unceasing dullness and solitude. I felt unbounded anger and pain and was beaten down, totally desperate, and frighteningly alone. Shortly after my daughter was born, my mother died and my husband's company folded. In our desperation, we picked at each other until every scrap of love and trust were destroyed. My co-worker listened sympathetically to my tales of woe and eventually suggested Al-Anon. I was divorced and living with my infant daughter at the time, but I didn't want to go.

I denied. I argued. I refused. I said, "Yes, but . . ." I ran away. I cried. I ranted and raved. I ignored. And I kept hurting. One day my friend said something that shook me to the core. He had listened, supported, nurtured, and been patient. He had watched my turmoil for a very long time, while I made no attempt to find help in the fellowship. Finally, as if washing his hands of me, he said, "Well, you must be getting something out of this. There's something in you that needs the sick satisfaction you get out of all the misery you're putting yourself through."

Imagine that! Putting *myself* through! How dare he say such a thing! I'd fix him! I'd go to his stupid Al-Anon meeting and prove him wrong. Instead, I got the jolt of a lifetime. Doors opened. Many things—in fact, *everything*—changed. Best of all, *I* changed.

I was too angry to understand much of what I heard at that first meeting, but one member suggested I try it for three months. She said if I wanted to leave after that, they would gladly give me back my misery. It's been ten difficult but rewarding years since that meeting, and I don't ever intend to take my misery back. Because of Al-Anon I have been able to walk through the tough times in my life. Most times things or events in my life don't change; I simply learn to handle them better. I have had to learn to stand up for myself. It was extremely difficult, but my self-esteem has skyrocketed as a result.

One of the most important things I have learned is that I don't know it all. The comforting truth today is that I don't have to, and I don't have to figure it all out alone. Day by day I work with my sponsor, or a reading, or I turn things over to my Higher Power. I always get what I need. Often, I have re-read something and have seen an entirely new idea. I scratch my head and wonder where those words were the last time I read it.

Today my eyes fill with tears as I try to find words for what Al-Anon has given me. There is a wonderful, classic children's story in which the author describes "realness" as something that only comes after you have been through a

great deal, become rumpled, and even worn bare from having
so much "loved off" of you. "Real" was something you had to
become, but once you became real, you could never be unreal
again. I feel that this is what Al-Anon is doing for me.
Through the rigor and honesty of the program, the care and
love of many members, and guidance from my Higher Power,
I am learning what it is to be thoroughly loved, and each day
I become a little more real.

part Two

BEGINNING TO RECOVER

SO WE'RE NOT PERFECT

AFTER ALL?

A long-time Al-Anon member recalled that one of his most valuable insights was the realization that "hurt people hurt people." This pithy statement helps explain how people who love each other can, nevertheless, unwittingly continue the destructive cycle of negative attitudes and abusive behavior even when they fervently desire to act differently. People who have been hurt or are hurting naturally try to get rid of the pain. In doing so, they frequently repeat what was done to them or fiercely try to do just the opposite, and, in the process, they hurt others. Unless recovery is found, blame, guilt, anger, depression, and many other negative attitudes can go on for generations in a family affected by alcoholism.

Individuals who do not obtain help for themselves will continue to suffer from their emotional wounds and will hurt others because they simply don't know how *not* to. As we become aware of these dangers, however, we can learn to protect ourselves and take care of ourselves, and, as we heal, we will hurt others less. Already overburdened with taking too much responsibility for other people, we may resist the suggestion that we focus on ourselves because it seems we will have to add ourselves to the mountain of problems we're already carrying. Nevertheless, we in Al-Anon have found that assuming responsibility for our own actions and our own happiness is the essential beginning of our recovery from the painful experiences of growing up with alcoholism. Focusing on ourselves actually allows us to release other people to solve their own problems and frees us to find contentment and even happiness for ourselves.

In Al-Anon we learn to replace negative thinking and behavior with positive alternatives, but it can be very tricky to do so without blaming ourselves or others for the pain we have experienced. We do not deny that we are wounded. We acknowledge our hurts, and the source of them, but we don't stay stuck in our anger or blame. The journey to recovery from the effects of alcoholism in the family may be longer and slower than we would wish, but many Al-Anon members have gone before us and have found paths that worked for them and can work for us. It is a nurturing, self-affirming, often rigorous journey we undertake together, sharing as honestly and lovingly as we can.

In Al-Anon we believe we are helped and guided in our journey toward serenity by a Power greater than ourselves. We do not define this Power, but we do share our experience of it with each other. We also share our common human experience, strength, and hope as we learn different ways to relate. In the beginning, some people found that the group worked as a Power greater than themselves, while others developed a God of their understanding.

As we admit that our lives and our families aren't perfect after all, we suspect that our present difficulties might stem from having grown up with problem drinkers. We look at our lives and decide, "This misery has got to stop!" We may be eager to change everything and everyone around us, but how? If we knew how, wouldn't we have done it already?

One of the results of growing up in a family where alcoholism dominated is that some of us have learned to believe we are helpless. We often feel a sense of futility even when we appear outwardly successful. Confused and suspicious, we've already tried every scheme and technique we knew for living happily, but have had little success.

Some of us have tried to hide from the terrible, haunting emotions we felt in our homes by studiously avoiding anything emotional. We've become quite intellectual, and we can analyze everything and everybody. Still, our relationships don't work, and prolonged analysis gets us nowhere. Alcoholism affects alcoholics and all those close to them emotionally, physically, and spiritually. Healing all aspects of ourselves is necessary for recovery.

Sometimes we feel sadly discouraged with our efforts to recover and are paralyzed by fear. Even beginning to try seems monumental. We want to do everything—including recovery—perfectly, but even taking the first step is difficult. Where should we begin? It is useful to remember that any kind of growth process, from learning to walk to learning how to be fully functioning adults, is progressive and is rarely, if ever, done to perfection. Stumbling ahead even one awkward step beats staying stuck. By taking small steps, we can lessen our fears and learn that no situation is truly hopeless, that we are not actually helpless, and that no pain is too great to be lessened.

Because we have varied needs, in Al-Anon we are encouraged to take what we can use from each other's ideas and leave the rest behind. No two people will work the program in exactly the same way. Newcomers often ask, "What should I do? How does Al-Anon work?" Most of us cannot answer the "How?" question without a lengthy discussion that might not be accurate anyway, since the process is unique for each individual. What each of us has learned has come largely through personal experience that must be felt to be understood; thus we encourage newcomers simply to come to meetings and see for themselves. This can be very frustrating for a newcomer because the message requires some trust—a commodity those from alcoholic families have in very short supply. But trust grows through the small acts of kindness from one another that we find in abundance in Al-Anon when we allow ourselves the time to receive them. Coming to Al-Anon without expectation or commitment in the beginning allows trust to build slowly and allows identification with other members to develop naturally.

Still, it is natural for us to ask what we should do. "Work the Steps," someone may say, or "Get a sponsor." Read pamphlets and books; volunteer to make coffee or put chairs away; talk to people. All of these suggestions are practical ways to get started. There is no single right path to recovery, nor is there an absolutely wrong way.

A variety of alternatives can feel very uncomfortable for newcomers who have lived with chaos, confusion, and with families that shifted directions in the middle of promised commitments. Many of our young lives were steeped in unpredictability and uncertainty. We want a road map. *Now!* What follows is *a* road map, *one* way to begin recovery. Some people will want the scenic route, others the straight and narrow. Feel free to tailor the path to your own needs and pace. All roads can lead to recovery if we walk them diligently. Whether you are sure or not, if you've gotten this far, you know enough to begin. Easy does it, but *do* it.

Chapter one

MEETINGS AS A LIFELINE

"There must be something terribly wrong with me" is a secret thought many of us harbor in the recesses of our minds. We suspect that we are flawed or sinful to feel so uncomfortable with ourselves and the world. Too often in our troubled families, if recovery has not altered the well-worn patterns, we will find confirmation of our worst fears. If we dare to admit any need or feeling of inadequacy, the finger is pointed and we hear, "You, You, You! The trouble with you is . . . The trouble with me is *you!*" Caught in the snares of the "blame game," even if we secretly suspect that all the trouble *is* us, we don't ever want to admit it to anyone. Then we could *really* be in trouble!

Under these circumstances, attending our first Al-Anon meeting may take an act of monumental courage. Sometimes we find that courage in desperation. We hope we will learn there how to control another person or situation we can't tolerate another minute. Sometimes we are gently guided to a meeting by a friend or counselor who sees our pain. Some of us sneak in under the guise of "researching" a problem "for a friend." Others of us read a book and decide Al-Anon is worth a try. We are almost all afraid that we will be accused, blamed, fixed, advised, or otherwise confirmed in our nagging suspicion that we are not O.K.

Attending meetings is a good way to start recovering even if we doubt that Al-Anon can help. In Al-Anon meetings, we hear many people grapple with life's often unfair demands. Because they are not pointing the finger at us, we can see our own characteristics revealed in other people as they tell their own stories. The honesty of fellow members who have struggled with the same doubts and hurts that we have inspires us gently to admit what we have been trying to deny. We were and are affected by the illness in our families. We have not escaped even though we have tried mightily.

If we attend enough different meetings or the same meeting often enough, we may hear parts of our own story in the sharing of others. We will find that although we are invited to share, we do not have to. No one judges us and says, "You, You, You, the trouble with you is . . ." We are not told what to do; we aren't criticized for how we feel. Not being barraged with advice may feel strange and uncomfortable, but it helps create a safe place. We learn that the best way to find out if Al-Anon can help us live richer, fuller, happier lives is simply to come, keep an open mind, and listen.

READING AND MEETINGS OPENED THE DOORS TO OUR HEARTS

I feared abandonment.

My father died when I was a year old, and my mother remarried by the time I was three. Both my mother and my stepfather are children of alcoholics. Today I can see that they too suffer from the terrible effects their parents' disease had on their lives. Until I joined Al-Anon, I struggled with continuing patterns of abandonment, abuse, and a pervasive feeling that I was not good enough.

My earliest memories are of my angry stepfather. I tried to escape his anger by being very good, not causing any problems, and dreaming of what life would have been like if my real father had lived. I was convinced that it would have been much better. My stepfather was utterly unpredictable. Sometimes he was loving, but he could change in a split second into a screaming monster. He frequently lost things and flew into a rage. He demanded absolute quiet while he watched television and yelled if I made a peep. I believed I had done something wrong.

When mother had a heart attack, I was catapulted into the role of family caretaker. Home felt like a quicksand bog ever pulling me under. I stayed afloat by compulsively cleaning the house, taking care of my sisters, and being an A student.

Fear of abandonment controlled all my actions. I thought that if I didn't keep things together and control the chaos, Mom and Dad would be mad, and might leave me. In my mind and my fearful little heart, I believed I had to take care of everyone so they would need me and I would be worthy of their love.

Yet no matter what I did, Dad still got angry and came after me. I hid in the closet. I ran down the street to a friend. Sometimes he yanked me out of bed at three A.M. to be punished again over a transgression for which I had already suffered. It must be me, I thought. There must be something terribly wrong with me.

My parents' messages were confusing. It seemed they were saying, "I love you/Go away!" or "I need you/You're a bitch." or "If it weren't for you, I'd have a good life." From them I learned three things about myself: I am nothing, but I am all powerful; I can fix anything if only I do it faster, harder, better; I'm the problem, but everyone depends on me.

I chose friends—alcoholics and people with unpredictable, hot and cold behavior—who mirrored back to me my feelings of worthlessness. When they didn't like me or treat me well, I again wondered what was wrong with me.

Six years ago, when my relationship with a sober alcoholic became unbearable, I tried Al-Anon. Though I felt a degree of peace after my first meeting, I had difficulty making a commitment to anything. When I shared my concern with an Al-Anon member, he told me to just keep coming back. I'm so glad I did, for wonderful changes have happened in my life simply through regular attendance at meetings.

Al-Anon meetings are an unending source of love, support, and recovery. I always hear something that I can identify with and use in my life. I have heard others share memories that triggered buried memories of my own.

In meetings I found a sponsor who walked a few steps ahead of me on the recovery path, lighting my way. As she listened to me and validated my feelings, I began to learn to trust. She taught me to do things differently, a little at a time. At last I had my very first relationship in which I felt unconditionally loved and accepted.

I had no formal religious training or concept of God or a Higher Power. I only knew that if there was a God, He didn't care about me and wouldn't help me. He never had before. In meetings, I met friends who suggested I act as if I believed, just to see what would happen. I did, and it was the beginning of my trust in a Power greater than myself. That trust was truly as small as a mustard seed. It has grown large enough to fill the great spiritual void I had felt most of my life. Every time I have cried out in pain, God's love and guidance have appeared to carry me through the pain to the other side and have nourished me until my trust returned.

My trust has been tested through the deaths of several people I loved. With each death, I slipped into crisis and doubt. I fell into a black hole. Even from that dark hole, God pulled me out when I was ready to let go and trust. With a relationship with a God of my understanding that I never imagined in my dreams, I no longer fear abandonment. With meetings, friends, a sponsor, and my Higher Power, I am no longer alone.

I listened carefully.

One of the first gifts I gained from Al-Anon was the ability to name feelings. Going to meetings, I heard others talk about the variety of feelings they experienced, and I tried to identify more clearly my own feelings. The sinking feeling in the pit of my stomach was fear. The lead weight on my chest some mornings I recognized as dread. I learned that fear and dread were not omens but feelings, and they would pass. When I woke each morning, I noticed what I was feeling. If I said, "Oh, yes. Hello, fear. I know you," the fear dissolved. Feelings came and went. I became able to distinguish the anguish of morning dread from other feelings such as discontent, frustration, or annoyance. Continued attendance at Al-Anon gave me hope and the strength to reach out for good feelings. I feel contentment gazing at the sun-dappled sidewalk under my favorite tree. Remembering summers with my Grandma in her garden evokes tenderness. Listening to bird twitters brings me gaiety. Joy, peace, contentment, calm—I now know and choose these feelings.

From listening at Al-Anon meetings, I learned to listen closely to people and hear what they were actually saying. I was able to listen to what my husband was really saying in the middle of an argument or when he called, long after dinner had been served to say he'd miss dinner.

I grew up with a screaming mother. She cursed blasphemously and colorfully until I was about eleven. Then Mother got religion and stopped cursing. She still screamed, belittled, found fault, ignored, scorned, and shamed. She did it sober. Dad was the drinker who had to have his pitcher of martinis in the freezer when he got home from work, but I thought he was the sweet one who loved me. He left for work hours before I got up, came home late, and rarely spoke, but when he spoke, I remembered it was with smiles, nice words, and gifts.

I remembered wrongly. Daddy actually claimed the post of arbiter in the family. A harsh judge, he dictated how we should treat Mother and how we should speak to her. He decided what we could do, often being shocked at what we did do.

Recently I phoned him and asked him to help me understand my second divorce—the bad divorce—the one with the three children, the fancy house, the executive husband. He told me I was only one of his four children. He had three others. He had his own life, his own bad marriage, his own poor health, his own problems.

It hurt, hearing that, but I listened. What I heard gave me some more recovery because I heard Daddy talk to me the way my fancy, executive husband talked to me. I heard Daddy shooting to kill emotionally, just the way Mother had. I heard myself asking for something and not only being refused, but also being put down and ridiculed for asking. I heard and I cried. I sobbed, but I didn't curl up and die. I didn't feel that cold lump in the center of myself that said I was wrong. Instead, I felt relief after crying. Now I understand why I picked selfish, empty, unavailable men to love. My "sweet"

Daddy was absorbed in his own pain, and I was alone outside the pain. I don't have to hate him; I can "live and let live," because through Al-Anon I have learned to live and to feel all the shadows and sunlight of emotions, and life is good.

Saying it aloud helped me.

Mother, I'm eleven and every day I wait after school for you to come. You said to wait, so I wait and wait and wait. The other kids have left. I stand with my head down. I don't want to see the way they look at me. They know I don't deserve your love. Where are you? Probably at the Friendly Tavern. You finally show up. You're mad. You'd probably rather be with your friends drinking beer. I'm so much trouble for you. I'm sorry.

We go to the beer joint. You order beer and get mad when I order a soft drink. I'm sorry, Mother. A man buys you a beer and asks if he can dance with me. I hate this! As usual you say, "Yes, but don't hold my baby too tight." But you're too drunk to see how tight he holds me or where he puts his hands. I don't tell anyone.

I wait for you. A man comes and says, "Your mom sent me." I get in his car and try to be invisible. That night you and Daddy fight. He's mad because a stranger picked me up. He says, "That man could have done anything to her!" You say, "Oh, he's all right. I've seen him around the bar a couple of times." Now I've made Daddy mad. I'm sorry.

You and Daddy divorce. I'm twelve. You remarry. I don't like him! He wants you all to himself. He says, "I wish you didn't have kids," and you say, "I know, I know, but I'm their mother." I wish you weren't my mother.

Daddy, I'm thirteen and you get married again. You say, "Come live with us." She seems nice. She has four kids, and her house smells like good things cooking. She cooks and cleans. Mother drinks and parties, so I don't always know when I'll have something to eat. I move in with you. Then you start making those early-morning-while-everyone's-sleeping visits to my bedroom. I don't dare tell anyone.

I'm fourteen and in *love!* You're sixteen. You quit school and have a job. You're nice to me and tell me you love me and want to marry me. I picture a house with a little, white picket fence and someone to love me. I tell Mother at Christmas. She says she got married at fifteen and if we'll wait till I'm fifteen, she'll sign for us to marry. I'm so happy! That's only three months away. I come back and tell you the good news, and . . . I think I'm pregnant. I'm so excited that I don't see you're not happy. I don't hear from you for two weeks, and a friend tells me you've moved away. My heart breaks. I'm not pregnant after all. I don't know if I'm sad or glad. I don't tell anyone.

I'm twenty-five. I've found a man I thought I could love. We've been married five years. We have a son. I'm tired all the time. You spend your time and money in bars and on other women. You yell at me for not earning enough to pay the mortgage and buy food. We fight every night. I know it's my fault. I'm sorry. My friends say, "Leave him! You don't have to put up with this!" I don't? It's all I know how to do, but I don't tell anyone.

You leave me. There are parties. There are men. I feel empty, hollowed out. I need help, but I don't know *how* to tell anyone.

I'm thirty-five and married again for two years. I stand by his grave feeling numb. He drank himself to death. I enabled him. I don't feel anything except relief. I *can't* tell anyone!

I'm forty-four. I've been recovering for four years in Al-Anon meetings for adult children of alcoholics. With your

help, I now own my past. I live in the present with a God of
my understanding, and I face the future without fear. I tell
you about the pain. I tell you about the anger. I tell you about
my shame. I tell you my secrets. With each telling, I heal. I
tell and tell and tell, and I'm not sorry. I'm grateful! You
accept me as I am, and I find the hollowed-out places fill up
with love. With each telling, my heart mends and I begin to
want to live again.

Sharing unveiled forgotten secrets.

I'll never forget that moment. I was sitting in a family therapy session at my sister's drug and alcohol treatment center
and the therapist turned to me and said, "Everyone else has
shared and you've been quiet, but it looks like you're in a lot
of pain."

"Me?" I asked, surprised.

I had been so wrapped up in everybody else's problems
that I had no time to look at my own pain. I was hurting a lot,
yet I felt nothing. I had numbed away all my feelings except
fear, guilt, and sadness. Happiness? Never. My mother
always said that only stupid people were happy.

When I first started attending Al-Anon meetings, I hated
myself and felt as if I had a black X slashed through my
soul. I felt guilty that my younger sister was an alcoholic and
addict. When I first heard the phrase, "you didn't cause it,
you can't cure it, and you can't control it," tremendous relief
flooded me. These "Three C's" were my first awareness that
someone else's disease and behavior were not my responsibility. Until then, I believed that her addiction was somehow
my fault, and my being a straight A student or popular and
pretty were more liabilities than assets. In my alcoholic
family, people took responsibility for everyone else but

themselves, and blame was always shifted.

The burden I had unconsciously carried began to lift. Next came the realization that my mother is an alcoholic and, more importantly, that I have been emotionally dependent on her for approval. I thought something was wrong with me that no matter what I did, I could not win her love. My sponsor suggested I detach from my mother and seek love within myself and from a Power greater than myself. At first it was difficult, but slowly I learned to stop turning to sick people for the unconditional love only a Higher Power can unstintingly provide. Filled with such love and learning to love myself, I feel less angry at Mom and am far less angry at myself.

The next awakening for me was with my alcoholic father. I sensed something was hidden between us. Eventually, when I was strong enough, I learned what it was. My father had sexually abused me. Facing this hardest truth of all finally set me free. Sexual abuse and my buried shame about it had created my self-hatred. With the support of Al-Anon friends and the Twelve Steps, I was able to face the horror of the memories, and the silent anguish I had carried for so many years began to melt.

Liking myself more has meant letting go of someone close to me. I can no longer live with my husband, who doesn't treat me with love, respect, or dignity.

Before I attended Al-Anon meetings, I was so numb I could hardly smell, feel, or hear. Today I am alive with sounds, aromas, and bodily sensations. I recognize and accept specific likes. Even my sixth sense—my intuition—gets stronger the more I rely on my Higher Power.

As crazy as it sounds, I am truly grateful that I grew up in an alcoholic family. Because of it I found Al-Anon and an exciting, adventurous life. I don't regret the past, because I am turning my painful history into today's blessings and strengths.

All I knew was bitterness.

Growing up in an alcoholic home devastated me far more than I knew. By the time I found Al-Anon, I was consumed with rage, resentment, and bitterness. I didn't trust a single human being, let alone a Higher Power. Fear had become my constant companion, and I teetered on the brink of suicide. One day, in a moment of desperation, I started to smash things. My brother and sister stood crying on the stairs. "My God," I thought, "I'm doing the same things to them that were done to me." Finally willing to go for help, I still resisted Al-Anon because I thought they taught you to be kind to alcoholics and I hated alcoholics! Nevertheless, desperation won the day and I went.

In my first meeting, I listened, amazed, as people shared their experiences of living with an alcoholic. Though my husband still drank, my thoughts kept returning to my childhood. Our family of thirteen children had suffered most of the abuses that accompany alcoholism, but I had never tied all those incidents to alcohol. In our coal mining town everyone drank!

Still suspicious and furious, I gave the group four weeks to cure me. I disliked the chairperson and let her know she couldn't tell me what to do. The only one in the room who made any sense to me was a young man who said he felt anger and hate. I thought he was the most normal person there. Because of him I came back the next week. That was fourteen years ago.

I was a tough case. When I heard some of the methods of detachment, I decided I could use them to "psych out" my husband, so I came back for more. Whenever a Higher Power was mentioned, I closed my mind.

It took a long time to melt my bitterness and defiance. I started noticing that the happiest people seemed to have a

Higher Power, but I didn't want happiness at that cost. I had decided many years before that God, who had never rescued me, had no place in my life, if in fact God existed at all. One day the Alateens came to our meeting and led me out of my self-imposed prison. I was "stuck" being nice to the Alateens, and the topic was Higher Power. As I listened to those young people express their deep belief in a God of their understanding, I was impressed. They literally took me by the hand and introduced me to God, and I'll be grateful forever!

With the gentle guidance of my Higher Power and conscientious application of the Twelve Steps, I have recovered scenes from my childhood and the more important part—my childish judgments, assessments, and feelings as I experienced the agony of life in an alcoholic home. I would like to share a few of these memory flashes with you, for I have learned that sharing my past drains the bitterness from my broken heart and floods the empty space with understanding and compassion for the child I was and for all of us who have suffered from the family disease of alcoholism.

I remember two people holding my drunken father against the door. Mother is crying. I kneel at her feet crying. My father, through clenched teeth, orders me to bed. I am terrified, but I won't go to bed. I know I must stay in control at all costs.

Who is this man? Why doesn't my mother do something? Why is she letting him get away with this? Why doesn't he grow up? He never looks at me except to scold. I hate him! He's always getting drunk and causing trouble. Why doesn't she leave him? I can take care of everybody. Someday . . .

My mother reads a story. My older sister and I sit peacefully on her lap, enthralled. Why can't life be like a storybook? When I am old enough, I am going to read all the books I can.

I watch a new baby arrive every year. I watch my mother dying by inches. I watch my father drinking. Cursing the new baby. Drinking. Cursing. I am helpless and angry!

It's my birthday and I don't know it. My cousin sends me a gift. Mother is angry. She wasn't going to tell me, as there was no money. I wish my cousin hadn't sent the present. I am always wrong. I wish my mother would notice me.

I am seven years old and have to take the younger ones swimming. The baby keeps crying, but I want to swim. When I pick her up, her diaper is full of blood. She has been sitting on a broken bottle. I feel terrible. Why didn't I pick her up sooner? I am selfish and horrible.

My new bathing suit is so pretty. I want to go swimming, but I have to take my little sister and I am afraid to make another mistake. I throw the bathing suit under the cupboard.

My teachers all say I'm smart. They don't really know how stupid I am. I hope they never find out.

My mother has been sick since the baby was born. The baby is only three weeks old. She has been crying, so I take her to bed with me. I call my sister to see how Mom is. "She's dying; do you want to come to the hospital?"

"I can't," I say, "because the baby is crying." Back in bed I shake. The whole bed shakes. I can't stop. I am a coward.

My mother is dead, and I have to help my father pick out the casket. He can't do anything. I ask God to help me not blame him. It doesn't work. He's drunk all the time. Right in front of them, he threatens to put my little brothers and sisters in a home. He particularly hates my brother who is mentally handicapped. One day he throws him against the wall. I run up the stairs, pick him up, and say, "If you ever touch him again, I'll kill you." Now my father will know he's not dealing with Mom any more.

"Come over quick!" a neighbor calls, "There's something

wrong with your father." I figure he's drunk again, but I go. He's dead. I feel a sense of relief because the worst kid is gone. "What a waste!" I think.

I marry an alcoholic. Now why did he have to get drunk on our wedding day? Life goes on in hate and bitterness. It's God's fault. He doesn't give a damn. I hate Him. I don't need all this misery! If the kids weren't here, I'd kill myself.

I don't kill myself; I find Al-Anon instead. Can I tell you what Al-Anon has given me? It's given me people who love me but don't want to run my life, and a *loving* God whom I can share when others are hurting. It's given me a chance to watch miracles happen over and over, and a sense of humor so I can even laugh at myself. It's given me a never-ending fountain of wisdom in the Steps and a love of life I never dreamed possible. My little brother who has Down's Syndrome is still living with my husband and me, and I don't always see him as a burden. In fact, he adds a new dimension of love to my life. I have learned to have the humility to say, "I was wrong" and mean it, and the courage to believe in my own gifts. I know now that my prejudices come from a lack of self-worth, and I can remove them slowly with help from my loving Higher Power, who has always understood.

I feel as if life is just beginning, and it all started in that meeting with the Alateens, when through their faith I heard a soft, loving voice in my own being whisper, "I am God, and I know what I'm doing." At last I know God doesn't hate me, and I can trust enough to let go and let God.

"**B**elieve it or not," said a member at a meeting, "it took me weeks in Al-Anon just to work up enough courage to ask, 'What in the world is an *ODAT?*'" Laughter erupted. Lots of us could identify with the fear of revealing any kind of ignorance: we're convinced we're flawed, but we don't want anyone to know it. We were also laughing ruefully at ourselves. How quickly we adopt a new language and expect others to know it. When she finally did ask, someone pointed her to the book, *One Day at a Time in Al-Anon*, which we affectionately refer to as "the *ODAT* ."

"One day at a time" is also a slogan. Each of the slogans represents a particular spiritual discipline. We use the slogan, "One day at a time," to help us practice Al-Anon principles in small, manageable doses. Practicing new behaviors can provoke all sorts of unaccustomed or unwanted feelings. In the past to avoid uncomfortable feelings, many of us have intellectualized, reacted physically, or escaped into a variety of addictions. These understandable defenses have damaged us further. We do not want to continue self-destructive behavior, yet we need to feel in order to heal. If our feelings had been acceptable in the first place, we would not have repressed them during childhood and continued to do so as adults. Learning to feel the full range of our emotions again takes trust, and we can only learn to trust in increments by doing it one day (sometimes one hour, one minute) at a time.

Slogans are very useful to newcomers and long-time members alike because they remind us to "Keep it simple" and are short and easy to remember. Some of us with well-developed intellects may resist what seem like simplistic platitudes, but we can remind ourselves to "Keep an open mind." No one has asked us to throw away all we have learned, or to accept ideas as true until we have tested them out in our own lives. In fact, in Al-Anon we are encouraged to take what we like and leave the rest. "Think!" and "Listen and learn" are also slogans.

In the beginning, it can be useful for the scientifically minded among us to view practicing the program as an experiment or a working hypothesis. We may not even be conscious of how many thoughts—how many *negative* thoughts—are already running around uncontrolled in our minds. Since only one thought can occupy the mind in any given moment, slogans are handy ways to substitute a positive thought for a negative obsession.

If we react physically to our stresses with ailments, tense muscles, sleeplessness, or exhaustion, focusing on a single idea can help us relax. We can "Let go and let God," or we can "Turn it over."

We should not underestimate the difficulty of trying to follow this counsel. The more agonizing the problem is, the harder we try to hold onto it. We are only too ready to admit we're desperate; what we fail to realize is that we are also powerless. We're afraid to let go. "What would happen if I did?" we think.

The answer is—nothing except what would have happened anyway, or perhaps something wonderful that we haven't even imagined. The reality of our powerlessness over alcohol and alcoholics must be accepted before any progress can be made. Once we stop trying to control the uncontrollable, we can leave it to God. We don't collapse and do nothing for ourselves; we co-operate by doing whatever we can and accepting that the outcome is not in our hands. Acceptance is a challenging but rewarding spiritual discipline.

Those of us who are perfectionists are often overwhelmed by the magnitude of what we imagine recovery to be. "Easy does it" and "First things first" help us to keep moving, but remind us we need only take small steps. Setting our goals too high can lead to frustration and despair. "Progress, not perfection" gives us permission to be human and a realistic aim to substitute for our unreasonable demands on ourselves and others.

Those of us who drown our feelings in alcohol or drugs, or bury them in food, work, or relationships, can start working with "Live and let live." We know at some level that we can't really live when we are driven by compulsions and addictions. Tolerance for others is tied to tolerance for ourselves. We can love the person without encouraging the disease.

If we attend meetings regularly, listen, and share our own truth, we are on our way to recovery. The Steps and Traditions provide the framework. Slogans are a handrail as we climb the steps toward serenity. "Together we can make it," says we don't have to do it alone. We have the group, our sponsors, and a God of our understanding to show us the way. Events in our lives will change, or they will not, but our attitude will surely alter if we practice these principles in all our affairs. Joy and peace of mind are among the rewards we seek when we decide to "Let it begin with me."

USING SLOGANS TO GAIN SERENITY

I longed for rescue.

Growing up in an alcoholic family, I found that many of my needs were not met. How could they be? I was raised by parents and siblings whose own needs had not been met. Consequently, I grew up feeling that I had to take care of everything myself. I didn't think I could rely on anyone else. Ironically, at the same time that I carried the weight of the world on my shoulders, I secretly waited for that "someday" when "someone" would come and relieve me of *all* responsibility.

When I came to Al-Anon and found the slogan, "Let go and let God," I thought that the "someday" and "someone" had arrived. Now I could sit back and let God take care of everything. Surprisingly, letting go was very difficult, for I had not yet learned to trust.

In time, I learned enough trust to turn over some things to God. I also learned that God would hand back to me that which was my responsibility. I didn't get a free ride after all, but I did get help.

Today we have a partnership. As long as I am willing to do my share and don't try to do His, God takes care of the rest. The responsibility I take for what God gives me to do provides me with a strong backbone so that I can walk straight and stand tall. I no longer break my back carrying the whole world on my shoulders—that's God's job. Neither is it permanently curved from spinelessly waiting for rescue. I can stand up straight and walk this path of hope.

I can speak up too, and I can listen. In my family no one seemed to hear anything but the sound of his or her own voice. I felt ignored and neglected. I didn't listen either, because I was always afraid of the negative things I'd hear. Though I longed for closeness and communication, I was terrified of letting anyone know me.

In the safe environment of my Al-Anon meetings, where I experienced unconditional love, I slowly let down my guard. Without the fear, I could listen, and I learned a lot.

Today, "Listen and learn" means I don't have to have all the answers. It means that God speaks to each of us and also through each of us. The humility I have learned in Al-Anon allows me to open my mind to views I had once stubbornly resisted. I can release prejudices and identify with others without requiring that they be just like me. No longer compelled to criticize those around me, I have lessened the compulsion to criticize myself. The punishing voice that once condemned me mercilessly is still. In the silence, I listen to myself and those around me and learn acceptance, tolerance, forgiveness, and love. When I am still enough to listen, I learn of God.

I felt unworthy.

After being in Al-Anon for almost three years, it seemed that it would be easy to turn everything over to God, but I have become an expert at turning things over only when they become a major problem. Hence, I was only able to turn my business and financial future over to God last year, when everything looked so grim that I couldn't think of anything else to do. What a surprise! The business and financial portions of my life became more comfortable.

In spite of that success, I still had difficulty letting go. I turned a portion of my life over to God, but I didn't turn over my entire life. I thought I could let God take care of finances, but I had to take care of my health.

I had somehow come to believe that I was not worthy enough to have God take total care of me. Maybe it came from my childhood when I was taught that God helps those who help themselves. I took it to mean that I had to do everything or nothing would get done. After all, I knew I could not trust my father to do anything for me, nor could I trust my mother to do anything but take care of my father. I didn't trust anyone but myself, and I didn't trust myself very much.

Thank goodness I finally came to Al-Anon, where members accepted and loved me whether I trusted them or not. Slowly, I began to learn to turn my problems over by first trusting God just a little at a time. Growing up with alcoholism had left me with a great deal of anger, resentment, and pain. I am learning how to let go of the resentment by letting my Higher Power handle my problems. I do this by writing whatever troubles me on a slip of paper, which I put in a small container that I refer to as my God box. Then, whenever I start worrying, I can look in the box and remember: I have already shared my troubles with One who can and will help. I try to wait patiently for guidance, but I don't just walk away; I still have to do what I am led to do. The difference is that I don't have to figure it out all by myself or do it all alone.

I am working on letting God into my entire life. I am learning to accept my worthiness with the help of all the unconditional love I receive in the program. I continue to make mistakes, but with Al-Anon support, I also continue to grow, learning to trust God, myself, and one day even "ordinary people"—if the wonderful people in Al-Anon could ever be called "ordinary."

I couldn't relax.

When I started this adventure called Al-Anon recovery, I felt shocked at first to realize my parents were alcoholic. Then I felt relieved as I saw hope for great happiness in my life. I noticed that eighty percent of my energy was spent worrying about people I couldn't control or change. I didn't learn right away how to stop the pattern. At first I used recovery as a new opportunity to direct my misguided family. I feel exhausted now just thinking of all the energy I used trying to convince people to recover who had no interest in what I was saying.

Finally I heard, "Live and let live." I began accepting differences in people. I let go of my need to change everyone else and had a surprising realization. I had many things I wanted to do in my own life. I started by organizing my house to please myself and by learning to have fun.

"Live and let live" for me means to live a full life and let others live their own lives. Having a full, happy life takes power away from alcoholism and helps me regain my own personal power. Now I'm no longer blown over when I come in touch with my parents, because I've learned to sway.

"Fake it until you make it" helps me take risks. When I first heard this saying, I was suspicious and felt insulted. What was I supposed to do? Become some false people pleaser or go back into denial? At the time, I was also depressed and angry. I wanted the ease and peacefulness I saw in others, but I wanted the genuine article. I didn't know how to get it, and I didn't realize it wasn't character I was supposed to fake, but new behaviors. I could fake confidence while practicing something new. I didn't have to deny that a problem existed or ignore my feelings. I just didn't let every little breeze of fear stop me in my tracks.

I wanted to feel free, so I decided to take some risks and try out new responses. When people asked, "How are you?" I tried saying, "Great!" They did double takes, then smiled. I smiled. Amazingly, inside I smiled too. Success led to other successes. Gradually I found positive, happy friends. I focused on the good in my life and it got better. Soon I actually felt happy. I didn't have to fake happiness any longer.

As the oldest of six children of two alcoholic parents, I am very responsible—too responsible, I have come to realize. For example, my children had always begged me to play with them. Play dinosaurs. Play dolls. Play outside. Play with Play-doh. It didn't feel natural, but I tried it and faked it. I pushed myself to play. I took adult roller skating lessons. Soon I was gliding along, feeling free. I played with my silly, fun-loving children. At first it felt awkward, then O.K. Now it feels great! I'm known as the "Fun Mom," and I love it.

I have pulled away from my original family. I faked self-confidence and told myself I was worthy, whether I felt it yet or not, as I reached out to new, healthy friends. Relationships in which reciprocity and unconditional love existed felt very strange in the beginning. But the feelings improved tremendously over time, and these new friends supported me through the many attempts of my unrecovered family to get the "old me" back. My family will recover or they won't, but I like the new me, and I'll never go back to the overly responsible sad sack I used to be.

Gratitude gave me power over moods.

Discovering that gratitude changes my attitude is one of the most wonderful gifts of my Al-Anon program. It reminds me that I am in charge of how my life feels. When I practice gratitude, my outlook improves and I become more positive. I have found that the key, as with so many disciplines, is practice.

While I am driving to work, I go through a mental gratitude list using the alphabet in search of peace of mind. A—Let's see—I'm grateful for my new Attitudes. B—Becoming an even Better person. C—Control! No, that's negative—how about Clarity? Yes, that will do. D—The ability to make good Decisions. I hum along, continuing my newly found ABC's as I negotiate the traffic. Amazingly, the terrible drivers along my route have become more courteous. Sometimes I can get all the way through the alphabet during my twenty-minute drive. Sometimes I don't. The result is always a more peaceful feeling. Driving to work and feeling closer to God, I am also more serene and ready for the challenges of my job.

My gratitude list changes as my moods change. Sometimes I choose to pair seemingly positive and negative attitudes. I match anger with acceptance, seeking to find a balance between the extremes I tend to favor when I forget to put serenity first.

Remembering to lighten up and be easier on myself helps me feel grateful. This morning I put on a jacket I hadn't worn for several months and was delighted to find my "magic" gloves in the pocket. Each finger is a different, vibrant color. It's hard to take myself too seriously or feel too glum wearing rainbows on my hands.

I was always aware of natural beauty, but, as a child of two alcoholic parents, I used it to escape the pain of my life. I lived in a fantasy world of books and nature. As an adult, I am grateful for my ability to see beauty, and I know that there is more to appreciate in nature and literature than just escape.

Recently I realized that acceptance also leads to gratitude. Finally, ten years after his death, with the help of the good people in Al-Anon, I have come to accept my father as he was. I had spent painful years agonizing over why he wasn't the way I needed him to be. It took a lot of sharing with others to understand his good points. I've had a complete reversal of my ideas about my Dad. Fortunately, it's never too late to have a happy childhood. I can be happy today.

Self-acceptance and acceptance of the world as it unfolds also produce ease and gratitude. I have a tendency to want to change everything at once. I usually have to remind myself I can live only one day at a time and that *all* the moments are valuable. Today I am even grateful for the silences and the voids, because I know they create space into which new riches and fulfillment will eventually rush.

Recovery crossed cultures and generations.

About two months ago, I had the opportunity to talk with a Native American man who said that the spouses of the alcoholics where he lived did not know how to take care of themselves. The active alcoholics in their lives had achieved some recovery, but the rest of the family were not getting any better. They were all very angry due to a lot of hurt. Issues went unresolved, and there was little recognition that alcoholism was a family disease. Ultimately they transferred the anger to their children, who then chose abusive people to be with or became abusive themselves.

This is largely what happened to me, but with the grace of God, my family and I are recovering today. Several years ago, I came through the doors of Al-Anon completely unable to communicate who I was or what was actually going on inside me. I had sidestepped this part of human development by choosing work and a lifestyle that required little or no interaction with people. The people I did know avoided intimacy.

As the youngest child in an alcoholic family, I learned I

had little or nothing of importance to contribute to a conversation or family activity. My mother had also been the youngest child in an alcoholic family. Her mother died when she was very young and her closest sister died in her teens. My mother had been raised by her father's sister, who resented being around her alcoholic brother. At the time alcoholism as a disease was little understood. My mother's father knew he had a problem. At one point he even requested he be put on the indictment list (the Indian list or blacklist they had in Canada at the time) so he would be refused liquor at the local hotel and would be forced to get some control over his drinking. He had the saying, "One drink is too much and one hundred drinks are not enough," long before anyone knew of Alcoholics Anonymous. He knew he was ill, but he didn't know how to find help.

I too cried out for help and found none. My father, who is also an alcoholic, worked with geologists, and he always had mercury around for testing rock samples. My brother and I played with it all the time. Somewhere I had learned I could die from the stuff. One night I decided I had had enough (at age ten) and drank from a bottle labled mercury. I was surprised and angry the next day to find I was still alive.

I was also confused and worried that I wasn't dead so I told the rest of the family what I had done. Being the traditional, unrecovered, secretive, isolated, sick family that we were then, they didn't react at all. In fact, they flatly did not believe me and didn't even bother to take me to a doctor.

After that I began to look at life around me very passively as I withdrew more and more from my family. Inside I focused on the day I could leave home.

People in terrific emotional pain reach for all kinds of soothers. I latched onto any form of human affection I could find, and I found it outside my family in men who sexually molested me. The sexual abuse and the desperation brought me very close to a completely corrupted world of alcohol and drugs.

I believe my first gift from God was a dog. Against my family's advice, I bought an Irish Setter before I left home. I might not be alive to write this had it not been for that dog. Because the dog was big, I had to move away from where I lived, right in the midst of the hard drug scene. The dog and I moved into the country, where I met people whose lifestyles were entirely different from those I had known.

I spent a lot of time there with aboriginal peoples. I *did* become a chartered herbalist and healer. I *did* live in a tipi for a winter. Later I *did* graduate with a college degree in physics. I *did* play the guitar and become creative in several media. I *did* and still do travel extensively. I emphasize "did" because the craziness and minimizing of everything in our family was so rampant, that no matter what I did, they patronized me to the point where I doubted my reality and wondered if, in fact, I had done anything at all.

Though I had left the hard drug scene in the city, I still found relationships with people who treated me much like my family. They talked love and in the same beat knocked me down with cruel words and actions. Sometimes they said white was black. I did anything I could think of to receive love, but I didn't know how to give it to myself or anyone else. I didn't awake from this nightmare existence until I finally found and lived with an active alcoholic. Only then did the problem get clear enough to send me through the doors of Al-Anon, where I could speak my truth and be heard at last.

Today I know that the unrecovered spouses of alcoholics had a more devastating effect on me than the alcoholic did. I must still be on my toes around them. Even though most of my family members have a Twelve Step program, unfortunately the need to victimize has not been completely healed. We still have scars and sometimes try to blunt the pain by passing it onto another victim. No one can throw me for a loop faster than someone in my family.

My family also keeps me focused on my Al-Anon program, for I don't dare take time off from recovery. Fortunately I was so ill when I came into the program that I immediately got involved with service so I wouldn't have to think too much. The more I gave recovery away, the healthier I got. I have led workshops where I combined recovery with my understanding of native spirituality. Intertwining two different types of spirituality helps me to "Keep an open mind." Serving Al-Anon gives me a way to "Let it begin with me," and along that way I have discovered that while my best may not be perfect, it is good enough.

My main motto is "Progress not perfection." My Higher Power keeps me well reminded—indeed, is reminding me at this moment. There is a church two doors down from where I live. Just now I felt sincerely furious because the five o'clock bells were distracting me from this writing. The bells invaded my quiet with Beethoven's "Ode to Joy," and I felt decidedly homicidal. The tune changed to "Faith of our Fathers," and suddenly I realized that if my own father hadn't put in the recovery time and service in Alcoholics Anonymous before he died, I might not have had the faith to be working this program today. Thank goodness, I can laugh at my annoyance and let go and let God.

Al-Anon gave me a life. I had lots of education, lots of training, lots of creative talents and gifts from God. I did not have a fulfilling lifestyle, connectedness, or comfortable humanness. Today after twenty years, every person in my immediate family, aside from one brother, is in a Twelve Step program. There are nine generations of alcoholism on one side of our family and three known generations on the other side. Recovery is long overdue.

Chapter three
PICKING UP THE TOOLS

A newcomer asked a long-time member, "Why isn't it enough to understand the concepts of Al-Anon in the literature? What is this 'working the program' you all keep talking about?" There was a long hesitation as the other woman grappled with the complexity of trying to explain something that can be done, and done well, in a thousand different ways.

Eventually, she explained it this way. "I know I am basically lazy, and I can live in my anger at having grown up in a disease that I didn't ask to be a part of. It's not my fault, I say to myself. I want a quick fix. Give me a shot and make me better! But there is no shot for the alcoholic, and none for us either. We have to change habits of behavior and thinking patterns that don't work and are actually self-destructive. Habits don't change just by reading about them. Even saying, 'Yes, that's a habit I have,' doesn't change it. Change comes through practicing something different. Working a program for me means taking one of the tools—a slogan, a Step, the Serenity Prayer, the phone list, my sponsor—and using it in my life. As I worked at making changes in myself, I found that where I used to react with anger and rage, I now react with love and compassion, and it feels good. I am no longer a victim of life; I am a survivor with choices."

As children growing up in alcoholic homes, we took ourselves very seriously. Often we did not learn how to relax and have fun. Life—sometimes even survival—was hard work. The last thing we want to hear now is that we have to work at recovery as well. Those of us who are already too responsible, serious, and overworked need to realize that working a program can be as simple as making a list of fun things to do and then doing one. We might want to start out by asking, "How important is it?" and letting something go, or leaving a task undone.

At other times, we who have suffered so much uncertainty or even chaos need the structure and discipline that a spiritual program provides. We wander in the land of pain where all exit doors seem shut. We need to do something to change our attitudes, but what? It can feel incredibly difficult to turn away from well established negative judgments. One member described her negative thoughts as a team of eight horses harnessed to her buckboard, galloping full speed toward a cliff. Turning that team, she said, took courage, strength, and firm determination. At times like this, working the program means picking up the telephone and calling someone, or reading a chapter on a Step and finding a way to apply it to the situation. We can say, "Stop!" to the negative chatter inside our heads, but then we must also replace it with a positive alternative, or the old pattern will rush back into the void as soon as we let our guard down.

The suggestions of the program are like a tool kit. Nothing changes until we change it. The tool kit just sits on the bench waiting for the master craftsperson to take it up. Selecting the best tool requires some skill, but we are not lonely apprentices left to our own devices. We can ask other members for help, read some Al-Anon literature, call our sponsor, attend a meeting, pray, or experiment with the suggestions on our own. As we practice, no lesson is lost and more is revealed.

We can help ourselves to any of the implements at our own pace. We can take what we like and leave the rest. We can dawdle along or charge at breakneck speed.

Eventually, many of us realize we are not going to get a quick cure. After some initial grumbling at the unfairness of it all, we discover that everything is just as it should be, for there is always more to learn and we find our serenity along the way rather than at the end of the journey. Friends come along the way. Fun comes along the way. Challenges? There are always some of those along life's way. Now at least we are equipped with new skills, loving companions, and spiritual support to help us meet them. Finally, love and self-esteem also come along the way.

PICKING UP TOOLS AND MENDING OUR LIVES

I couldn't just inherit Al-Anon.

Though my father had been sober in AA for fourteen years and Mom had been in Al-Anon ten years, I didn't really join Al-Anon until I had been away from home for almost a decade. They had taken me to some open AA meetings when I was younger, and I even attended Al-Anon for a while with Mom. At that time I was involved with a man who never wanted to do things with my family, and we never seemed to get beyond the cocktail lounge when we went out to dinner.

I had spent many hours as a child, waiting for my Dad to finish drinking, and I felt a familiar discomfort with my boyfriend's behavior, so I wrote him a letter explaining my feelings. He wrote back saying that when I was around those "crazy women," I got crazy. I chose to believe him and quit attending Al-Anon.

That relationship eventually ended, and I married a man who didn't drink. Nevertheless, I found myself focusing solely on my husband. I tried to "help" him and love him enough to fix him, while my two little children sat in front of the television. One night this picture of my neglected children and my obsession with my husband hit me between the eyes, and I realized my priorities were messed up. Because my parents had continued to work their respective recovery programs, I could see that, even though they had been crazy, they now had sanity and serenity in their lives, and I knew where to go for help.

I had watched them change throughout the years, as they chose recovery and I chose sickness. The first time I can recall being aware of a change was while I still lived at home. I was twenty-two and my sister was twenty-eight. With both of us totally out of control, we got involved in a terrible swearing, kicking, punching fight. Dad, who had a friend visiting, calmly walked out of the house and continued talking to his friend on the front steps. Even in the middle of that huge fight, I recognized that something had shifted.

The following week, Mom wrote my sister and me a note asking one of us to move out of the house because our behavior was threatening Dad's sobriety. Resentfully, I moved. Today I can see it was very good for me. When I left my family, I took "me" with me. I got to live with all my character defects and had no one to blame for my feelings of depression and anger. Though I no longer lived with an active alcoholic, I still managed to find unhealthy relationships.

I am grateful to my father for naming the disease and leading the way into AA. My mother helped me face up and begin to work the Steps when she told me, "Many of your problems may have my name on them, but the solutions all have your name." She was right. She may have hurt me, but she couldn't give me what I needed, which was self-esteem. I felt I was less valuable than other people. To regain my sense of self, I had to accept help from my Higher Power, call other people, and work the Steps. Today my anger and rage are melting into grace and human dignity. I have completed college and started graduate school. Today I know I am a valuable person, and when I forget it, I know that in Al-Anon I will find people who will remind me until I can remember again.

Though we all are recovering, heaven hasn't arrived and we still have to work at peace of mind, day by day, here on earth. My family is still my greatest challenge to working the program. One night on the way to an Al-Anon meeting, my sister-in-law said, "Do you realize we have twenty-three years of recovery in this car?"

"Wow!" I replied, "Just think how much we'd have if the whole family was here."

"About two minutes!" quipped my brother.

We all laughed, and we keep trying, one day at a time. Life in recovery has had some big challenges—a divorce, the foreclosure on our house, my son deciding to live with his dad—yet the God of my understanding has helped me through them. The people in Al-Anon have held me up. Recently I heard someone say, "God's will will never take me where His love cannot protect me." I use this saying daily to remind me that all I have to do is rise each morning and step out in faith. So far it's worked.

Detaching was kind.

I had only been in Al-Anon nine months when I got my first potent lesson in detachment. It was eleven o'clock on the night before Thanksgiving and I had just gone to bed. My mother, who had been asleep after drinking through the evening, woke up and burst into my room. "Get up and clean out the refrigerator!" she demanded. In the past, I would have been in the kitchen, cleaning, before she had finished her sentence.

This time words from my Al-Anon friends whispered in my head. "Don't react," they reminded me. Gritting my teeth, I decided to try a suggestion I had heard in meetings. "Mom, the refrigerator can wait until morning. I'm going to sleep. I love you. Good night."

She repeated her command, louder this time. I remained calm (at least on the outside) and stated again that I would handle it in the morning. On the inside, I said the Serenity Prayer over and over as fast as I could. My heart pounded. I had always put the needs of everyone else first; standing my ground was a tremendously bold action.

She raised the volume and the force of the furious language, demanding I get up immediately and clean the refrigerator. I focused on members of my Al-Anon group and remembered how they urged me not to buy into crazy thinking. I have a choice, I remembered. "Good night, Mom," I said.

It wasn't what she wanted to hear. She pulled out all the stops. She knew my weaknesses well and jabbed at every emotional hot button I had. I winced, but fortunately those wonderful people at my meetings had told me that when we lash out, it is because we are in pain. I could clearly see my mother's pain as she screamed at me. I did not want to add to it or take it on as my own, so I remained silent.

She stormed out of my room. Soon there was a commotion in the kitchen. She reappeared in my doorway and said, "Well, son, you've done it now. The turkey and the rest of the

food are all on the kitchen floor! You'd better go put it away."
She retreated to her bedroom, slamming the door.

For a moment, my detachment crumbled. "Oh, no!" I
thought, "Tomorrow the family will be eating peanut butter
and jelly sandwiches for dinner, and it will all be my fault!"
The Al-Anon members in my head countered: "Why is it your
fault? You didn't put the turkey on the floor." Caught up in my
guilt, I pushed the voices out and hurried into the kitchen,
where I began putting food away. With a nudge from my
Higher Power and too many meetings under my belt, the voices came back: "As long as you clean up her messes for her,
she'll never have to. Your 'kindness' could kill her."

I left the turkey on the floor where I had found it and went
back to bed. I turned my mother, the turkey, and the potential
peanut butter sandwiches over to God.

The next morning everything was back in the refrigerator.
Mom had taken responsibility for her own actions.

Today my mother is not drinking. Although I did not cause
her sobriety any more than I caused her drinking, I feel good
knowing that, by detaching with love, I at least did not enable
her to keep killing herself. She has my love and the dignity to
take care of what she creates. Both of us have more positive
lives.

The Serenity Prayer lit my path.

My father drinks, but while growing up I didn't really
notice it. I am the eldest daughter in a family of five
children. Our family lacked physical closeness and any
semblance of communication, but I didn't equate it with
alcoholism. In fact, I thought it was normal. Estrangement
defined us all so much that, when I was eight and my older
brother ordered me out of his room, I vowed never to speak

to him again, and I didn't until I was married at twenty-one.

My father was distant, seeming to care only for my brothers. He dominated my mother, and I didn't want to be a doormat like her, so I tried to fit into the circle of men by being a tomboy. Once, when my father discovered I had a packet of cigarettes, he stamped on it and hit me hard across my face. I heard my mother saying, "Hit her! Hit her!" I was so hurt by her words, all I could do was cry.

I began to rebel, sneaking out my bedroom window and smoking *dagga* all night long. I spent my time on South Africa's streets with downtrodden people who were the outcasts of society. Eventually my parents caught me. Though that part of my life is extremely shadowy, I did stop taking drugs.

At seventeen, I fell in love. For the next five years, we were reckless, irresponsible, and drunk a good part of the time. I wanted to be somebody, anybody different. I acted, made a fool of myself singing at a night club, and rode at high speed on a motorbike. I enjoyed losing myself—and at last being popular.

On my twenty-first birthday, we got engaged. It seemed the thing to do. We carried on as before, but I began to feel that we should be growing up and acting like a couple. He didn't understand my change at all. We bought a house, and, as I worked for an attorney, I took on the burden of attending to all the paperwork. I was scared! Scared of marriage. Scared that we seemed to be drifting apart. Scared of being alone with all the house-buying responsibility.

Our families busily prepared for the wedding, and I was too scared to disappoint them, so I decided to go ahead with the wedding and get divorced later. Before I ever walked down the aisle, I had accepted that the marriage wouldn't work.

It didn't. We returned from our honeymoon to find all our

friends waiting in our new house with the now familiar bottle. Without the restrictions of parents, everyone drank with wild abandon. I often woke up in a house full of people I didn't even know. After a few months I asked my husband for a divorce. I was surprised at the tears of anguish he shed, but I wouldn't budge.

One thing kept me going. My cousin had given me a copy of the Serenity Prayer for my twenty-first birthday. It hung on my wall like a ray of light. I glanced at it occasionally and the words became familiar. When something happened or I had a problem, I would ask myself, "Can I change this or can't I?" If I couldn't, I turned my attention elsewhere. I survived the troubled sea of my marriage with the Serenity Prayer as my lifeline.

After the divorce, I returned to reluctant parents who didn't really want me home. I felt terrible when I found I was also pregnant, and they reacted with shock. My mother came around and supported me, but my father pretended my condition didn't exist. I felt so guilty, I struggled not to bring up my food in the early months of morning sickness.

Only the Serenity Prayer provided any glimmer of hope during those dark months. I repeated it over and over whenever I could remember. Soon people began appearing in my life who talked to me about God's love.

My mother stood by me through the birth of my baby, and, for the first time in my life, I felt close to her. After my baby's birth, a kind friend of mother's noticed how depressed I was and guided me to Al-Anon.

I bounced into and out of Al-Anon meetings for a long time. Surely my father wasn't an alcoholic, I told myself. Then I watched him one Saturday afternoon as he stood in the road with a hosepipe glaring at two boys who were laughing at him and throwing stones at our dog. He looked pitiful. I could see that he had been drinking, and shame engulfed me.

I returned to the Al-Anon meetings but soon found other excuses to leave. I decided they weren't talking about alcoholism enough and were talking amateur psychology too much. With compassion and patience, my mother's friend encouraged me to keep trying. My next excuse was my fussy baby, who made it difficult to concentrate. Even when my nerves snapped and I landed in a psychiatric hospital, where another patient thought *I* was *her* baby (and I realized I could become like that), I had difficulty sticking to the program. One night my father's furious behavior at the table scared me so badly, I went to a new meeting just to get out of the house. The warmth of the fellowship surrounded me again and again, as I made my way through all my excuses until I finally decided to stay.

The Serenity Prayer had been my anchor before I came into Al-Anon. Seeing it at my first meeting was like finding a long lost friend. I have a long way to go before I fully understand all that alcohol has done to me, but as I make my way along, I know that Al-Anon and God *as I understand Him* will help me accept the things I cannot change and give me the courage to change the things I can. Al-Anon shines a bright light onto my life and its challenges, and helps me find the wisdom to know the difference between what I need to accept and what I need to change.

My sponsor taught me to be good to myself.

Why did I always feel so bad? Impatience with minor frustrations brought me to the point of rage every day. I yelled at my husband and two sons. I often woke in the morning feeling the "black mood" which I knew meant everything would go wrong for me that day. I cursed. I swore. I slammed doors.

Sometimes I locked myself in the bedroom or bathroom for hours, hovering close to tears.

Friends and relatives thought I was a great manager and really had it together, but I was only a competent impostor. My perfectionism and compulsive hard work had them fooled. I did my household chores with a vengeance! I shopped, cooked, and cleaned with grim determination. Every day I felt a little more miserable.

By the time my sons were teenagers, I was in so much pain that I knew I had to do something. My nephew had been sober in AA for five years, and because of him I had read some books about alcoholism. I finally called a friend of his who counseled alcoholics and who already knew a lot about our family. I told her I didn't know what was wrong with me but I felt like I was going insane. I couldn't say no to anyone, and I always ended up doing things I didn't want to do. She suggested Al-Anon.

I'd never considered it. I knew my sister was an alcoholic, but I thought I didn't belong because I didn't think my husband was an alcoholic. Oh, he drank, but he always provided for us, and my life wasn't like those I'd heard of with beatings and drunken rages. He was a very critical person—but an alcoholic?

I started attending Al-Anon meetings and reading Al-Anon literature anyway. Gradually, I began to learn about myself as I listened to others, but something was missing. I called my nephew's friend again. "Do you have a sponsor?" she asked.

"No," I answered.

"Then get one."

At one of my meetings I heard a woman I admired mention that her sister was an alcoholic. She didn't say anything about her husband. It took several weeks to build up enough courage to ask her to sponsor me, and when she replied enthusiastically, "I'd love to!" my life changed. No matter how rotten I felt, no matter what awful thing I thought I had done, my sponsor said it didn't seem so bad and pointed out how much better I was getting. I could be honest with her and still be accepted. Only then did I realize how dishonest it was to always say "yes" and then resent it.

"Don't be so hard on yourself," she said often in those first months. I didn't know I was hard on myself. I'd been that way all my life. "Take care of yourself. You're worth it!" she said. What a concept!

In my family, where criticism flowed like water, I had been the "sweet" one while my sisters were "pretty" and "smart." I came to believe I had so much power to hurt, or disappoint, or anger others that it might kill them. I used my sweetness to make everyone like me, and I succeeded so well that I was the favorite niece, cousin, and sister, but the price I paid was never to say "no" to any request or demand. I lived every waking moment for others and felt I had no right to care for myself or think about what I wanted.

Frantically active, with no time for myself, I was utterly out of touch with my own needs. Always pleasing other people left me feeling angry, resentful, and victimized. The notion that caring for myself wasn't selfish but life affirming came as a big surprise. Focusing on myself was very difficult. I felt guilty and had no idea what I wanted. I learned to feel the guilt and do it anyway.

I hadn't recognized my parents' alcoholism because they seemed too perfect. Extremely religious people, they attended daily services and dragged us children along. My father had given up drinking on his own when I was very small, but he remained angry and unhappy. In Al-Anon, I began to realize that my father has suffered from being a "dry drunk" for more than thirty years. My mother had a few stiff drinks every night before dinner. Even when she slurred her words and talked loud, I didn't connect it to alcoholism. Deeply buried awareness takes time to surface. I heard the Twelve Steps hundreds of times before the day came when the First Step actually made sense. I really *am* powerless over their alcoholism. Not to be responsible for my sister's, my parents', or indeed, my husband's drinking brings great relief, and I hadn't even realized how responsible I felt until Al-Anon.

When I started Al-Anon, I was sure it was too late for my sons—I feared I had been so abusive that they were damaged for life. It hurt to even think about it. One day my sponsor said to me, "Remember the struggles you had when you were a young adult, needing moral support but not someone telling you what to do and what's best for you? Now that you know better, your sons will have the support they need without your meddling in their lives." I have to admit I'm not a perfect mother and I don't always know what's best. I'm relieved that I don't have to be a perfect mother to love and support my children in their growth.

I cannot begin to enumerate all that I have gotten from working the Al-Anon program. When I have a slip and start saying "yes" when I want to say "no" or trying to fix other people, I can call my sponsor and she will lovingly help straighten me out. A sponsor who loves me enough to tell me the truth with compassion is a priceless gift.

Love is an inside job.

I was born in a place I fondly refer to as "The Rock." Until three years ago, when I found Al-Anon, this was the one and only thing that gave me any sense of who I was. If nothing else, I was from "The Rock," and I could be proud of that.

My home as a child was just like everyone else's, or so I

thought. I had a Dad who drank daily and a Mom who was deeply affected by it. Whenever Mom and Dad got together for more than five minutes, there was a racket. When I was young, I did everything I could not to rock the boat because I feared that some of the garbage might fly my way. I thought Mom had the problem. If only she would leave Dad alone, everything would be just fine. I was terrified I might grow up to be like her.

The most potent lessons I drew from my family situation were to stuff all my feelings deep in my subconscious and to become adept at the art of non-communication. I decided that surely there was more to life than this, and I charged out to find it.

My serious quest for love and acceptance began at age fourteen. I hung around with an older crowd, where I met a guy who paid a little attention to me. I felt so lucky to have my first real boyfriend that I didn't look too hard at him. If I had, I would have gotten a clue about what kind of men I would choose for a long time. The lady he had been involved with before me was four months pregnant at the time, but he said it was over between them and I was the one he cared for. I ate it up and closed my ears to everything else.

Already having been introduced to booze and drugs, with him I added sex. It was a heady combination for one so young. I thought that losing my virginity made me a grown-up. I equated sex with love and maturity—a big mistake.

He also introduced me to a bunch of guys in the bike club on "The Rock." They weren't exactly the Hell's Angels, but they weren't angels either. My so-called boyfriend started spending time again with his old flame, so I spent my time with the *b'ys* in the club. I started dating the club's president. With him I felt protected and also felt that I was *someone*. I rationalized away the fact that he had a live-in girlfriend, and

I learned how to lie effectively the few times we were caught.

Being with the president did give me the status of "no one messes with her," whether we were at a bar, a party, or the clubhouse. At home with my parents it wasn't much help. My parents gave me lots of flack about my choice of friends. So I solved the parent problem by moving in with a girlfriend. Even though I was just sixteen, I worked at a bar where the bikers hung out. Sometimes I went to school.

I spent the better part of ten years in an on-again-off-again relationship with one of the *b'ys* whom I thought I loved. Every time I was convinced I had him out of my system, he'd show up again, and I'd climb back on that emotional roller coaster. I visited him in nearly every jail in that part of the country. Without ever stopping to think of the consequences to me, I smuggled drugs into jail for him. He ran and I followed across the continent.

When we finally broke up, I found another alcoholic and jumped on another emotional roller coaster. We moved from place to place, and each time we moved, I thought we had left his drinking buddies behind and could get on with our lives together. I somehow missed the point that there were always new drinking buddies in every new town.

He called me a fat, hoggy dog, and at 215 pounds, I hated myself. One night I snapped. I pounded on his chest with both fists like a maniac, shouting, "Your purpose in life is to drive me crazy! Well, are you happy? Look at me! I'm nuts!" That night *I* started to look at me and to look for help. I found it in Al-Anon, where I learned I didn't cause alcoholism, I couldn't control it, and I sure couldn't cure it. Even though I wasn't drinking it, booze controlled me. The things I swore I would never do, I did. Things that had gone on in my home as a child now happened in my own home.

For the first time in my life, in Al-Anon I fit in. The only thing they wanted me to do was to keep coming back. I did. The people in those groups showed me the love I had never known but had searched for all my life. They gave me tools I could use to help me recover—Steps, a sponsor, meetings, friends, and slogans. On a daily basis, I clung to the slogans "Think," "Easy does it," and "Live and let live." I learned the Serenity Prayer and said it over and over. I found a Higher Power I could entrust with all things, even the most personal. As I worked the Steps, I learned to clear away the wreckage of the past and live every day for all it was worth. I even began to believe I was worth something.

All the things I had wanted and searched for in other people, I finally found in myself. What a relief. I could stop searching, sit back, and enjoy life on life's terms. It's a simple concept, but I have to work at it to keep it.

I leave the door open for good things to happen. I met the man who is now my husband. My parents traveled six thousand miles to attend our wedding. I now have a relationship with them I never dreamed possible. I am a lot like my Mom, but today I am proud of it. I can accept that they are real people with problems, not just my parents.

My husband and I are real people too. We have problems, but we share a set of principles that helps us deal with them. Acceptance of my husband's worth as a human being, and thus my own, is one of the greatest gifts I have gotten from Al-Anon. When I forget my right to be, or another's, I remind myself I am God's child in God's universe and I have a right to be here. I keep coming back because it works!

Chapter four

WHEN CRISIS STRIKES

A member chairing a meeting commented on how often in early recovery she tried to skip over the word "sanity" in the Second Step. "I really didn't like the part about being restored to sanity," she said, "because it somehow implied *I* was insane. I figured it applied to the alcoholics I knew. Now *they* were insane, and I certainly didn't want to be associated with them. *Their* insanity was what put me here. I believed that my life was littered with crises not of my own making. I had no idea how to stop them all, since I hadn't created them. Then one day I heard someone define insanity as doing the same thing over and over and expecting different results. I squirmed in my chair, for the definition hit me rather close to home.

"Not long after that, in another Al-Anon meeting, I heard a similarly uncomfortable definition. 'Sanity' was humorously described as 'what we get when we quit hoping for a better past.' How often did I secretly whisper to myself: if only my parents had loved me, if only they could at least love me now, if only I hadn't been so terrified. If only, if only, if only—on and on it went, as did my various crises and inability to deal with them. I hadn't even seen it as living in the past. That's when my recovery began in earnest."

Insanity is often as subtle and confusing as the insidious disease of alcoholism itself. Just as we come to realize that one doesn't have to lie homeless and jobless in the gutter with a brown paper bag in order to suffer from the disease of alcoholism, we eventually come to understand that one doesn't have to be admitted to a psychiatric ward or slash any wrists to have certain behaviors that are not models of ideal rationality. Anger and resentment accompany the abuse and excessive responsibility of living with active alcoholism, and they block our serenity just as they do the alcoholic's. Since many of us are "model citizens," our irrationality is often hard to grasp.

Sometimes society even lauds and supports our martyrdom because that behavior keeps the messes created by the disease "off the street." Unlike the recovering alcoholic, who may find people grateful that at least he or she is not drunk, we may find little support in our families when we begin to recover. When we quit cleaning up others' messes or filling in with extra responsibility, sometimes things get worse, and not everyone is comfortable. Starting and staying with a recovery program in the face of opposition or even hostility is difficult. We need lots of new ideas and lots of support from each other. It is a hero's journey of a different order than we are used to, but it can literally save our lives.

Negative responses do not disappear simply because we have broken through our denial and can now recognize them as negative. We have found that substituting a positive thought, word, or action for a negative one works better than simply trying to block out or stop the negative. In the past, we used our old responses, whether they were denial, blaming, keeping busy, being perfect, or raging, because they were the best skills we had. In order to give up these reactions, even after we have learned that they don't work, we need something else to grasp.

Al-Anon gives us new alternatives to replace the ones we

used and misused. They may not produce all the results we want. We sometimes do not even know what results are actually best for us, but at least if we try something different, we may get different results. In the midst of a crisis, any new idea may be better than the ones we already know don't work. With practice, we learn which ones are effective for which situations.

Repeating a slogan can quell rising panic. Reading Al-Anon literature can provide new perspectives on a difficult situation. Calling a sponsor or an Al-Anon friend can provide love and compassion when we feel attacked or rejected. Working a Step can straighten out our obsessive thinking or calm our fears. Going to an Al-Anon meeting can reduce our isolation and the sinking feeling that we are again alone with the problems that go hand-in-hand with alcoholism. Saying the Serenity Prayer can connect us to help from a Power greater than ourselves.

We cannot stop other people from creating crises. We may have to accept that some unexpected difficulties are a part of life. Nonetheless, as we apply Al-Anon principles to our lives we discover that we do not have to face the difficulties alone and unarmed.

FACING CRISIS WITH SERENITY

I helped my daughter and myself.

My husband was out of town when I woke at two A.M. with my heart pounding from a horrible, terrifying dream. I could barely breathe, and I was only dimly aware of what had awakened me. Awake in the night as well, my daughter called out for solace and a back rub. I struggled to roll out of bed, reminding myself I was awake and safe right now. Though I felt shaky, I remembered an Al-Anon member's suggestion about how to cope with fear. "To cope with strong emotions, get the body moving," he had said. I went to my daughter to rub her back, and I consciously refocused my mind on the given moment. We were not in danger at this moment.

As I rubbed her back, I asked God to help me rid myself of the thoughts of the dream. It occurred to me to ask my daughter if she wanted to talk about why she was awake. She too had had a scary dream. Talking about feelings had never been practiced in my abusive, dangerous, alcohol-dominated childhood home. I had learned to deal with feelings by talking in Al-Anon meetings. When she finished telling me her dream, I prayed over both of us, reminding myself of the "short version" of the first three Steps: "I can't. God can. Let Him."

I began to calm down. My daughter drifted off to sleep, and I reached for my journal. When it is too late to call someone, writing works as well. As I wrote, it dawned on me that I had the terrible dream because I had felt like a mean witch when I was coaching soccer that day. I had pushed the slower players, snapped others to attention, and made them do lots of ball drills. I had felt inadequate as a coach, because my husband, the "real" coach, was out of town, and we had lost our last game. Projecting my own feelings of inadequacy onto them, I had driven them rather hard.

Through Al-Anon, I have learned to take my black and white thinking and look for the shades of gray. It's good for the team if I encourage them to get in better shape, to keep developing their skills, and to pay attention. But I also need to work on my tone of voice by handling what I feel inside. It was my feelings of inadequacy that day as a coach that had prompted me to drive them so hard. Writing about it helped

me re-balance myself. I really was a good coach. I am human
and I make mistakes. Trying too hard to work my Al-Anon
program and become the perfectly recovered parent and perfect coach is as crazy as expecting every youngster to be a
world class soccer player.

Today I realize that the fear that used to have total power
over me is receding. As I chisel away at fear with insights
from Al-Anon, the part of me that was repeatedly abused as a
child feels safer and I have power over it. My fear melted
away; I laid down my pen and went back to sleep.

Daily practice was my key.

When I joined Al-Anon I was in an emotional panic.
Though I had been an honor roll student, spent four years of
active duty in the military, and found considerable fulfillment
helping families who had children with birth defects, I barely coped with my own roller coaster emotions. A voracious
reader, I had read about the disease of alcoholism and easily
recognized my family in the literature. I was not an alcoholic,
yet I began to suspect I had some alcoholic behavior tenden-
cies and it alarmed me.

If it hadn't been for the slogan "Easy does it," and very
accepting Al-Anon members in the meetings I attended, I
might have driven myself crazier yet, trying alone to use the
program to blot out the negative characteristics I feared I had
absorbed from my cruel father and self-pitying mother.

Alcoholism awaited my birth and may have affected me
while still in the womb. My alcoholic father and my mother
had a baby a year during the Great Depression until my mother threatened suicide if it continued. Years later I appeared.

Pregnant again and living with a man who bullied everyone
sexually and physically, my mother increased her own drink-

ing. Drinking did not make Mother as nasty as Dad, but it did
encourage her self-pity. To make matters worse, I had the gall
to arrive on Christmas Eve. She truly minded missing all the
holiday get-togethers, and I heard about it throughout my
boyhood. She also told me she was sick every day with me.
Born at 12:06 p.m., I heard that that was the last time I was
ever late for lunch. My medical conditions (I was born with
birth defects) cost my parents more than they could afford,
and I kept everyone awake for the first three years by crying
all night, every night.

My father's capacity for alcohol and cruelty was known to
all the neighbors. He had vicious nicknames for all of us. My
mother was "Suicide Sal"; I was "Freak."

I thought I could escape by being unusually good or by
leaving home, but until I found Al-Anon, I could never
escape the excruciating feelings that nothing I could do
would make me acceptable and worthy to be wanted. I continued to suffer daily from loneliness and grief until I found
love and acceptance in Al-Anon. Now I practice the program
gratefully every day. The First Step has been a great comfort
to me, because it allows me to ask for help without feeling
guilty about it. I am most grateful for my home group (the
meeting I attend regularly). Though I have attended other
meetings and been made welcome, in my home group I have
finally found for the first time in my life a loving family that
wants me there. This is the greatest gift I have received from
my Higher Power.

In turn my group has given me an ability to have a loving
relationship with my Higher Power. Before coming to Al-
Anon, I had rejected religion as shallow and hypocritical
without replacing it with anything else. I had no Power
greater than myself, and I had no comfort. Al-Anon has

helped me realize my need for and willingness to accept a very deep feeling of spirituality. My gratitude is boundless.

Acceptance brought me peace.

Step One, the Serenity Prayer, and acceptance all overlap for me because they all speak of powerlessness. When I came into Al-Anon, it was an admission that both of my parents were alcoholic and that this had made my life unmanageable.

Before I can accept something, I first have to acknowledge that it exists. Admitting my parents' alcoholism meant revealing the family secrets and breaking family loyalty. It was a beginning step toward accepting some of the things I cannot change.

Slowly, as I admit that things like unpleasant feelings and events exist, and as I allow myself to experience and accept them, peace results. For me, acceptance doesn't mean I have to pretend I'm happy about all the facts of life. Acceptance means I acknowledge reality as reality and accept my human feelings of loss or frustration and my human limitations. I am not in control of reality. Nor am I always in control of how I feel about reality, which is sometimes decidedly furious, but I *am* in control of how I choose to act on my feelings about reality. My behavior and my attitude are mine to choose, and that knowledge has brought me a much deeper peace than I used to know.

Practicing acceptance, I have worked my way through many major and minor crises. What types of things have I accepted that I cannot change, control, or make disappear? My parents were alcoholics. My parents neglected me. My parents died. My brother died. My other brother is mentally ill and a sex abuser. My parents abused my siblings, who in

turn abused the younger children. I myself was sexually
abused. My body doesn't produce an important enzyme.
Traffic lights don't change because I will them to. Other drivers are sometimes rude. I am sometimes rude. My students
have difficulties. Other people in the program whom I care
about suffer pain and sorrow. Life hurts sometimes. Life
ends.

If I can accept life on life's terms, it becomes much more
manageable. Like a river, life moves on whether I agree to it
or not. I can choose to ride the river as it flows. I can paddle
upstream. I can float downstream. I am not in charge of the
river, but I do have choices. I feel more peace, joy, and relax-
ation today. I call that serenity. When I am willing, God does
grant me the serenity to accept the things I cannot change.

Understanding powerlessness relieved my guilt.

At an Al-Anon meeting chaired by a young woman, I discovered a meaning of powerlessness that worked for me. She
explained the concept as "it doesn't matter!" "It doesn't matter what I do, say, think, feel, or believe. I cannot and will not
make anyone stop drinking," she said. "It did not matter how
many times I bailed my brother out of jams, or believed he
was right, or covered up for him, he is still in jail today. I
could have been spending all those precious moments on me,
and perhaps I would have more happy memories than sad
ones if I had detached with love from my brother. Today, I rescue myself."

Her sharing about powerlessness made me take a good
hard look at my relationship with my own brother. The years
preceding a motorcycle accident that paralyzed him were
spent chasing him, protecting him, checking on him, and

supporting him. Nevertheless, he held onto his drinking and
drugging.

The whole family was involved with his life. My parents
gave him jobs and money. My mother cooked for him, bought
him clothes, and worried about him constantly. My older sisters pulled him out of bars and city jail cells. I fed his problems by telling him he was a good guy with a few small
problems. We all gave him cars, at one time or another, that he
wrecked because he drank. When he bought his motorcycle,
he drove it unregistered and without a license. We all knew he
drank too much, but we were too busy rescuing him to help
him face his real problem. He was crippled by alcohol.

The whole time, we were powerless. My denial of my own
powerlessness flashed before my eyes. I had kept busy rescuing because it was too painful to accept that I couldn't stop
someone I loved from destroying himself. My brother's twisted body and his electric wheelchair are tangible evidence of
our total powerlessness over alcohol.

If a way had existed to help my brother, to keep him safe,
to make his life the way we wanted it to be, we, a determined
family of nine, would surely have found it. We didn't. Al-Anon
brought me an understanding of my own powerlessness. I still
feel the pain when I look at him, but at least I don't have to
feel guilty. I have a right to my own life, as he has a right to
his.

Love works.

Though I could not understand why or how the program
worked, I kept coming back to meetings because I felt a deep
sense of need. One night I heard a man say, "Al-Anon is a
perfect program. It is we who are not perfect." He lowered his

head and then looked up at us with eyes twinkling. "And we don't have to be. Love. That's it. Love, my friends, is what we find here. That about covers it. Love is the reason it works." It sounded so simplistic and downright syrupy that I almost laughed. Then I did laugh, because I knew he was right.

When I arrived at my first Al-Anon meeting, my repressed feelings were erupting and I thought I was going crazy. I remember those early days. The first year contained endless painful days that I felt would never pass. I thought the deep hurt from my alcoholic childhood home would never be healed. The Al-Anon members loved me when I was unable to love or accept myself. Their hugs were so important. I felt safe. I was not judged as either good or bad. All that seemed to be required was my presence. It was fortunate that nothing more was asked of me, for I had absolutely nothing to give at the time. I made it from one week to the next by depending on meetings. It wasn't too difficult to go, for I found in the fellowship my first taste of unconditional love.

Today I celebrate my fifth Al-Anon birthday, and what a wealth of precious birthday gifts I have. The Steps taught me how to forgive my past, to live in the present, and to leave the future to God. Today I realize just how much love God has poured into me through the Al-Anon members. The love is so abundant, I am filled to overflowing. I can share it with others. I can share it with hugs. I can share it with service. The more I share it, the bigger it gets, so I'm almost never out of it.

I receive so much joy working on Al-Anon events and serving my group. No one seems to criticize my efforts. What a blessing it is to know that I can do some things right.

I have learned to please myself. I try not to read other people's minds. I value myself as a person. Al-Anon taught me that others can only respect me if I first respect myself. Today

I have opinions. I don't have to prove them right or wrong, and I can allow others to have opinions. We do not have to agree on everything in order to live in harmony.

I am not infinite. I don't have to be. I can set limits on what I will do. I no longer feel I have to be all things to all people. I don't even have to be all things to the people I love.

I continue to grow. Today I am facing my difficulties with intimacy. I feel vulnerable and sometimes afraid as I lower the walls that protected me from the pain of my childhood. Before Al-Anon, I thought love, sex, and intimacy were three words describing the same thing. Today, I am learning, they are words that describe either emotions or behavior. They are interrelated but not dependent on one another. Slowly, as I mature in Al-Anon, I realize the depth and variety of human relationships.

If you asked me today how Al-Anon works for me, I would answer, "Very well, thank you."

I feared my anger.

When I was six months old, my father decided there was something wrong with me because I was left-handed. So he fixed it. I do not remember the period consciously, but I did remember it emotionally. As an adult, I had to get help for clinical depression. In counseling, I discovered the damage changing my handedness had caused and I also found that my father was an alcoholic. With my therapist's encouragement, I joined Al-Anon, where I learned about alcoholism and my reactions to the disease.

In the Al-Anon group, I found something I needed very badly—permission to get angry. I had been afraid of my anger, particularly because as a woman I had been taught it was dangerous and ugly. With the support of my group and my sponsor, I learned how to handle this potent emotion in a healthy way. I found ways to release my anger without hurting anyone, including myself. As I learned I could express anger without fear of hurting or being hurt, I also dared to identify why I was angry and with whom. I hadn't wanted to think I felt angry at those I loved.

Over time, my repressed anger had hardened into rage, and often the unexpressed rage caused my whole body to tense painfully. With the help of an Al-Anon friend who listened to me talk about my dark feelings, I discovered a method to deal with the rage concealed in my body. Talking and writing about it helped, but most of all I found the courage to release rage in vigorous physical exercise. Today my whole body is more relaxed, and I feel mentally and physically healthy.

Now, as I work through problems, I find that more is revealed to me. I have come to understand that the event, however abusive, is only part of the problem. The rest of the problem is my reaction to the event. It was my anger, lingering long after my father "fixed" me, that caused me the difficulty as an adult. I cannot go back and undo the events of my childhood, but I can alter my attitude toward them. I am powerless over the past, not helpless in the present.

Before I started dealing with my anger, I could only tolerate one good friend at a time, and I wanted to virtually own her. I didn't want her to have time for anyone else. After dealing with the anger, I found I could have lots of friends and share them. I felt more love for my brothers and mother. I could even love my dad.

Being accepted where I was and not being judged by the members was the greatest gift Al-Anon gave me. It was hard to admit my tremendous fear and anger to myself, because I wanted to believe I loved my family. In Al-Anon, I found out I can love someone very much and yet still feel fear and anger at the awful things that person does. I don't have to ignore my feelings to convince myself I love my family today, because I do love them, and I can have many feelings, both positive and negative, without judging them or being judged.

Learning to trust enough to let go did not come easy for me. It felt a lot like trying to "make the mountain come to Mohammed." Fortunately, as I tell new members today, in Al-Anon when we take it easy, we can bring the mountain to Mohammed one pebble at a time. As I began to turn my problems over to my Higher Power, I started doing it five minutes at a time. Eventually, I could do it for longer and longer periods. Before I knew it, my Higher Power had the whole problem handled, and I discovered it was only a molehill and not a mountain after all.

No situation is hopeless.

The day alcohol began destroying my life was the day of my birth. I don't figure anyone was overly happy about my birth. I was my 25-year-old alcoholic mother's seventh child. My alcoholic father had disappeared.

I remember huge booze parties at our house with lots of people drinking and cussing. At one of these parties, I got drunk for the first time when I was about two. The room spun and I couldn't stand up. My head buzzed. I felt frightened and sick. No one held me. No one consoled me. I was in a room full of drunks—utterly alone!

A street-wise manipulator by age three or four, I had learned to steal and lie quite well. My younger brothers and sister and I were referred to as "the four babies." As long as

"the four babies" stayed out of everyone's way, we were toler-
ated. We'd get up in the morning and leave the house, and
we'd stay out until after dark. No one ever came looking for
us. We stole from stores for food and went to people's houses
and begged for water and sometimes food. Sometimes they
called the police and we ran.

Two weeks before my sixth birthday, my fifteen-year-old sister got married, and I became the oldest girl and head child
care provider. Mom, really sick in her disease, wasn't home
much. Dad wasn't home at all. When Mom was home, she usually had a man with her. One night when I was sick, I went to
look for her and found her having sex on the couch. I didn't
know what was happening, but it scared me to death. I hurried
back to bed.

When I was eight, my mother married my stepfather. We
moved far from where we had been living and had a nice four-
bedroom house. He didn't drink, and Mom quit drinking. We
went to church and school, even ate regularly. It felt good and
I liked him, but he had his own sickness. At night he made
my sister and me into his sexual playmates. We were devastated. We finally told Mom, but she didn't do anything except
say he was sick and we'd all have to help him.

Finally, he was sent overseas on duty. I was glad for that,
but before he left, he filed for bankruptcy. We lost everything,
and Mom went back to drinking. I had problems with several
of Mom's men and felt scared all the time.

When I was ten, my mother got in trouble with the law and
we ended up living in a car and a U-Haul trailer. We were all
constantly sick and none of us went to school.

Somehow my stepfather got an emergency leave and came
home. He and a friend of his found us, and we stayed together until he had to return to his overseas assignment. We were

then declared wards of the state, and my stepfather's friend
and his wife took us in as foster children. We were a wild
bunch. We all cussed. We all stole and lied. We didn't know
how to cook, clean, bathe, or do anything properly. I was a
ten-year-old infant.

Our foster parents provided a small, warm house, regular
meals, clothing, and sent us to school, but they were young
and had two children of their own, as well as their own problems. He was an alcoholic who abused his wife. She took her
frustration out on all of us kids. Soon my two younger brothers and sister (all of "the four babies" but me) were kicked
out of the home. They were all I had to love, and I felt like I
was being ripped apart. My foster parents told me it was their
own fault. I wasn't allowed to say goodbye. I couldn't hug
them. I couldn't cry. The next year my two older brothers left,
so I had lost my whole family and I wanted to die.

I didn't die, but I did discover that marijuana could drown
out painful reality. I spent nearly my entire senior year of high
school stoned.

Soon after I graduated, I met a man who drank and did
drugs. He even sold drugs, but he treated me like royalty, and
I loved him very much. I was happy when I became pregnant
with his child. He said he was too, but in four months he
abandoned me. My foster parents, insisting I was just like my
real mother, disowned me.

Though it was one of the lowest points of my life, I was
determined to have this child. It would be my family. My
blood. I wanted it badly enough to suffer through the accusations of being a whore. I have never regretted the birth of my
oldest daughter.

Two years after her birth, I married my husband. He was a
hard worker, and he loved us both. He was also an alcoholic,

but I thought I could love him into sobriety. I couldn't, but with three children and eleven years behind us, we are still married. And I have found a program that *literally* saved my life—Al-Anon. As our lives deteriorated with the disease on both sides of our marriage, suicide began to be the only solution I could see to end the pain. Fortunately, again I did not die, and this time I found a therapist who directed me to Al-Anon.

Since that day my life has changed drastically. For the very first time in my life, I have found that serenity is possible and that happiness comes from within. I have found ways that I am blessed, and I have a connection to a Higher Power. I always thought God was keeping tallies of all my wrongs and I would never make it to heaven. Al-Anon showed me how wrong I was. Instead of a vengeful, judgmental God, I have found that God loves me just as I am and I deserve to be loved.

Recovering people are Al-Anon's treasure. Because of the people in this program, I have found acceptance, support, and a love so warm I can hardly describe it. I didn't know unconditional love existed. Now I know it exists in abundance.

I've learned that it is much more harmful and painful for me to carry grudges and resentments than it is for me to go through whatever grieving process I may need to go through to forgive my past and forgive myself. I've learned that I'm not perfect and I don't have to be.

For the first time in twenty-two years, my mother and all seven of us kids were recently reunited. It felt like a miracle. Everyone in my family has their own version of the sickness, and I admit it hurts to see it and know that I am powerless and cannot rescue them. But I also know there is a program and a Power greater than I am waiting for them, if any of them decide they want to heal. It is also available for my foster parents, who have gone their separate ways. It helps me forgive them and appreciate what they were able to give to me despite their own limitations.

I am far from well, but I am also far from where I was. Changing my attitude has allowed love to flood in from everywhere. It is a great way to live, far better than anything I had ever thought possible.

I wouldn't be alive to write this without the help I received from every single person who held my hand along the way. They say the best way to keep this program is to give it away. I hope by sharing my story I can help someone. I really want to help someone, because of all the wonderful "someones" who helped me.

Suggestions for Getting Started

When we begin anything new, we feel sensations of excitement and anxiety. We are excited to think there really may be solutions to life experiences that have hurt and baffled us. We feel excited to try new knowledge because learning is exciting in itself, but we also feel anxious. We may believe we're at the end of our rope and fear that this too will not work. We might worry that, although it may work for others, somehow we are so damaged it won't work for us. We may simply not know what to expect, and since change in the past has often been for the worse, anything different can feel threatening. The key to getting started in an exciting but perhaps frightening new adventure is *willingness* and having other people to en*courage* us.

The sharing of our experience, strength, and hope with each other at meetings and over the phone makes it possible for newcomers and long-time members alike to learn from each other and support each other in trying new behaviors. While newcomers may draw much-needed hope in a dark moment from members who have recovered from similar situations, they also contribute, for many long-time members have found new areas of personal growth opened for them as they listened to new members. The axiom that we must give it away in order to keep it is a well-worn truth in Al-Anon recovery work, where newcomers are both needed and welcome. The first movement toward recovery may simply be to bring our bodies to a meeting so we can listen and learn. Time is needed to heal deep wounds; patience with ourselves allows our minds to follow at a pace we can manage. As one member put it, "If you're thinking about going to a meeting, go to the meeting and think about it afterwards." For some of us, learning to discipline ourselves with kindness and gentleness will create a whole new world, in which long damaged self-esteem can finally blossom and grow.

Once an alcoholic has recognized the disease of alcoholism, the prescription, however difficult to apply, is fairly obvious. The alcoholic cannot take a drink without triggering the disease. For those of us affected by someone else's drinking, the triggers and prescriptions are less obvious. Unlike drinking, behaviors of excessive responsibility or caretaking are not necessarily characteristics we want to wipe out entirely. Caring about someone else and offering help is admirable unless it is carried to an extreme. Often we suffer from an excess of a good thing, which we must manage in order to live healthy, loving, balanced lives. How do we know when we are slipping into destructive behavior and need to take up an Al-Anon tool? Which principle should be applied in a given situation? There are no easy answers; there is no one perfect program suggestion for each situation, but with willingness and perseverance we have learned that we are all capable of finding solutions which lead to serenity.

If you are wondering which aspects of life need Al-Anon suggestions, or when to reach for the phone, write out your feelings, read some Al-Anon literature, or spend quiet time seeking help from a Power greater than yourself, the following questions on pages 142 and 143 may help you recognize the need for recovery work.

1. When difficulties occur, do you need someone to blame even if it is yourself?

2. Do you feel uncomfortable or draw a blank when asked what it is you really want?

3. Does a dark cloud of despair or a creeping depression sometimes seem to appear from nowhere to weigh you down?

4. Do you feel guilty or selfish whenever you say "no"?

5. Are you lonely and isolated? Do you feel like an outsider in the midst of a crowd?

6. Can you identify only one or two extreme feelings, such as anger or fear?

7. Do you think in black and white terms? Is life either wonderful or miserable, with little in between?

8. Are you numb or flat, with no extremes in your feelings whatsoever?

9. Does your memory fog out or have giant holes where you remember nothing?

10. Do you feel suicidal or have a need to hurt yourself or others?

11. Do you tolerate unacceptable behavior even after you have said you won't?

12. Do you have difficulty relaxing and having fun? Would you not recognize fun if it hit you in the face?

13. Are you frequently impatient with yourself or others?

14. Do you think you are the only person in the world you can depend on?

15. Do you feel compelled to do things for other people that they could do for themselves?

16. Do you do things you don't want to do, rather than risk disappointing other people?

17. Do you have difficulty trusting your own perceptions and need to prove you're right and others are wrong in order to convince yourself?

18. Do you feel embarrassed or ashamed because of someone else's behavior?

19. Do you startle easily?

20. Do you think the best way to take care of your needs is not to have any?

If you notice yourself feeling this way once in a great while, it is probably not significant, but if several questions are uncomfortably familiar, or one or two are constant companions, Al-Anon principles might help you.

Learning to detach from other people with love allows us to place a healthy emotional distance between ourselves and our loved ones without abandoning them. In the simplest terms, we find out where we leave off and others begin. It may come as a surprise to discover that we are not responsible and thus need not be embarrassed because of someone else's behavior. The society in which we live often does not understand our detachment and may still convey the message that we are at fault if our loved one drinks or acts unacceptably, but we need not accept this point of view. The key to detaching can be willingness to call our sponsor or another Al-Anon member who will recognize our powerlessness to control another human being, or it may be to pick up Al-Anon literature and read about detachment, or it may be to ask our Higher Power to help us detach. The signal that we need to reach for an Al-Anon tool is often simply feeling uncomfortable. Learning to recognize and trust our feelings is one of the great gifts we get from practicing Al-Anon principles. In the process, we discover that even very negative feelings we have tried to avoid or suppress in the past may be important keys to our recovery. They make us aware of our shortcomings or tell us when something unacceptable is occurring and remind us to reach for recovery.

Recovery is a process of learning to know ourselves. As a process, it is never completed, and change continues to occur. It's part of being fully alive. As certain problems are solved, we are led to deeper levels of consciousness. At first this may seem discouraging, but long-time members have found it a blessing, because even after a crisis has been overcome there is always growth and ever-deepening serenity. Finally we come to feel gratitude for the very agonies that brought us to these rooms and acquainted us with Al-Anon, for we recognize that ours is a lifelong journey, and all the tasks and support we need are here for the taking.

In the meantime, as we journey, we want to know which tool to apply to which problem, and it can be very frustrating to be groping around in the dark. Wise members tell us what worked for them; they cannot, however, guarantee that it will work for us, for although we have a common struggle with the disease of alcoholism, we are also individual people who must find our own unique blend of solutions. We can learn what works for us only by trying it out in our own lives. If you do not know which tool to apply, try one. Pick the one that seems best to you. Ask someone else what worked for them. The key is willingness; the goal is to achieve progress, not perfection. Eventually, like any student who starts with little skill and proceeds to mastery, you will become adept at using the skills and insights of Al-Anon. And for those times (which happen to all of us) when nothing seems to fit and, even after years of practicing the program, we feel like newcomers again at our first meeting, it is important to remember to return to the beginning, attend a meeting, talk to someone, and realize that all your work has not been lost. Instead, a new level of recovery is being offered, and more will be revealed as we journey together on this wonderful adventure called life. The key is willingness.

part Three

CLIMBING THE STEPS TO RECOVERY

Living a life rich in human caring, fulfillment, and inner peace is a challenge. It is a worthy goal to live life wisely and well—one that many of us seek in Al-Anon. We are not proclaiming that we have solved these most difficult riddles of life, but we have found that practicing the Twelve Steps of Al-Anon helps us approach life from a spiritual perspective that has brought progress in learning to define our own idea of fulfillment and to realize we are worthy of a healthy, happy life. Few of us came into an Al-Anon meeting because we had decided it was time to take the philosopher's journey into the nature of truth and beauty and learn how to live a fulfilled life. More than likely, we arrived bristling with anger or sagging with depression and convinced that our misery was all someone else's fault, or—worse yet—that it was all our fault. Many of us came desperately seeking a way to stop the alcoholic from drinking. Though others of us no longer lived with active alcoholism, we arrived surly and martyred, eager to get fixed and get out. In truth, we would have much preferred going dancing to sitting in an Al-Anon meeting.

When we first walk into an Al-Anon meeting, we often have so much pain and crisis in our lives that the notion that our goal is actually happiness and fulfillment seems remote and practically impossible. Long-time members who declare that they are grateful and that they will practice this program for the rest of their lives seem crazier than the alcoholics we have known. Who in their right mind would want to suffer as we are suffering? If we notice they are not suffering the way we are suffering, we may simply decide they have not experienced what we have and dismiss them, but if we stay and listen long enough, we will hear their true stories and discover they have in fact experienced much of what we have but somehow are able to laugh, hug, smile, and enjoy life anyway. Their stories are our stories, and since they've found a way to be happy, we may also find the secret of happiness that has so far eluded us. We come to want the serenity they display and become willing to take hesitant steps along the path they are walking. To walk the walk, rather than telling someone else to walk the walk, takes courage and action. It is helpful, but not enough, simply to attend meetings. At some time (the time when it is right for us) we recognize we must work the Steps to continue recovering.

In Al-Anon we learn self-respect by respecting each other. We come to realize that everyone has the right to seek their own solutions even when their choices differ from ours. The First Step, which tells us, "We admitted we were powerless over alcohol—that our lives had become unmanageable," is essential to giving up trying to control others, even if we believe we are doing what we do for their own good. It is also simply a statement of reality. After some time in the program, it becomes obvious that if the alcoholic cannot control his or her drinking, we certainly can't; in the beginning, however, this fact is not so obvious. The crises in our lives may be so devastating that we fear that if we do not somehow take charge, no matter how impossible the task may be, we will perish or be destroyed. Crisis brings us in, hope keeps us coming back, and serenity in the midst of both turmoil and joy rewards our efforts.

Once we have begun to experience serenity, we realize that

Al-Anon is not just a program where sick people get well, but a way of living that is rewarding in itself. We may not look eagerly forward to new challenges, but we know that together we can handle them, and we feel grateful to have a program that grows as we grow and fits us for the duration, as well as a loving Al-Anon family to accompany us on our life journey. Loneliness and despair still visit us at times, but we do not invite them to dinner and fix up the guest room. Instead, we go to a meeting or review a Step, and eventually they are replaced with fellowship and hope. We smile more often.

Working the Steps does require climbing, effort, occasional breathlessness, and willingness. Some members compare the Steps to a handrail on a staircase. They are placed there lovingly by those who have gone before, for us to hold onto as we make the effort to grow into the human beings we wish to become. Such an uphill journey can seem daunting when viewed from the bottom, but fortunately, all we are asked to do in Al-Anon is to take the First Step. We have found that when we do, all manner of help appears. Someone, perhaps our sponsor, hands us a map, we're outfitted with slogans and companions, and we feel anticipation, excitement, and anxiety as we move toward recovery. Fear not, the journey is worth the climb.

Chapter five

FINDING AND HEALING
SHATTERED FAITH

The first three Steps in Al-Anon are the spiritual foundation of recovery. Without spiritual help, living with an alcoholic or even having lived with alcoholism was debilitating and often disastrous for us. As we struggled with the family disease of alcoholism, many of us lost our faith and felt alone and abandoned in a hostile world. Naturally, we tried to control that world as best we could to make it safe, but even our best efforts made no impact on this devastating disease. We longed for help, but the effects of alcoholism on our families made trusting a Power greater than ourselves very difficult. We often wondered where that Power was when our young lives were being shattered. Many of us felt betrayed and abused. Fear made surrender appear dangerous. In order to even consider believing in the loving help of other people or a Higher Power, we first had to try everything we could to handle the situation ourselves—and finally face defeat.

Even after many defeats, some of us came into the Al-Anon rooms still hoping forlornly for a way to stop other people from drinking. It seemed a bitter pill to swallow to admit powerlessness over alcohol and the alcoholic, but gradually it dawned on us that this was really the only way to obtain our freedom. Step One, "We admitted we were powerless over alcohol—that our lives had become unmanageable," requires us to humbly face our human limitations. Who among us eagerly wants to embrace limitation? Yet we found that accepting that we were not in control of another human being brought with it relief from the burden of assuming responsibility for others' behaviors. Understanding that we did not cause the disease, could not control it, and could not cure it lifted the ever-present guilt we had carried unconsciously for so long. Finally, we found the permission and the courage to focus on ourselves and the pleasures, hopes, and dreams that had slipped away while we were concentrating so much energy on others. Admitting powerlessness does not mean we are totally helpless; it means we are not responsible for everyone else in the world.

We are a varied lot. We come from many religious backgrounds and from none. We bring our religious beliefs and disbeliefs with us, but we leave them outside the door and concentrate on keeping an open mind and remembering that the Steps are suggestions, not dogma. There is no requirement that we accept a specific belief in order to belong to Al-Anon. The Second Step, "Came to believe that a Power greater than ourselves could restore us to sanity," is written in the past tense, as are all the Steps, because they state what happened for us when we practiced the program. For some of us a Higher Power has been the only source of love and solace in a long, painful journey. Others of us have prayed for so long without result that we are bitter and suspicious. There are also those among us who have never thought much about whether a God exists, and others still who have experienced abuse and alcoholism within organized religion. Though many members choose to call their Higher Power God, some members may find a Power greater than themselves in the natural world or in the deep caring of their group.

We avoid discussions of particular religious beliefs because they tend to hamper unity and divert us from our primary goal, which is recovery from the effects of another's alcoholism. We do share with each other our experiences with a Higher Power, but each of us is encouraged to take what we like and leave the rest. At least in meetings there is a forum for our own individual spiritual questing, as well as acceptance of our right to find a God of our own understanding to aid our recovery. With human support and spiritual guidance, it comes as a great relief at last to find we are not alone in our pain.

As our faith in a Power greater than ourselves begins to grow, we need to become willing to act on the guidance we receive. Action requires a decision. Step Three, "Made a decision to turn our will and lives over to the care of God *as we understood Him,*" asks us to let go of control and allow our Higher Power to help us. Letting go of control (or the illusion of control) feels very risky for those of us who have grown up with the loneliness, chaos, disappointment, and sometimes outright terror of alcoholism. Fear of surrendering the defenses that we managed to create during our formative years— after all they at least kept us alive—can make the Third Step appear quite perilous. Fortunately, no one rips our security from us by demanding we surrender everything we know and take on a whole new philosophy. Rather, we learn to practice Step Three a day, perhaps an hour, or even a minute at a time. If we are not even willing to do that, we can return to Step Two and gather more confidence or ask for the willingness to try.

Slowly, little by little, we release our fierce grip on control and discover that surrender is not suicidal. When our shattered faith in God, other human beings, and ourselves begins to mend, we are ready to move on toward accepting responsibility for our own lives. We know that if our faith falters, we can always return to Steps One, Two, and Three.

STEPPING OUT ON THE JOURNEY

Al-Anon was the last resort.

Giving up the power I never really had has been quite a challenge for me because I keep believing I can do it myself—and, worse, that I have to. About a year before I came to Al-Anon, I read an article about research on children of alcoholics. I didn't identify with anything, so I decided my mother's alcoholism hadn't affected me. Later I saw someone on public television talking about adult children of alcoholics, and I did recognize a similarity when I heard, "we're as sick as our secrets." My family regularly admonished us not to "air our dirty linens in public." Actually we didn't air them in private either. We just pretended problems didn't exist. The man on the television suggested Al-Anon meetings, but I thought that now that I knew about the problem, I could handle it on my own. Was I wrong! Fortunately, I visited my younger sister, who invited me to go to her Al-Anon meeting. As soon as I got back home, I hunted up an Al-Anon meeting; the topic was control, and I knew I was in the right place.

But I still wasn't ready to really sign up and work a program. I live in a world of drive-through windows, microwave ovens, and movies where people solve mammoth problems in an hour. I came looking for a quick fix. I hated hearing that it took me forty years to get where I was and I wouldn't change overnight. Sometimes I still catch myself waiting to hear the magic word or phrase that will make me well. Then I know it's time to work harder on my program and remind myself to expect progress rather than perfection.

At first the First Step seemed easy. I had already tried everything possible to keep my mother from drinking and had given up. I also felt that if my life were manageable, I wouldn't be coming to these meetings. What was difficult to accept was the concept that alcoholism is a disease. I could drink one or two drinks and stop. I thought she could too, if she wanted to. When I got in touch with my own addictive/compulsive behaviors, I understood the disease concept.

Being addicted to relationships had never entered my mind, but as I examined my life in Al-Anon, the compulsions became obvious. My first marriage had lasted less than six years. After nine years single, I married again—to a man who drank and smoked himself into a fatal heart attack just two years later. By the time I arrived at Al-Anon I had been single again for four years, and I looked down self-righteously on all women who had to have a man around. Were my cheeks red when I realized I had always had a man around, just never the same one for very long! At the time, I was in a relationship with an alcoholic, workaholic, married man. With the help of Al-Anon, I ended that destructive relationship and decided to take a few months to get to know myself. I'd heard a year suggested, but I figured I was smart enough not to need that long. Wrong again! It's been four years and I'm still getting to know myself. I had changed so many times, matching myself to whoever I was with, that I had to do a lot of digging to find the real me under all the many-colored skins I wore. Today I am willing to wait for God to choose the next man in my life.

I discovered I can also make compulsions out of positive traits. I am a compulsive reader. I block out the world with books the way my mother blocked it out with alcohol. I am compulsively good. It isn't a real, conscious choice to be good, but a feeling of being driven by need, as if not being good will bring immediate disaster. After I took the First Step, I found myself often sliding back into the "good girl compulsion." I was still trying to be good enough to deserve a sober mother. To alter this deeply rooted belief, I take the First Step daily.

I knew I needed to be restored to sanity, but I didn't believe the first half of Step Two. It bothered me that meetings closed with the Lord's Prayer, but I'd heard the words, "Take what you like and leave the rest," so I left the Lord's Prayer. It also bothered me how often Higher Power or God was mentioned. I was a rational human being who *knew* there was no higher power. I thought the universe had evolved out of chaos and my life was proof of it. They said, "Keep coming back." That I could do. Gradually, I came to believe in a Higher Power. I'm not sure how it happened, but I'm glad it did. The God of my understanding has nothing to do with my childish God who made lists of my bad deeds and never noticed my good ones. Now I can see that, even when I believed in a God of fear or no God at all, a Higher Power still watched over me. He kept me unharmed all the times my mother drove us around drunk—even through two accidents. While I ran around in bars picking up strangers, God protected me. When I finally was ready for recovery, God led me to Al-Anon, even though He had to use newspapers, magazines, television, *and* my sister to get my attention. Patiently, He watched over me while I tried to do the whole Twelve Step program in sixty minutes. Thank God, today I do not have to live my life as if I am a sound bite or thirty-second commercial.

I am the sum total of all my experiences. The bad ones have made me strong. The sad ones have made me compassionate. In Al-Anon I am learning to treasure all of me one day at a time.

> *Powerless is not helpless.*

Alcoholism can turn triumph into tragedy, and love into grim determination. Recently, I realized that even years of faithfully practicing my Al-Anon program did not protect me from the tragedies the disease creates. I became angry at the program and felt betrayed, much as I had felt betrayed by God, as a small boy trapped in an alcoholic home. Then, in my child's mind, I had reasoned that, if God gave me an alcoholic father who beat me and threatened to murder my mother, either I deserved it or God was cruel. Neither option left me any hope.

Al-Anon gave me hope and taught me of a loving God who walks every step of my life with me; yet, today, as an adult still facing the periodic alcoholism of my father and willful martyrdom of my mother, it is very easy to slip back into my childish reasoning when events are particularly devastating. How quickly I slide into despair and the compulsion to do something, anything, to fix it. When nothing I do yields a positive result and all I can accomplish is to make the best of a bad situation, it is time to revisit the First Step, but first I still seem to slip into a dark tunnel of hopeless, helpless anger. Such a situation occurred this year.

A year ago, I came home from New York triumphantly carrying my first book contract, eager to tell my friends and savor the beginning of an accomplishment I'd worked for and desired for more than ten years. While in New York my father, who is not in recovery but hadn't had a drink for four years, called me, desperate for help with my increasingly dependent, demanding, frail mother. In spite of his own disability (he is 85 and has only one leg) he had been trying to care for her, but she was beginning to require daily care, and he felt frantic. I rushed up there the very next weekend.

He wanted me to hire a live-in caretaker for which they clearly didn't have enough money, not to mention the difficulty of hiring someone to live in a house with a man who had in past alcoholic episodes pulled out some of his numerous guns and threatened to blow us all away. I tried to break it to him gently and suggest daily help. That wasn't what he wanted to hear. By afternoon he was drunk and abusive. Trying to practice my Al-Anon, after one warning, I left the house. As I pulled out of the driveway, I could see my mother, wild-eyed, peering out from the curtains.

All my life I had wanted to protect my mother from my father. As a child, I had felt ashamed that I was not man enough to protect us. As an adult, I felt revolted by Mother's obvious plays for Dad's attention by fawning over me—her little man. She wouldn't leave him, but she heaped guilt on me if I didn't come running whenever he drank. Though no longer physically afraid of my father, the whole scene wrenched my gut. I felt nauseous. I knew I could not live with my mother, even if I could have afforded 24-hour care in my home, which I couldn't. Neither could I leave her there, needing medicine in the form of shots twice a day, toilet care, feeding, and watching (for she had begun to wander and fall down). I collected myself and returned. My father was raging and staggering around the house; she had disappeared. Finally, I found her cowering like a terrified animal under the bed.

I removed her from the house that night, but since she required daily nursing, I had to find her a nursing home. Though it was the newest, nicest facility in town, Mother was inconsolable. The nurses told me that each day she packed her bags and announced she was going home. She pleaded with me, "Can't you afford your mother even a small corner in your house? I won't be any trouble. I won't eat much." With my heart breaking, I tried to console her via long distance. My father got sober, but not before he broke the only leg he had. It was unlikely that he could provide care, but before he could get well enough to even consider taking her home, she broke her hip and died of complications from the surgery.

All humans must cope with the death of their loved ones, and I doubt if it is ever easy, but alcoholism layered my mother's death with guilt, betrayals, and recriminations that increased the pain for all of us. Mother's death was as hard as her life had been. Her bitterness at the last indignity of being stuck in a nursing home, while Dad drank in the house she had worked, saved, and scrimped for all her life, allowed her no peace. I longed for love, forgiveness, understanding, and connection in those last weeks, but the disease still held too much power in our family. At one point she managed to tell me I had been a good son, and that maybe she should have gone to Al-Anon. It was the only moment of comfort in a long series of angry, pathetic complaints that I had not saved her. I wanted to save her, but I was powerless. Through the whole ordeal, I clung to that moment of comfort and repeated the Serenity Prayer.

Serious crises still catapult me back into my character defects like a stone flying from a slingshot. Before I have time to practice my principles, my thoughts race pell-mell toward negativity and control. I find myself thinking, "What kind of a program is Al-Anon if coming, and working hard, and being good still leaves me with an unrecovered family, where all the choices are painful?" It is my childish mind speaking—the child who kept believing that if only he was good enough, the horror would stop and Mommy and Daddy would love each other. I still have difficulty realizing that my

being good has nothing to do with someone else's alcoholism
or someone else's reaction to alcoholism. I still have difficulty not feeling betrayed by God and Al-Anon when life
seems almost too sad to bear.

But if I put one foot in front of the other and go to enough
meetings, read some literature, and call my sponsor—even if
my trust that anything will come of it is meager—eventually,
I will hear something that will help me. So it was with this lat-
est crisis. Eventually, it dawned on me that it was time to
revisit the First Step. I am powerless over alcohol. Al-Anon is
a wonderful group of people like me, but even as a group, we
are powerless over alcohol and alcoholics. It is a very painful
fact to have to accept powerlessness over something that
destroys people we love and is brutal to watch. No wonder we
often slip back into our own form of denial and try yet again
to find some way to fix the situation. No wonder I often
repress my grief until my eyes brim with tears, my shoulders
ache from hanging onto control, and I wonder why I am
depressed again.

Though it may sound grim, I am actually very grateful for
a sponsor who, when I tell him how it all happened, can say
to me, "That's awful! That's a terrible, painful experience!" In
my family, no matter how awful it was, I was told, "It wasn't
that bad." It is comforting to have another person realize it
really was that bad, because even after many years in recovery, I still sometimes need another human being to give me
support and permission to feel as badly as I do. In Al-Anon I
am allowed to feel and to be real.

Al-Anon has taught me compassion, and as I practice the
program (pretty mechanically during the dark times), slowly
my compassion extends even to myself. Today I can forgive
myself for not being able to save my mother from her pain and
can realize that it was not for lack of love. Today I am learn-

ing to accept that it has taken me a year to begin to grieve my
mother's death and to understand that sometimes I still need
physical pain to remind me to take time to feel. Today I can
forgive myself, when family problems loom, if I slip into feelings of anger and betrayal toward those very Al-Anon members who are loving me into recovery, because I know they
will understand. Today I know that even in Al-Anon I will
often trip, but if I keep walking toward recovery, even though
I can't see why or how, I will arrive once again at Step One,
and eventually relief, serenity, and the love of the fellowship
will triumph. Yes, even over this.

I blamed myself.

Like so many of us, I needed Al-Anon long before I found
my way to my first meeting. The first eight years of my life
were spent with an alcoholic father and a mother who desperately needed the solace of Al-Anon but never found it. No one
ever talked about why there was so much yelling, screaming,
and hitting in my house. After my father left, I saw that
Mother had problems too, but I thought the real problem was
me. I tried desperately to be a perfect daughter, but I could
never be good enough to relieve her anger.

At eighteen I married and left home, vowing to be a perfect
wife and mother. Though I lived in a nice house with two lovely children, and a husband who didn't drink, I was so miserable that I left them all.

I then spent years wandering in and out of alcoholic relationships until I finally found a wonderful man with three children. He had custody because his former wife was an
alcoholic. We managed quite nicely until the children reached
their teens and the problems began—truancy, fighting, and
arrivals at the front door of a slightly tipsy teenage son. What

I later learned was denial kicked in—I ignored his alcoholic behavior and convinced myself that I just needed to spend more quality time with the children to fix everything.

All the quality time I could manage didn't avert near tragedy. The youngest child overdosed. She was rushed to the hospital in an ambulance, her blood level of alcohol twice the legal limit for drivers. I still didn't consciously admit the possibility of alcoholism, but her father and I knew that something was wrong. We admitted her to a psychiatric hospital. At that point I believe God stepped in, through a wise doctor who bluntly told us she was an alcoholic. Cutting through my denial, he informed me that I needed help as well and I could find it in Al-Anon.

Though it has been seven years, I remember clearly how I felt, walking into that first meeting. I was furious with my daughter, scared she wouldn't get well, and so sure it was all my fault that I believed no one could possibly understand. The people at Al-Anon told me it was all right to feel those things that day, but in time I could change if I'd just keep coming back.

Step One wasn't a problem for me. I felt powerless because I had tried everything to change my daughter's behavior. Step Two was a different matter. I didn't believe I would or could have a sane life. I was sure my Higher Power was punishing me for getting a divorce and for being a bad daughter, mother, wife—you name it, I was being punished for it.

The people at those first meetings just listened, and listened, and hugged me, and told me to come again. I got a sponsor, went to the same meetings she went to, and listened to her. Eventually, I started to pray again. I had stopped in despair and because I was afraid of God, but now I prayed in a new way—not only when I was desperate, but every day.

Ever so slowly, sanity came creeping into my life. When I

realized that the other children had problems with alcohol, I was able to seek help for them.

I began to look at my childhood, and I found out that the secret in my house was alcoholism. I learned to put names on my feelings, acknowledge them, and let go of the ones causing destructive actions that brought me pain.

Thanks to the program, my daughter and I have a relationship again after almost five years of no contact. One son hugged me on his wedding day and said, "I always know that you love me, Mom, no matter what I do," and another son recently told me he loved me. If I had to pick one gift that has been the most healing, it would be the one I received in my relationship with my mother. You see, she died recently, and I was there with her. The love and forgiveness I felt for her as I held her hand is beyond words. I felt sadness too, for she never accepted the gifts of Al-Anon, but I also felt grateful that I had. The pain caused by alcoholism went back forty years, but in seven short years, I was able to change that pain to love, forgiveness, and serenity.

I don't have trouble with Step Two any more, because whenever I feel a little crazy I know that my Higher Power can help me get back to sanity and I thank Him every day for that blessing.

I banished shame.

Because of the fellowship of the Al-Anon Family Groups, I have hope today. I have hope that, if I continue to use the tools and practice the Steps and Traditions as a *way of life,* my life will continue to get better. Through all of the wonderful gifts of this fellowship I continue to be restored to sanity. Last week I took a big step for me. I raised my hand to speak about the meeting topic, which was Step Two.

Recently, some workmen and artists restored some of the great art work on the ceiling of the Sistine Chapel at the Vatican. The work was already beautiful. All they were doing was restoring and bringing out more of the beauty that was there. I feel much the same thing happening in my relationship with my Higher Power and the fellowship. I do the work, but my Higher Power helps me see the beauty that has been here from the time I was born. How do I begin to say thank you for a gift like that? I attempt it by living life as fully as I can and by carrying the message as well as I can.

Because of Al-Anon, I am able to ask for help; that was not always the case for me. I grew up in a family deeply affected by the disease of alcoholism. An uncle I loved very much died, partly as a result of his drinking. He was murdered by someone he knew, probably over something related to alcohol, drugs, or money. I grew up in a war zone with a violent father whose drinking bothered me. Many times police came to our house, responding to a domestic abuse call. They never arrested my father; they just asked him to leave the house for a couple of days and come back when he had cooled down.

My whole sense of reality was distorted from living in that house. I couldn't trust my own eyes. Today I understand why. I remember a very violent episode, when I was five or six, during which my father assaulted my mother. Sure that he was killing her, I yelled and screamed at the top of my lungs for him to stop. After it was over, my aunt came to me and told me my parents were only playing. Talk about destroying a child's sense of reality! The whole family denied and minimized the regular, horrible violence until I could not trust what I saw or what I felt. The violence continued until my parents broke up when I was in my teens.

With caring teachers, neighbors who tried to help, and a wonderful pastor, we survived the war zone. I believe that, having lived through it, my sisters and I got some skills that benefit us in life, but many of the skills we learned in order to survive in an environment like that did not help us as adults. The mistrust and insecurity I carried cost me jobs, relationships, and precipitated many "geographic cures."

One geographic cure *did* work for me. As soon as I could, I left home for college. College was wonderful! I was safe for the first time in my life. I made some great friends, learned a lot, and did a lot of growing. Thanks to Al-Anon I can look back today with gratitude toward all the people who helped me ride out my childhood and grow up in college. With some of the pain ebbing away, I can once again see how full my glass was despite the many traumas. The Twelve Steps are helping restore me to sanity and improving my attitude by teaching me that people do not have the ability to ruin my day unless I let them.

I remember hearing someone in the fellowship describe the Twelve Steps as follows: One to Three—Clear up, Four to Nine—Clean up, Ten to Twelve—Grow up. I identify with this description. I went to my first Al-Anon meeting filled with shame, and I tried to hide so no one would see me. Thanks to working my program, a wonderful sponsor, and my Higher Power always being on the lookout to restore me to sanity, today I can believe the Al-Anon literature that says, "There is a confident and radiant personality in each of us." Slowly, I begin to see more and more of that confident and radiant person that God wants me to be. The fellowship helped restore my cultural pride in my Puerto Rican heritage. Before Al-Anon I was terribly ashamed of it, as well as having grown up on welfare for a period of time because of the disease. Al-Anon gave me the courage to become a musician, albeit a novice. I've discovered I don't have to play music perfectly to enjoy making music. Like music, the more I practice Al-

Anon, the better I will get at it—and the joy is in the practice. Today I love life and am looking forward to more of it, and you, my Al-Anon friends, are the reason. From the bottom of my heart, thank you!

I didn't trust God!

My baby book records that my first word was "da-da" at age six months. It's interesting that I should first identify the alcoholic member of our family—probably because I learned to fear him early on. My siblings confirm that they too feared him and concentrated on doing whatever it took to get out of the home and become independent as soon as possible.

Though my father drank to excess even when courting Mother, she never expected him to become an alcoholic. All of their friends drank too, and she attributed the excess to the stress of World War II. Of course, the war came and went, and Dad kept right on drinking.

Dad was loving and protective of us as far as necessities were concerned, but we always knew him as an easily angered, somewhat abusive personality. My earliest memory of this was when I was five. My mother warned me to be quiet so I wouldn't bother Dad, who was upstairs feeling ill. When he came downstairs, I sat on the couch eyeing him wide-eyed, having stopped my play and chatter so I wouldn't disturb him. He must have sensed the tension and felt condemned, because he growled fiercely, "And what the hell are you so goddamned quiet about?" I was too young to understand his foul moods. Mother once told me that when I cried from colic, he used to pick me up out of my crib, in frustration, and slap me until my nose ran profusely. Later she retracted that admission. I remember him shoving my brother against the wall and beating him in the face. When he caught me watching, he sent me to the kitchen unless I wanted to be next. Once he sat on me and beat me until my nose bled. To this day, my parents are united in their opinion that I deserved it for becoming impatient with one of my father's drunken remarks.

Besides pervasive violence in our home, alcoholism created an atmosphere of mistrust and disappointment. My father often showed up very late to pick me up. He was so late picking me up from school on the night of a dance at which I was supposed to be a member of the Queen's Court, that the hairdresser didn't have time to fix my hair. I had to walk out onto the floor in my dress and shoes with my long hair wet and disheveled. I felt humiliated.

I endured, thinking that once I left home my problems would be over, but I was in for a surprise. At school and my part-time job, people thought it strange that I seldom went home and didn't stay long when I did visit. I blew off their inquiries. The performance evaluations at my first real job should have alerted me. They described me as somewhat compulsive and afraid to have fun or take a break from work to do things with co-workers like decorate the office Christmas tree. They didn't know the worst of it. I was anorexic in my teens and was headed for a nervous breakdown. Eventually, counseling was a mandatory requirement to keep my job. Thank goodness, this requirement finally put me in touch with a counselor who knew about alcoholism and its effects on the children in the family. She referred me to Al-Anon.

Because I was somewhat paranoid and suspicious of people, I had difficulty trusting anyone to really be there for me. My repressed neediness strained the friendships I did manage. I also felt very suspicious of God. Step Three came very hard for me. It asked me to turn my will and life over to the care of God as I understood Him. I felt I had suffered quite enough pain and injustice in His "care" and trusted only my own will to run my life. The group taught me to reconsider how I understood God, a definition I came to realize was colored by my associations of God with my father—the most powerful and abusive figure in my life. With the help of friends in Al-Anon, I could see my parents as the biological instruments of my existence and two people gravely affected by a disease. I learned to think of myself as a survivor rather than a victim and to recognize God's hand in my survival. There were people and circumstances in my life who helped me survive, and a loving God to guide me toward health in even the darkest, most self-destructive hours. When I could focus on those who had helped me instead of all the pain, I began to feel some gratitude and some relief from the pain.

Putting the focus on myself rather than the alcoholic helped me to see that most people do not hurt others intentionally. They act out of their own pain, just as I acted out of mine. Even the alcoholic did not set out to hurt me; his actions were the symptoms of a disease that had progressed, just as red spots are a symptom of measles. Nevertheless, I do not voluntarily expose myself to diseases, and I no longer allow anyone to abuse me, nor do I abuse myself by starvation or withholding from myself life's pleasures.

This program is a way of life, and it comes in handy every day because others in the world come from poorly functioning families, and interpersonal difficulties don't end when you leave home. Dealing with my family is still the greatest challenge. I'm the only person in my family in recovery, and sometimes I get criticized for it. My siblings, who left home before the later stages of the disease, wonder why I can't just forget the past and do without the program. I know I can't, and I don't want to do without Al-Anon. When their need to deny the problem causes them to accost me, I first turn my will over to the God of my new understanding. Then I turn them over as well. Everything isn't perfect. I don't always have exactly the right answers, but it is much better than when I was doing it the hard way all alone, using my own will power.

I've read that in scientific experiments, when electrodes are applied to certain areas of the brain, past memories can be recalled and almost re-experienced in the present. I have news for those researchers. Such experiences do not require strategically placed electrodes to reproduce them. From time to time, things that happen in the normal course of my life cause an old resentment or reaction to surface, and I have to work through the issue yet again. I've been told this is normal. I have to work the Steps daily; they aren't done once and for all. Those of us who grew up with alcoholism tend to overre-act to situations over which we have no control, for they have proven consistently painful in the past. I take this into account when the present seems unaccountably alarming, and I remember that this is not God punishing me forever for having had a painful childhood, but rather God allowing me to bring the memories up a little at a time, now that I am strong enough and have enough support to heal them.

Knowing these things about myself helps me extend the compassion to others. I take into account how affected I am by my past when I meet people who seem difficult, and I try to give them a break. Instead of throwing a mistake in some-one's face because I have to be perfect to avoid an alcoholic's wrath, I can choose to promote healing by responding with tolerance. I am grateful that I have a program of recovery that my parents' generation generally did not know about. I am grateful that I do not have to right all the world's wrongs before I can recover and that there is hope and help available, whether my parents recover or not. The experience, strength, and hope I have to share is that I survived, and life looks a lot better from today's vantage point.

The program stayed with me.

I have read that we humans tend to mark with ceremonies significant events that indicate major life changes, because these events leave marks upon our lives. Religious rites of passage are one example—circumcision, Bar Mitzvah, Confirmation, Baptism. We hold commencement ceremonies to honor academic achievements and marriage ceremonies to recognize the union of two people in loving relationship. When someone dies, we attend memorial services, or sit Shiva, or, in New Orleans, parade through the streets to mark their passage. Whatever the occasion, we want to observe it, to recognize it, to support it with prayer, song, dance, silence, or community celebration.

Reflecting on my Al-Anon recovery, I see that the markers which led me into the program were very much like the Steps. I grew up surrounded by alcoholism and the sickness that affects everyone who comes in touch with it. I will not dwell on incidents in my childhood, for they are variations on what each of us have experienced. I will say this: we were dysfunctional long before the term was coined. Though we had the basics—a decent home, food, clothing, even an excellent education for which I am very grateful—we were emotionally disadvantaged. My brother likes to say that we were denied our birthright: the expectation that we would be loved, accepted, and nurtured by the people who brought us into the world. He is right.

How could we feel lovable if the significant people in our lives could not express love for us? How could we feel accepted if they continually pointed out our shortcomings and rarely rewarded our accomplishments? Could we be nurtured if our family members were always drunk or angry or retreating from reality? We grew up feeling like burdens to our parents, "bad" children who had to earn love and were never accepted as is.

We chose various behaviors to deal with our environment. I became super-responsible (yes, I'm the oldest), while my brother sought attention through outrageous behavior—always challenging and violating authority. We left home with little self-confidence or emotional maturity to guide our life choices.

When I was thirty, a friend persuaded me to attend Al-Anon. Because I wasn't ready, I guess, to see my emotional emptiness as a result of alcoholism in my life, I didn't stay with the program, but, as I found out later, the program stayed with me and marked my life even before I recognized its full significance.

Step One. I recall the moment vividly. I had stopped by my parents' home to inform them of a major decision I had made which I knew they would not receive well. Their response reflected only how this decision would affect them, not how it would affect me. Not only did they not offer support, they basically disowned me. It was a measure of my own foolishness that I came seeking acceptance and love from them in the first place, deluded (as so many of us have been) that "maybe this time things will be different." However, that moment was an "Aha!" for me. As much as I wanted their love and acceptance, I knew I could not count on it. My search for serenity and sanity began that day. I believe that "Aha!" was my first Step One. I admitted I was powerless over parental approval and that my life had become unmanageable.

Step Two. Two years later I took a long trip with a friend whose behavior became increasingly distressing to me over the weeks. In a small town in Nevada, I blew up, completely out of control. Walking back to the lodging alone, I recalled the words of the Serenity Prayer from Al-Anon meetings years earlier. The words comforted me and lulled me to sleep. That night I took Step Two as I came to believe that a Power greater than myself could and did restore me to sanity.

Step Three. In October of that year a family incident left me so angry I feared I might do something to myself or someone else if I didn't get some understanding and control of my behavior. Though I did not yet make the connection between alcoholism and my sorry emotional state, something within me whispered that Al-Anon would help. The very next day, I attended a meeting. I sat and listened to others share their experience, strength, and hope, and suddenly the events of all those years had a context and an explanation. More importantly, I recognized that Al-Anon, which I had rejected years before, had nevertheless continued to provide me with the tools and road map I needed. Surrender happened at that meeting, but you could say that it had been happening on a subconscious level for seven years. I made a firm decision to turn my will and my life over the care of God *as I understand Him.*

In the years since, I have lived the Steps, Traditions, and slogans, and I have grown spiritually, mentally, and emotionally. People who meet me today cannot believe I once lacked the self-confidence to speak in even a small group of people. They cannot conceive that I was fearful of decisions and incapable of loving, nurturing relationships, but then they didn't grow up with alcoholism either. Only those of us who have been there can truly appreciate the miracle that is recovery through this sane and simple program.

Chapter six

REALISTIC ACCEPTANCE
OF RESPONSIBILITY

"**I**'ve discovered something," a member commented at a meeting. "I really am like my mother. I take responsibility for everybody in the world except myself. I often felt angry at Mom for making me responsible for her happiness and laying guilt on me whenever I didn't meet her expectations. She worried incessantly about my children and always let me know that she sat miserably at home waiting for me to call, but she never called me or created fun for herself. When, as an adult, I refused to come over and share the misery when Dad drank, she was furious, but she wouldn't leave and take care of herself. I, too, take responsibility for everything except my own happiness. When our nation started a war recently, I felt guilty and responsible, but when my husband says, 'What do you want to do tonight?' I draw a blank. I cater to others while secretly waiting and expecting them to finally get it and take care of me. They don't. The hardest thing I've had to do in Al-Anon is ask for what I want, because I usually don't know what I want and I think asking for it proves I'm selfish, just as my parents always said I was. This method of trying to get my needs met just didn't work."

In a family affected by alcoholism, sorting our appropriate

responsibility from inappropriate accusations, blame, and guilt aimed at us by sick relatives is a thorny task. Family members coping with the severe illness of one member frequently take on roles and jobs that would normally be assumed by the sick member. With a disease such as alcoholism that is chronic, progressive, and often of many years duration, responsibilities that belong to the alcoholic are shifted to others, a little at a time, until the whole family becomes distorted. Children, who naturally have many needs, may be accused of selfishness for having *any*. Partners of alcoholics, expected to carry far too much responsibility, may be so overwhelmed that they unconsciously attempt to shift some of the burden to their children, or they may be too tired to pay attention to the children.

When we were children we naturally loved our families, were dependent on them, and tried hard to help in any way we could. Trying to fill the holes left by an adult who is not available either literally or emotionally creates overly responsible children whose thin veneer of maturity overlies a great void of unmet needs. Some of us performed heroically while inside we were driven, frightened, empty, and felt we were never good enough. Some of us demanded the attention the family was unable to provide by acting wild, rebellious, and alarming, as if to scream, "Look at me!" Inside we felt shame, guilt, and pain. Some children of alcoholics sought to divert attention from the real problem (the drinker) by joking, talking compulsively, or being the life of the party, while others shrank into a corner, becoming utterly invisible by choice. Though these adaptations may originally have been outgrowths of natural aspects of our personalities, they can become so overblown and compulsive that they eclipse our real selves. To tell the difference between our true selves and the rigid roles we play, we must learn to listen closely to our feelings and examine our behavior and motives with clarity and compassion.

Self-examination can be terrifying for people who have been blamed, shamed, criticized, and abused. Convinced that we are deeply flawed, and frightened that we are not worthy of love and acceptance, we often have no idea how to treat ourselves gently. We may have had no models of kindness at all, and the notion that we should examine ourselves with kindness might be completely foreign. Approaching Step Four, "Made a searching and fearless moral inventory of ourselves," we sometimes want to run right out of Al-Anon, or we grab the inventory with the zeal of a ferocious bulldog, convinced that we will finally find out what is wrong with us and fix it. Though both extremes are common to those of us who tend toward black and white thinking, neither works very well.

When taking an inventory, we might first want to find a sponsor or at least begin to talk with other Al-Anon members in order to provide ourselves with support, encouragement, and perspective. We need someone with experience in working the Steps to give us balance and remind us to use self-knowledge for personal growth rather than further self-abuse. We need a lot of reminding to treat ourselves with the empathy and tenderness we are so quick to extend to others. If we don't know how to treat ourselves gently, it may help to think about a best friend or some child we love very dearly. How would we treat this person if she or he were admitting deep secrets? We can then treat ourselves the same way.

Sharing the secret shames we have carried is the task of Step Five, which states, "Admitted to God, to ourselves, and to another human being the exact nature of our wrongs." Many of us approach this Step with even more fear than we had doing the inventory, for we suspect that no one in the world is as shameful as we are. Perhaps we have been told that we were the cause of all our parents' woes. Perhaps we came to feel, deep inside, that we must have done something despicable to deserve all the pain we suffered. Or, we may have developed an image of a judgmental God, just waiting to punish us as soon as we admit we really did "it"—whatever "it" is. Sharing is important to the cleaning-up process, because only through sharing can we unburden ourselves of the darkness we believe lurks within and begin to live in the present. Many of us are surprised to find that our faults are not earth shattering. We may even come to understand how egotistical it is to believe that we are the worst human beings; we may discover we are not bad people but people who made imperfect choices, perhaps because they were the only choices we could see at the time. Even our worst behaviors were attempts to cope with long-held pain and can be understood in the light of compassion. With great relief, we attain a realistic view of ourselves as human beings with limitations and capabilities.

Once we have discovered our character flaws and assets, there is still work to do. Step Six, "Were entirely ready to have God remove all these defects of character," reminds us that changing is a collaborative process. We don't need to dig into ourselves and root out every flaw and every characteristic we deem unworthy. We accept responsibility for ourselves and the choices we made. We become willing to *let* God remove those aspects of our character that no longer serve us. We supply the willingness, then trust our Higher Power to do the rest. Al-Anon teaches us to sort our responsibilities from those which others should assume. It also reminds us that, as human beings, we are not gifted with the vast universal view that is the realm of a Power greater than we are. We cannot even see from all the various vantage points a group affords. Sometimes we may not know what is best for us. Characteristics we find totally unacceptable may have a useful purpose in the universe. Along with a developing sense of appropriate responsibility comes humility, which can be defined as knowing what is ours to do and accepting realistically our appropriate place in the universe, then letting God do God's job.

In order to let go and let God, we may have to expand our sense of trust in God, ourselves, and other people. Most of our character defects served a purpose at some time. We might have learned control to ward off chaos, or judgment to reduce our own overwhelming shame. We may eat, buy things, or give gifts we can't afford in an attempt to assuage loneliness. We may laugh and joke, even inappropriately, rather than cry uncontrollably. We may rage to cover up terrifying feelings of helplessness or refuse to take any chances rather than risk failure. To become willing to release a character defect, we must come to believe that we can find a positive alternative to our old defensive behavior. We gain this faith by seeing others bravely growing before our eyes in meetings, and we develop trust by turning over small issues to our Higher Power. As we practice Al-Anon principles, we notice a slowly growing pile of our own successes, and as we listen to the strength and hope of those who go before us on the path, our faith expands.

When we have gathered enough courage and faith to trust that we will survive change and can conceive that we may even find our new life better than any we have yet known, we are ready to take Step Seven, "Humbly asked Him to remove our shortcomings."

There's that word "humble" again. Haven't we suffered indignities enough? Been criticized and humiliated way beyond our faults? Won't we lose the small edge we had on survival and become weak if we embrace humility? It is easy to misunderstand many of the concepts in Al-Anon because spiritual practices are both simple and profound. In other words, practicing Al-Anon principles is easy to say but hard to do. Humility, to those of us who have been abused over the years, can sound like once again bending the knee to a tyrant, but it is something much kinder and more beautiful. Humility doesn't mean loss of self-esteem but rather esteeming ourselves for who we really are and loving ourselves enough to want to grow into even better, happier, and more useful human beings. Once again we find ourselves in relationship to an Other.

We may have asked and asked God to stop someone else's drinking only to feel abandoned and betrayed when the drinking continued. If we asked for attention from an adult already overwhelmed with the demands of the drinker, our needs could have been seen as impossible additions to a strained situation, and we may have been attacked as selfish and spoiled for wanting anything. If we then whined, cried, or demanded, some of us were even slapped and told, "You asked for this!" We were too young to realize how sick these adults were and perhaps concluded that the very act of asking was itself perilous.

Because relationships have been the source of all our pain and disease, we are leery of them even as we long for them. Healing all our relationships is a fundamental goal of Al-Anon, as is accepting that there is a Power in the universe greater than we are. We cannot be in relationship with a Power greater than ourselves if we cling fiercely to our own self-will, our self-righteousness, and our stubborn conviction that only we know what is best. To embrace humility does not mean to say we know nothing and have accomplished nothing; it means we accept that we do not know everything—we are willing to become teachable.

If we are willing to be humble, we may still find ourselves

tripping over the word "asked." Many of us learned the danger of asking in our alcoholic families. We discovered that when we asked for something, it might be promised but never delivered, and then we felt piercing disappointment. For those of us who have grown up with alcoholism, asking for anything often requires immense courage and trust, qualities we have been slowly building up while working the earlier Steps. Eventually we do work up enough courage to ask.

Even our shortcomings may be difficult to release. After all, they are ours and they are familiar. Change is never utterly predictable, so it is tempting to settle back into our old routines with the comforting thought, "Better the devil I know than the one I don't know." At this point in our recovery, all the pain we suffered and the failures we endured that brought us into the Al-Anon rooms actually become assets. If we allow ourselves to be honest, we remember how it worked (or, rather, didn't work) before we decided to try this thing called recovery. Some of us revert to the old way of functioning for a while just to make sure it really was "that bad." But soon we are back in a meeting, ready to attempt Step Seven, prepared to regard change as a challenge rather than a disaster. Once more we step out bravely on our Twelve Step hike; our knees may quiver, but our lungs are full of fresh, clean air.

RELEARNING RESPONSIBILITY

The key was resentment.

I joined Al-Anon as a tag-along. My husband finally admitted his need for Alcoholics Anonymous. One day he came home and said, "I am an alcoholic, but you are at least as sick

as I am, and you need help too!" He then took me to an Al-Anon meeting at the same time and place as the AA meeting he attended. I don't know which part of that first meeting frightened me most, going through a room full of alcoholics or through the door into the Al-Anon room. Fortunately, he was there to give me the courage to pass the AA's, and since I was too cowardly to admit that I feared the other door, I began recovery.

Though the first three Steps were very easy for me, the Fourth Step blocked my recovery for some time. I was afraid of what I would find if I took a *thorough* look at myself, so I put it off for nearly two years. When I did try, I had a terrible time finding a way to do it. I tried unsuccessfully to write it out, using our *Blueprint for Progress*. Someone proposed the Alateen Fourth Step workbook. Again, I made no headway. My husband suggested I follow the AA literature. I tried that too—and failed. Someone else suggested I write my life story. Unfortunately, I have a very good memory. I wrote for days and days without reaching my third birthday, and, frankly, I bored myself to death.

Finally, I found a solution that could only have come from my Higher Power. I had heard it said many times, "If something bothers you about someone else, it's probably something you're doing yourself." I decided to try this key to unlock the door to myself. I picked the person I resented the most—my mother—so I could get the most issues dealt with at once. Gleefully, I took her inventory with painstaking detail. When I had her character defects picked to pieces, I started a fresh paper and worked down the list to see if these things really did apply in my life. They *all* fit! There wasn't one tiny little defect I could leave out. I felt so embarrassed and depressed, I could hardly stand myself. I shelved my inventory.

My Higher Power was patient—but not willing to let me slide forever. I had begun the practice of kneeling daily to ask for guidance. One day, purely as an afterthought, I went back down on my knees and asked to find the time to finish my inventory. Almost immediately I could hear the words in my head, "If you'll get up off your knees, you have time right now." Sometimes prayers are answered more quickly than I want! I went to the table, unfolded the pages and reviewed what I had written. Even after months, I didn't have a lot to add to my defects list, so I thought hopefully, "Am I already done?" Again that little voice in my head answered immediately, "No, you haven't listed your strong points. You need to know them too." In a few short hours I finally had the terrible deed completed and felt almost euphoric. I had plusses as well as minuses and a place to begin to grow.

After the Fourth Step, the Fifth was almost easy for me. Having looked at these issues myself, and *knowing* that God still loved me, sharing them with someone else didn't seem too awful. It wasn't.

Shortly after that I worked on my amends list and discovered something wonderful. I realized as I wrote out my list that I no longer resented my mother. Working the other Steps had resolved those bitter resentments for me and had given me freedom.

Working on myself helped heal the breach with my daughter as well. Today we communicate on a level neither of us ever knew before. Detaching from her life with love has brought fantastic rewards.

Working the Steps takes time. They may not be easy, but the growth, freedom, and peace they afford are absolutely worth the price!

Progress was enough.

As a child in an alcoholic household, I believed that if I worked hard enough I could make up for the feelings of abandonment, sadness, and isolation that were my constant, though mostly silent, companions. When even my best efforts failed to leave me feeling secure and close to my family, I always concluded that my best efforts simply weren't good enough. I decided I could achieve happiness by fixing everything outside and keeping too busy to notice any lurking unhappy feelings. I had no idea what a price I paid for this belief until I finally did my Fourth Step in Al-Anon.

Contemplating the Fourth Step filled me with dread. Also confusion, fear of failure, impatience, and self-righteousness. It took a long time to realize I could take a "fearless inventory" with the help of my Higher Power. Even after I completed the inventory and delivered it to my sponsor, I felt a nagging uncertainty and had the recurring feeling that I hadn't done it right. Try as I might, the feeling would not be put to rest until I realized with surprise that the miserable, nagging feeling was more than an assessment of my Fourth Step efforts— it was my underlying assumption about life! I felt that nothing I did was right or enough. Put another way, I had never learned to feel satisfaction with my efforts and let them go.

As I sought to act differently—to accept that I had done my Fourth Step as well as I could at the time and that I deserved some satisfaction—I realized that my feelings did not spring from my work or my essential nature, but from a self-destructive perfectionism I had learned as a defense against criticism. If I enumerated my own shortcomings first, I had reasoned, I could avoid the pain of another's criticism. While it did take my attention off of others, I flogged myself mercilessly and hurt constantly.

Somehow, enjoying my accomplishments seemed dishonest. In Al-Anon, I began to realize that expecting perfection in everything requires a great deal of pride and self-will. I had to give up the false pride in my own perfectibility, but now I get to take pleasure in the fruits of my labor. To keep my perspective, I have replaced the battle cry of my youth, "Perfection or nothing!" with "Progress is enough!" I also use another old saying with a new twist. I remind myself, "Anything worth doing is worth doing badly." For me this means, I can clean up one room adequately rather than being stuck doing no rooms because the prospect of having to clean the whole house perfectly overwhelmed me. Writing a poem can be useful, even if it is a very bad poem. If nothing else, I may uncover some feelings and be able to write a better one another day, or I may be able to appreciate someone else's good poem.

Taking the Fourth Step has helped me replace perfectionism with fun and experimentation. I have discovered the joy of goofing off. With a decreased sense of always having to do something useful to justify my existence, I now allow recreation, enthusiasm, and delight into my life.

It has taken me many years to realize that my Higher Power does not expect more from me than I am able to give. I know now that I can never earn the love of those unable to love me, but I can find others who *are* able. When I admit their love into my life, the old, nagging fear, that I can only be happy when all aspects of my life are going as well as I can possibly imagine, disappears. I haven't succeeded in changing my past, of course, but the present is filled with promise, and, amazingly, I am discovering that it is fun to be me.

I "caught" my mother's illness.

As a very young child of three or four, I realized that my father, whom I adored, needed protection from my mother, who was intolerant, demanding, and seemingly unloving. My father called my mother every day before leaving work to let her know he was on his way home. We didn't have a car at the time, so he took the bus. By the time he got from the bus stop to our apartment, my mother was always angry, yelling, and crying. I decided to meet him at the bus stop so I could be with him when he got home to protect him. Today I realize there was a bar at the corner where the bus stopped. Every day he went to that bar and drank before going home. When I met him, he had probably only had one or two drinks, and the times he got in so much trouble with mother were the times when he had had quite a few and arrived home very late. I can see that I tried to control alcoholism when I was very young, though I had no idea exactly what I was doing.

When I was six or seven, my parents divorced, and I hated my mother for sending my father away. For the next thirteen years I fought, cried, and screamed at my mother. Criticism colored everything I did; nothing I did was right; I could never be good enough! My self-esteem plummeted and my resentment toward my mother soared. Determined to do what I wanted, when I wanted, and how I wanted, I refused to fit into her mold. After all, what did she know? She had made my daddy leave. I even took care not to eat or drink after her because I feared I would "catch" what she had—that's how much I hated her.

She could not tolerate the first man who came along in my life, so I married him! He turned out to be gone more than he was home. He never came straight home from work (when he worked) but stopped off to have a few. He might leave to buy a pack of cigarettes and return two days later. How could he be so irresponsible? I had dinner ready, and his son, who adored him, waited and waited. I didn't recognize the familiar pattern until I had attended Al-Anon for quite a long time.

We divorced and I remarried. My new husband didn't go to bars; he found the "nineteenth hole" at the local golf course. We did nothing together as a family. I divorced again and spent the next twelve years as a single mom. My son refused to do what I told him, the way I told him to do it. We screamed and yelled and fought. Actually, he usually stood shaking while I screamed and yelled. I actually told him he was lazy, fat, and worthless, and let him know how much easier my life would have been if he weren't around. One horrible day I realized that, although I had never eaten from my mother's plate or drunk from the same glass, I had nevertheless "caught" what she had. With no recovery to help me, I blamed and hated both of us.

Something must be terribly wrong with me, I decided. My life was unbearable and I attempted suicide. This was not my first attempt—my first had been at age eleven—but this was my best. I landed in a mental hospital, where they diagnosed my depression and told me it was hereditary. My grandmother had also suffered depression, but she was dead so I couldn't talk to her about it. I did have a cousin living in another state who had been hospitalized for depression, so I called him, thinking it was for his sake, so he would know he wasn't alone.

He asked me about my drinking habits and determined I wasn't alcoholic. He revealed to me that he was an alcoholic and that depression was part of his disease. Then he pointed out the obvious point that I had completely missed—both our fathers seemed to drink a lot and spend more time in bars than at home, and both my husbands had acted the same way.

He not only recommended Al-Anon, but made a special trip halfway across the country to take me to my first meeting.

The people at the meeting seemed to be talking about me. They knew how I felt and where I had been. They understood how much I hurt and told me I didn't have to hurt any more. They told me it wasn't my fault. They gave me hope. Hope was something I couldn't remember feeling—ever!

After about a year in Al-Anon, I married again, but it lasted only twelve days. My mother came over to console me. She commented on how well I was handling my situation, and I began telling her about Al-Anon. She said my husband's unpredictable behavior and change in personality reminded her of my father. Amazed, I turned to her and looked at her squarely for the first time in my life, in the light of love and compassion. "My God, Mother," I said, "you lived with an alcoholic. All these years I hated and resented you for how you were and for sending Daddy away."

She replied, "I know, but I showed you how much I loved you the only way I knew how. I could keep a roof over your head, but I couldn't put my arms around you. I could keep clothes on your back, but I couldn't tell you I loved you. I was afraid to let you make any decisions on your own because you might be disappointed by failure and attempt suicide again, and you were all I had to live for."

I realized at that moment I had indeed caught something from my mother: the effects of another person's alcoholism. The alcoholic wasn't around, but the disease continued to spread—from mother to daughter, from daughter to son.

With the loving understanding of Al-Anon members, I have been able to take a Fourth Step and see the things I did to others rather than dwell on what others did to me. I have continued working the Steps and have made amends to my mother and my son. I am learning to allow all three of us to make mistakes and still share love. I might not have been the one to start the spread of this disease in my family, but I can help to start the spread of recovery.

So that was it!

I was conceived, born, and raised in a home suffering from the sickness of alcoholism. As an adult, I married, conceived, and raised five children in my home, which also suffers from the sickness of alcoholism. The first part I didn't know until very recently.

I came to Al-Anon five and a half years ago, by God's grace, for I was desperate and ripe for an insane asylum. It took a long time and many meetings, but each day I became less dizzy, as my blood pressure (which had been stratospheric) began to normalize. I know from personal experience that living with alcoholism can make me physically sick.

One subject almost always made me sick each time someone brought it up—the idea that alcoholism was a family disease. I raged at my husband for making me part of the illness and doomed to live in a black future.

The Al-Anon way is slow but sure. A few months ago, a pamphlet written for adult children of alcoholics fell into my hands. I read it and then I understood! I had never related the kind of life we lived—full of conflict, jealousy, rage, immaturity, loneliness, and lies—to my father's drinking.

Today my elderly father needs liquor to take a plane, to be happy at a party, and even to eat. He needs alcohol daily to blunt his inner desperation. My mother denies his alcoholism, and there is very little respect, privacy, or kindness in their home.

Twenty years ago, I married a young, good-looking, hard worker who was desperate enough to need a drink to have a good time. Sometimes, I now realize, I hate certain conduct in my husband only because my mother or father used to do the same thing when I was small. My husband is also the child of an alcoholic parents, and I can see how unfair my intolerance for him is.

I no longer get sick to my stomach when the family disease of alcoholism is mentioned. Now I realize my husband did not infect me with the disease. I had already been touched by it when I met and married him, choosing for myself a pattern of life familiar to me. When I accepted the truth of my family of origin, a great weight lifted off my shoulders.

Now when I get a surge of hostility, I know I need to take my own inventory. Then I resort to the Fifth Step and call my sponsor, wait it out, use the telephone, or read some literature until I can admit to God, myself, and another my part in the rage. Sometimes, when I have done all the Steps around the hostility, I can try to lovingly explain to my husband what I am going through, not what he caused. By God's grace, he too is in recovery and can sometimes listen.

My goal now is to form an Al-Anon group for adult children of alcoholics here in Costa Rica, so that others too can get release from the burdens they carry through their lives.

I had choices.

If I were to find a single word to describe my experience of growing up with the family disease of alcoholism, that word would be loneliness. Until I came to Al-Anon, my loneliness was so intense and all-encompassing that I assumed it had always been with me. I thought I was, *by nature*, a shy, quiet, withdrawn loner who was better off not even trying to communicate with anyone.

Al-Anon taught me to separate the disease of alcoholism

from the people who suffered from it and to separate myself
from the distorted self-image I had from living with alcoholism. Looking at old photographs and home movies, I
became aware of the bright, playful, rambunctious boy I once
was. I searched to find what changed this little bundle of
energy into the sad, frightened hermit I had become.

Though the fourth of five children, I was my mother's first-
born. My father was a widower with three daughters when she
married him, and I became the mortar expected to hold these
separate individuals together as a family. They were big shoes
for a baby's feet to fill.

Recently, my aunt recounted to me an incident that
occurred when I was an infant. My mother, hurt and upset
over a disagreement, stormed out of the room. My aunt found
her later, rocking me in her arms and comforting herself by
saying, "At least I'll always have you. You'll never leave me.
You'll always love me." The message whispered to me from
the start was that I existed to meet the needs of others. The
burden was subtle enough that I didn't recognize it for a long
time.

As my mother's alcoholism widened the cracks in our family structure, forcing my older sisters to shoulder adult
responsibility, they relied on me to stay out of the way and
look after my baby sister. I made sure they never had to worry
about us.

By the time I was six, I already wished constantly that life
could be like "the good old days" when I was three or four.
My only sources of peace and comfort were a vivid imagination, an ability to draw, and my relationship with my
younger sister. Withdrawing into fantasy cost me a tremendous price in loneliness and isolation. My sister was my
only relief from it. Yet as close as we were, my need to protect her kept distance between us as well. I couldn't let *any-*

one, even myself, find out the truth I knew inside.

Ironically, the most painful and confusing aspect of all about my upbringing was that I knew my family loved me. I never doubted it. They continually proved their willingness to help me in any way they could. Unfortunately, they were severely limited, both by the disease and by my lack of communication, so things got worse, and I blamed myself and distanced myself more.

When I was ten and my mother left my father, despite all the hopes and promises to the contrary, things got worse yet. I became the "man of the house," and the fighting continued among the three of us who were left. My older sister's death from a rare disease convinced me anew to retreat from life, for I mistakenly reasoned that she would have lived longer if she hadn't been so vivacious and taken so many risks.

I spent my young adult life alternating between hiding from the problem and trying to force a solution, until my utter desperation finally brought me into Al-Anon. The fear of continuing the familiar finally out-weighed the fear of trying the unknown. Nevertheless, in a life full of difficulties, going to my first meeting was still the hardest thing I had ever done. It meant breaking many of the rules I lived by. It meant facing reality. It meant reaching out for relationships. It meant taking down the "everything's fine!" facade. Worst of all, it meant revealing family secrets. Though I didn't know it yet, breaking those rules would save my life.

I felt better immediately after my first meeting. Al-Anon did not, however, magically erase the effects that this hideous disease had had on me. Each new suggestion challenged some old defense, but slowly I took them up. When I talked to people with whom I felt safe, loneliness receded. Listening connected me to my feelings, which I thought didn't exist. I had always done things alone, so asking for help and using the phone were not easy. In time I even asked someone to sponsor me, and my capacity for intimacy greatly increased.

Speaking at open meetings helped me begin to change not only myself, but my perception of myself as well. I received validation for my courage. I was speaking out! Perhaps I wasn't really quiet and shy after all. People who met me certainly didn't think so, and others who once did were changing their minds. My sponsor suggested I take a new look in the mirror via the Fourth Step.

While all the Steps helped me, the most beneficial were those I resisted most. The Fourth looked particularly intimidating; all my life I had avoided anything that might reveal who I really was. My sponsor and Al-Anon friends actually suggested I might like the man I would find. Another fact that made it easier was that the Fourth Step, like the three before it, could be done primarily between my ears. No one else needed to be involved.

Step Five was a different story. Taking it became my biggest Al-Anon challenge. Sharing my findings with my Higher Power wasn't too hard, for I had replaced the punishing God of my childhood with a loving, benevolent Creator. But surely another human being would not be as accepting as my Higher Power—that's what made this Power *Higher!* Despite my fear of rejection, I did it. The result truly amazed me. For the first time that I could remember, I felt I was *truly* a human being. It took my Fifth Step to really teach me I was no Martian or changeling, but a person who belonged on earth, at one with humanity.

If I had not risked admitting my characteristics to another human being, I would not have healed an important part of my life—my relationship to other people. My inability to relate to and trust others created my loneliness, isolation, and the incorrect belief that I was shy and doomed to a solitary life. Now I can risk knowing my real self and being real with others. Loneliness rarely haunts me today, and I do not wander any more as a lost soul, frightened of my fellow human beings. Today I have lots of friends and lots of opportunities to share myself with others.

I can feel all *my feelings.*

For as long as I can remember, I suffered deep and regular depressions, usually lasting for two weeks out of every month. I learned to cover them up in public and earned a good living. When I arrived home at night, however, my only defense against despair was numbing my mind with television, losing myself in books, or obsessing over other people.

When I turned forty, my depressions deepened. I had not become the famous author I so badly wanted to be. I thought if I were famous, I could say I had risen above my alcoholic parents and it would prove that their abuse had not affected me.

At first I poured effort into my writing, but the intense rage and violence that erupted in my stories frightened me. Eventually I couldn't write at all—a terrifying loss, since writing was my escape route out of depression and my instrument of revenge against my parents. When my beloved dog died, feelings overwhelmed me. A voice inside said, "Give it up. Give it up!" and I thought it meant I should kill myself. Before actually doing myself in, I consulted yet another therapist.

He listened to me for ten minutes, then gently asked if there were any alcoholics in my family. No one had ever before connected my depressions with my parents' alcoholism, but I now realize I had practically recited to him the Al-Anon pamphlet, "Did you grow up with a problem drinker?" He handed me a meeting list and urged me to go as often as possible. That night I went to an Al-Anon meeting for adult children, where I was so overwhelmed by the honesty I heard, I could do nothing but weep. People spoke about *their* childhoods and *their* own characters, yet they seemed to know me better than I knew myself. I had only a dim awareness of these truths, but I felt tremendous relief and gratitude, which I realize awakened me spiritually. Just when I had given up hope, I found a home.

Because I was so frightened and desperate, I willingly committed myself to the program. I attended five meetings a week, got a sponsor, and devoured the literature. My depression lifted almost immediately. This miracle, however, did not make me humble. When I heard other people say they had been in the program for years, I decided they must be slow-witted. I would get my life together in six months, or so I thought.

For three years, though I committed myself to work the program, I was blind to an unconscious ulterior motive. I thought if I worked as hard and fast as I could, God would at last make me the great writer I wanted to be. In time I realized my hidden agenda. Then I finally surrendered to my Higher Power not only my life and will but my writing. In the years that followed, I finished my college degree and guided my life with the prayer in the pamphlet, "Just for Today." The desire to write never left me; the desire for fame and revenge did. Eventually, God restored my ability to write, but now I try to express God's will in both my writing and my life.

During those years while my writing had stopped, my awareness of my past increased tremendously. My alcoholic mother died, and I began recalling my alcoholic father's incestuous behavior towards me. I could never have faced this shaming truth without a Higher Power and the Al-Anon fellowship. I erroneously believed I must have caused the incest. I kept believing, even as an adult, that if only I were good enough, I could have prevented it. I had not yet learned "the Three C's." The belief that somehow I could control another's anger or penchant to hurt me was so deeply ingrained, I had to reword the First Step to remind myself that I was powerless over people's responses to me and that my attempts to control their responses made my life unmanageable. Now I am learning that I am responsible only for my own behavior.

My sponsor and many other people supported me lovingly as I worked through the excruciating pain of incest, but I owe my continuing recovery to Steps Six and Seven. These two Steps helped me place my anger, hurt, resentment, and self-righteousness into the hands of my Higher Power. I had a right to these powerful feelings, for my childhood had indeed been awful. Nevertheless, I came to see that holding tight to my very justifiable feelings hurt me spiritually, emotionally, and physically. Trusting God to judge my parents' behavior, I humbly asked to be relieved of these painful emotions. I coupled willingness to forgive my parents for their alcoholism and incest with willingness to forgive myself for not being able to overcome all the terrible effects alone. Today, six and a half years later, I am no longer weighed down, dragging my past behind me.

Everything that has happened to me is useful when I sponsor others. The unconditional love Al-Anon gave me so freely has allowed me to extend it to others, even my father. At first I was ashamed to admit that I cared for him at all after what he had done to me, but forgiveness brought with it the freedom to love others even when they are sick and fallible. Without the grace of God, I too might have become an alcoholic and child molester. Without Al-Anon, I might never have tapped into that grace and the ability to love myself and other people exactly as we are at this minute in time. It is a glorious freedom indeed to be able to love.

I learned in laughter.

"Be careful what you pray for—you may get it!" I'd heard that often enough, and earlier in my recovery, I'd answered it cynically in my mind, "Oh, yeah? Well, I prayed and prayed for Daddy to stop drinking, and I never got it!" I was not one to appreciate the wisdom that all prayers are answered but sometimes the answer is "no."

Nevertheless, I had survived my childhood, and once I dared to pray again as an adult in Al-Anon, I had seen enough "coincidences" to convince me that prayer was powerful and should be used judiciously. I'd also experienced getting my prayers answered in decidedly uncomfortable ways. Sometimes I could see the answer to my prayers only after a roller coaster ride of loss and dizzying change that left me shaken and wobbly. One thing was sure: it was wise to take care what I prayed for.

When it was time to work Step Seven, I decided to practice a little uncharacteristic moderation by working on only one character defect at a time. It had become increasingly clear to me that I was a bit judgmental, and I thought that might be something I could live without, so I decided to ask my Goddess to remove it. Being mindful of past experiences, I hastened to add, "and could you please teach me with happiness or fun instead of clobbering me this time?"

I've heard others say ruefully that, whenever they ask their Higher Power for removal of something, all sorts of events conspire to give them lots of practice, which is a positive way of saying, ask for removal of a defect and it will confront you at every turn for as long as it takes to release your death grip on it. Sure enough, within a week, I got a potent lesson in my own judgments, but I must also gratefully add that She heard my addendum prayer too, for this lesson came with laughter in its wake.

For several weeks, I had been talking over the phone to an Al-Anon member whom I only knew by voice. The more I talked with this wise, humorous, caring man, the more I wished to meet him. We were both single, and it would be disingenuous not to admit that I hoped our Al-Anon friend-ship might blossom into something more intimate. Apparently he felt the same way, for although we had never discussed meeting face to face, one day a stranger appeared in my classroom. When all the students had filed out and I went to see what he wanted, he handed me an apple for the teacher and announced his name. At first I stood there, startled and disbelieving, trying to place all the men I knew with that name, but finally I realized he was my telephone list friend.

Before me stood a tall, very handsome man with big, kind eyes. My immediate response was an earthy, clearly erotic attraction. So far the story sounds like a perfect fantasy. There was only one hitch—he was obviously ten to fifteen years younger than I was. I fumbled around, trying to mask my feelings, which I thought surely must be written in flash-ing neon all over my face. I felt somewhat relieved when he beat a hasty retreat, mumbling some banality about catching me at a meeting.

As soon as he disappeared, I felt disappointed and assumed the worst about his reaction to my age. Nevertheless, I tripped through the rest of the day quite elat-ed and buzzing with newfound energy. I told myself that even if I never saw him again, it was worth the surprise to feel alive once more. Then . . . I ran into a colleague who marveled at how fresh I looked that day and how happy and *young* I was, and my lesson crashed into consciousness. This man was one of several of my male colleagues who were notorious for chasing after *young* female students. I had judged him an immature jerk on more than one occasion. There I stood, before his admiring gaze, flushed with the same feelings he may have felt many times for those coeds. My cheeks turned as red as the apple in my hand—at least that's how hot I felt!

I must have gained some recovery along the way to Step Seven, for after my colleague left and the heat had receded from my cheeks, I could laugh heartily at myself, knowing that embarrassment is not the same as shame but merely an acknowledgment of my own generous share of human foibles. Being judgmental is still a challenge to me, but today I take care not to be too quick to assess the romantic involvements of others—especially since that handsome young man with the great eyes just kept coming back until at last I gave in and married him.

Steps are my garden tools.

I suffered seriously from stuffed feelings, and I had had very bad backaches for eight years, even though I thought I had everything in life I wanted—a job, house, security, and a multitude of other *things.* I had managed to control every aspect of my life except my humanness. I couldn't imagine accepting life on life's terms, and I totally lacked appreciation of the richness available for human expression, just for the asking. Control meant I could not trust in the security of my future unless I managed every detail. I was deathly afraid, so I did everything I could not to repeat the experiences of my childhood in an alcoholic home.

Unfortunately, managing and controlling every aspect of

life and living entirely in your head is painful. I needed to learn to trust, to follow my heart as well as my head. Thanks to Al-Anon, I went on a journey which, like Dorothy's in the *Wizard of Oz*, began a bit like a tornado. Like Dorothy, I found in the program true friends. Together we found strength, as did the Scarecrow, and courage, as did the Cowardly Lion. We even found our hearts, like the Tin Man. In our little group, we were all different, yet we found our common humanity, which like the Wizard's was more precious than any magic. Yet there was magic as well, for we each got what we needed from each other and from our Higher Powers.

Unlike the story of the *Wizard of Oz*, this program is not a dream. I was in a dream before I came to Al-Anon—a dream of denial in which my ego (that stands for Easing God Out!) hid what real life was all about. Life is much too grand for measurements and comparisons. It *cannot* be controlled. Through accepting my powerlessness and surrendering my ego, I gained real power to farm my life and see it grow into a profuse, wild garden.

Everywhere I look I see analogies between nature and human beings. A seed is planted and something grows—a flower or a weed. Roots and growth appear aided by sunshine, water, and food. The flower sprouts, buds and blooms, and sometimes must be transplanted. Wind brings surprising transformations to the earth, and spirit does the same for me.

In Step Four, I learned to look at the seed of where my character defenses began and to accept and love myself for creating survival tactics. As the flower grows and sprouts new buds, my Higher Power gives me courage to recognize behaviors that no longer work. Sometimes, I must just pinch it back, like an unruly plant growing straight to the sun with no branches. Other times, I must examine the roots to see how far they go and begin to weed the garden. When in Step Six I agree to weed, and I ask for the Master Gardener's help in Step Seven, I find the defense removed, and sunshine pours over me.

I may even be transplanted to a new location from which to continue my growth. I recognize that even in the new, sunny garden plot rich with dark earth and fertilizer, new weeds will sprout and some plants will forever need pruning. The Steps equip me with weed control and garden manuals. Just as old weeds, given enough time in the mulch pile, break down into new fertilizer, no part of my life was a waste. Instead I view it as part of a plan devised by my Higher Power.

Step Four showed me my dark side, where light and sunshine were never allowed. My denial covered like a spreading oak, shadowing my past of growing up in an alcoholic home until it was barely visible. But like the oak in the night, not seeing it didn't mean it wasn't there. Looking back today with gratitude reveals my background as a rich garden of human possibility just waiting for the gardener with the right wheelbarrow full of tools—the Twelve Steps. The program works; miracles do grow, and I am one of them.

Chapter seven

TAKING ACTION ON OUR OWN BEHALF

Forgiveness and making amends for our own mistakes are essential tasks in the process of recovering and beginning to live vividly in the present. To admit error and take the actions necessary to rectify the situation is never easy, however. Growing up with alcoholism creates its own set of confusions that sometimes confounds our best efforts. To assuage the tremendous remorse and guilt that accompany alcoholic behavior, members of an alcoholic family sometimes dump their feelings on whomever is available and least able to defend themselves. Guilt is twisted into blame and spewed forth to land on any handy unsuspecting victim. The available scapegoat is often the child.

Those of us who grew up with alcoholism were often the innocent victims of others' misbehavior and projected guilt. For adults who may still feel like innocent victims, facing our own culpability in harming others is both shocking and confusing. Since we were often blamed when we were innocent, we have trouble sorting out our actual responsibilities from those exaggerated ones we assumed or had imposed upon us. Extremes of too much and too little responsibility are the great weights hanging around our necks. We swing wildly between these two extremes, with little practical ability to distinguish reality from what we have been led to *believe* was reality. Many of us have marched bravely through the so-called "hard Steps" (Four and Five), only to find ourselves tripping over Eight and landing flat on our faces. It is never predictable which Step in our growth process will be the "hard" one for us, but we have found that the ones that seem "hard" usually yield the most growth and the most freedom, once accomplished.

Step Eight asks us to "make a list of all persons we have harmed and become willing to make amends to them all." If we suffer from an exaggerated sense of responsibility, our lists become endless. We think we have managed to harm nearly every person in the world we ever touched. It is certainly important in Step Eight not to avoid putting someone on the list simply because doing so is embarrassing or particularly painful, but it is equally important to remember Step One, in which we admitted our powerlessness so that we don't assume we have superhuman power to hurt others just as we once believed we could control and fix them. Some of us struggle with people who claim we harm them whenever we refuse to rescue them or to live according to their dictates. Choosing to set boundaries and create wellness for ourselves is our primary responsibility, and it may not make our families comfortable. Releasing our responsibility for the feelings, reactions, and obligations of all those we love is as important as admitting when we have in fact done harm.

Those of us who tend to feel victimized may be angry, feel self-righteously that we are never at fault, or be afraid to admit fault to the perpetrators who have hurt us, lest they use the admission for further abuse. "No way!" we say. But in the spirit of progress, not perfection, we can perhaps divide up our lists into "yes," "maybe," and "no way!" and make a start on

the "yes" list. As we find the willingness to take small steps
toward our own relief from guilt and our improved mental
health, more is revealed to us about what else we need to do
to continue on the path, and we gather rewards to make the
journey more attractive. Let's walk a few steps together but not
flog ourselves with the bullwhips of perfectionism and self-
righteous judgment that we acquired in our unhealthy homes.
We have joined this fellowship to heal, a result which cannot
be accomplished by slashing open our wounds and pouring
salt into them. It does, however, sometimes require taking
strong medicine that doesn't taste like chocolate truffles.

As we examine those we have harmed, we may find that
most of our offending behaviors were "sins of omission"
caused by paralyzing fear. We will need first to forgive ourselves for the fears that resulted in an inability to act in our
own behalf or perhaps to protect our children. Victims create
victims. Fortunately, recovery works the same way—recovery
creates expanding recovery. Through the same intimate
process that connects us so firmly to those we love and those
who have greatly impacted our lives, the family disease of
alcoholism can become the family healing of recovery. It may
take a while, but if we wait and work, it will spread.

Once we have a list, we face Step Nine, "Made direct
amends to such people wherever possible, except when to do
so would injure them or others." We are asked to use judgment, courage, and willingness in Step Nine. We may have
developed lots of courage, surviving in an alcoholic home, but
suffer from impaired judgment, nonetheless. How do we know
if we will injure others? Did we remember to include ourselves in the "others?" How do we distinguish between
wounding ourselves further and the healthy discomfort that
accompanies any admission of error? Experience suggests
that, by the time we reach Step Nine, we have found ways to

evaluate our thinking realistically. Instead of charging out to make amends, we take the time to consider the consequences of our actions. If we can't anticipate the broad consequences, we call our sponsor or an Al-Anon friend to discuss our doubts and confusion. We become willing and then ask our Higher Power to provide the opportunity and the guidance, praying for the result to be for the highest good of all concerned—and remembering to include ourselves in "all."

Then, once we have reduced our task to manageable stages, we bravely step out to clean up our past. We accomplish one amend at a time and before we know it, the path to tomorrow is bright and shining. Old, festering mistakes and regrets no longer keep us hiding inside ourselves, wishing life were not so dangerous. Life is certainly not without challenges, but the challenges are manageable when we live as adults in the present, with all its possibilities, rather than as frightened children in our traumatic past. When the frightened part of ourselves peeks out—and it will from time to time—we know we can soothe ourselves, care for ourselves, accept all our feelings, and continue to grow up, for we ourselves are becoming the mature people we lacked in our childhood homes. Knowing how to care for ourselves properly also allows us to care for our loved ones without becoming overbearing or overwhelmed.

With the help of Al-Anon friends, sponsor, literature, and our Higher Power, we learn to distinguish the real from the imagined, the harm from the legitimate boundary, the deed from the fallible human doer—and perhaps we can eventually polish the tarnished past into a treasured antique. Many of us feel that in Al-Anon we found the healthy family we had missed and, in the Steps, the reasonable guidelines toward maturity that were lacking in families distorted by the disease of alcoholism. By the time we complete Step Nine, serenity and gratitude don't seem like such loony ideas after all.

MENDING AND AMENDING THE PAST

A Higher Power helps.

Every time I approached Step Eight, I got stuck. At first my sponsor told me I wasn't ready to work it. The relief of not having to drive myself to accomplish, as I had done all my life, loosed a flood of affection and appreciation. You mean I don't *have* to perform and bring in those A's to be accepted in Al-Anon? I wallowed happily in much-needed, wonderful, unconditional love.

Eventually, however, I was back bumping up against Step Eight. I felt stuck in my program, a familiar, discouraging feeling I had known in therapy when I'd gotten as far as I could go but still wasn't happy. Though I tried not to, I compared myself to other glowing Al-Anon members who were announcing their triumphs regularly at meetings. They felt so good! Love blossomed in their lives. They knew their parents did the best they could. How I hated that phrase! It was as if it made everything O.K.—the verbal assaults, the violence and threats of violence against me and my mother, the incest, and, worst of all, the denial by my mother that anything had happened, her insistence that I had imagined it all. I could tell myself that alcoholism was a disease, could even rationalize that my father was blacked out when he raped me, his five-year-old daughter, but how could I exonerate my mother? She wasn't drunk, or at least she usually didn't drink. Frankly, I don't know where she was.

Although Step Eight merely suggests that I list those I had harmed, I got hopelessly tangled in blame, denial, accusations, counter-accusations, and, I now realize, my own towering resentment. I can get apoplectic at the thought of having to clean up other people's messes, and I find it incredibly difficult to forgive people who claim they did nothing wrong yet are still doing it. When I try to clean up my own messes, as Step Eight and Nine require, I feel paralyzed trying to sort out my actual guilt from all the guilt my sick parents heaped on me, not to mention my tendency to absorb any available guilt like a thirsty sponge.

I do not want to harm myself further by taking on the unreasonable expectations of my mother, who always claimed I harmed her whenever I tried to set any kind of boundary. If I asked her to call before she arrived on my doorstep, she said, "I have never been so hurt in all my life!" When I suggested that it wasn't a good time to entertain her when she arrived unannounced one early Saturday morning, she said, "What are you doing that is so shameful that your mother isn't welcome." When I tried to put her on my list (I knew she felt I'd hurt her terribly), I couldn't seem to determine what I needed to amend with her and what I needed to amend with myself, which would undoubtedly wound her further.

A friend suggested I try listing only people with whom I felt uncomfortable, and I managed to do that, but surely my parents belonged at the top of such a list. I could barely spend two hours with them without having to take two days to recover from the resulting depression. I knew I had hurt my children. Being divorced and half-crazy, I was certainly no model parent, but even here the sorting of my responsibilities was difficult. Was it harmful to be depressed and emotionally unavailable, or more harmful to feel so guilty about depression and my necessary self-centeredness that I taught my children to manipulate me with my own guilt? An Al-Anon suggestion that changing my behavior would be a better amends than an apology helped somewhat with this one.

I often feel victimized, yet watching my mother and my first husband, both of whom always played the victim, demonstrated to me that people who believe they are victims actually do great harm. Both of them were such self-pitying martyrs that they never had any room for my pain or my needs. I, the strong one, the guilty one, was left without comfort, drained, and exhausted, but how could I focus on my own needs without becoming just like them? I thought, "Aye, there's the rub!"

I kept getting stuck because I felt that most of the people on my list had harmed me much worse than I had harmed them (children excepted, of course). Since they all assumed that I was the only problem and since none of them were in recovery, I couldn't figure out how to make amends without opening myself up to further assaults. Though I have still not discovered how to do this, I did learn something about myself in the process. I have difficulty forgiving and tend to carry grudges, even though I know that carrying a grudge is harmful to my health. Now I understand that I carry grudges because of fear. Until I learn how to protect myself from those who continue to abuse me, it is difficult to forgive them and admit my part in the errors. My anger—in the form of the grudge—provides some protection. In Al-Anon, however, I have learned better methods, such as detaching and stating the truth of my feelings whether they are heard or not. Eventually, I believe I will achieve safe forgiveness.

Today I am still working Step Eight. My progress is slow,

but it *is* progress. I have three new tools to help me—my Higher Power, practicing moderation, and focusing only on my part in any situation. I was so busy trying to do it right and sort it out, that I forgot a basic tenet of our program—if we ask, our Higher Power will do for us what we cannot do for ourselves. Today I can ask my Higher Power to help me tell my errors from my abuses and show me what I need to amend. I also ask to have my old, inappropriate fears removed, while retaining those that let me know when I need to protect myself. I have learned in Al-Anon to moderate my black and white thinking, so I no longer have to be entirely fearful or utterly fearless. I know that my family, the source of most of my fears and of my need for recovery, is the greatest challenge to me in making amends. I can understand and forgive myself when I find the Eighth Step difficult under such circumstances of extreme love and fear. Then I remind myself of something I heard in a meeting. Even in the unusual situation in which another person is ninety-five percent at fault and I am only five percent, I am still responsible for my five percent. Knowing that, and that I am not responsible for everyone else's part, I inch toward recovery, making my amends list in God's time rather than mine. This is one time in recovery that this impatient child of an alcoholic, who usually chafes because God works so slowly, has been willing to let God take Her own sweet time.

I acted like a child.

I am the child of three alcoholics—my father (who died of acute alcoholism), my mother, and my stepfather. By my thirtieth birthday, I had become keenly aware of how deeply I felt repressed by my history, but I had no real idea what to do

about it. Someone suggested Al-Anon, but after trying one
meeting I left in disgust. I wanted to talk about my mother;
they told me to talk about myself. What a ridiculous idea! I
would be fine if I hadn't grown up with an alcoholic mother,
or an alcoholic stepfather, or if my father hadn't died of alcoholism. It took another three years before I tried Al-Anon
again and stayed.

"I would be fine if . . ." just happened to be the story of my
life. Everything I had ever wanted had always been prevented from happening because of someone or something else.
Poor me! This is not to say that the alcoholism of my childhood home had nothing to do with the pervasive futility in my
life. If nothing else, I learned thoroughly how to have a bad
attitude. I always felt negative and hopeless. Nothing ever
worked out in my life. In Al-Anon I learned that I had developed this philosophy through necessity as a child.

What exactly was it about growing up with alcoholism that
affected me? For me it was a system of lies, distortions, half-
truths, and manipulations that began when we, as a family,
tried to make sense of, control, and excuse the behavior of
persons in the family who were frequently drunk. This system
of deceit perverted my sense of what was real and left me
without the ability to live comfortably with myself and others.

As children, we did whatever seemed to work to protect
ourselves from the rage of the drunken parent. Both my mother and my stepfather were usually drunk at the dinner table.
My mother's drunkenness showed itself first in slurred
speech, glazed eyes, and slow, careful movements. She
repeated statements two or three sentences behind the conversation or responded inappropriately, not seeming to have
heard correctly. Pretending there was nothing wrong with
this, my sisters and I carefully repeated what she had missed

and avoided revealing by any action or word that anything was wrong. If we revealed in any way that we knew what she was trying so desperately to hide, she became testy. "Why are you looking at me that way?" she would bristle.

"Nothing, Mom. I'm not looking at you."

"Yes, you are! I can't seem to do anything right around here any more!" On and on she'd go, angry and self-pitying.

By that time, my stepfather would have had four or five scotches and his anger would flare. He'd rage through gritted teeth about his pet peeves and the absurdity of the world in general, while we sat in stony silence, eyes cast down at our plates, not daring to look up. As soon as dinner ended, we fled the table and pretended nothing had happened.

My parents weren't drunk in front of other people. Both of them appeared to be good-natured, agreeable people who seldom drank in public. Before the disease progressed they were loving, affectionate parents. I remember my stepfather, particularly, encouraging my imagination and being very gentle with a little girl who had lost her father only a few years earlier. My friends thought my parents were "neat" and didn't understand my complaints, so I stopped talking.

The front we presented to the outside world was seamless. Inside, however, life was ripped apart at every seam. Sarcastic and jealous, my sisters and I competed for the meager attentions mother could give in the scanty hours between work and her third scotch. After the third one, she became so inebriated that her caresses and coos disgusted us.

Because both my parents drank, my oldest sister literally raised me. She made my dinner, drove me to after-school events, and dried my tears. Sometimes, however, she created my tears. Only seven years older than I, with her own angers and frustrations, she wasn't a great mother. We lived on a farm, and one day she insisted that I play "cowboy" with her: she would be the cowboy and I the cow. Trying to rope me from her horse, she chased me around the pasture until the game ended when the horse ran over me.

I learned to view the world as a negative, untrustworthy place. Afraid of my parents, I never mentioned that my sisters regularly beat me up. Since I could never predict anyone's reaction—and sometimes members of my family became very hostile—I learned that asking questions was dangerous. I stopped asking.

When I left my parents' house, I began a long series of short-term enthusiasms, bouncing from one place to another and one job to another. Highly adaptable and being an approval seeker, I became a great employee. Winning points at work with my perfectionism was easy, but it got me into trouble because I could never admit to making a mistake. My whole self-esteem was built on out-shining everyone, and a mistake threatened to reveal my imperfection. Rather than suffer such a humiliation, I quit and moved on, blaming the situation or other people.

As one episode followed another, the numbers added up on the wrong side of the scale. Common sense told me that it wasn't possible for every situation to be unredeemable. I had always known that my childhood wasn't quite right, so I switched from being a victim of the world to being a victim of my upbringing. It was all their fault!

Talking with my friends about my horrible childhood, I discovered they all had something wrong in childhood. In fact, most of them had parents who drank! A couple of my more mature friends had gotten help, one from Al-Anon and one from AA. I smiled to myself at their weakness and congratulated myself on my own superiority. I didn't need to sink so low. I decided I could get help from the many books appearing about children who grew up in alcoholic homes. I bought a few but could never bring myself to finish them. I could read the part that identified the problem, but when the book began to focus on solutions, I quit reading.

Though I wasn't bouncing around as much, the cycle hadn't stopped. I had two volunteer positions and a very demanding job working for a boss who drank heavily. After a particularly stressful day, I narrowly avoided a car accident on my way home. My heart pounded so heavily I thought it was a heart attack, so I called the medical emergency telephone number. The nurse listened and replied, "It sounds like you're having an anxiety attack." I hung up the phone and burst into tears. I had come to the end of my coping skills and knew I needed help, but I still wasn't ready to admit I needed Al-Anon. That would be my last resort. Instead I sought therapy—and found a therapist who kept telling me I should go to Al-Anon! Nonetheless, I kept making excuses until I ran out of money for therapy. Beaten and broke, I walked in the door of my first Al-Anon meeting.

It was an adult child focus meeting and one person after another spoke aloud the thoughts I had never dared tell even my therapist. People talked of the shame they felt from growing up with alcoholism, of rediscovering their feelings, of coming to terms with anger and finding their way to forgiveness of alcoholics, who after all were sick and suffering too. And these people were happy! I wanted what they had, so I threw myself into the program. I got a sponsor and bought literature, which I read faithfully. I spoke at meetings and volunteered my service. Slowly, I began to find some of that joy that had so astounded me at my first few meetings.

My group emphasized the tools of recovery and examined

a specific topic each week. They encouraged me to work the Steps. It didn't come easy, but Step work brought me most of the peace that has finally grown around my childhood.

Recently, I gained some great gifts by working Steps Eight and Nine. I had a long talk with my mother last year that lifted most of my resentments toward her and brought light to dark corners of my childhood. We discussed all the questions I had never dared to ask. Not only did I learn more about my experiences, but, for the first time, I realized what devastation my mother suffered when my father died of alcoholism. Until then, I had believed I was the only victim of alcoholism in my family. My amends to her truly began on that day and have continued in a new attitude toward her and her disease.

Last spring I wrote an Eighth Step list which revealed that I particularly owed amends to my oldest sister. What a change of attitude that experience created! I harbored terrific resentments against her for what I perceived to be her controlling behavior whenever I visited her. Working the Eighth Step revealed that I had an unrecognized expectation that she would always take care of me, and I carried that expectation with me whenever I entered her house. What a set-up! I walked into her house with a child's attitude and then resented her for treating me like a child. So, like a child, I cut her out of my life. It's been two years since we have had any normal contact. Today I have her at the top of my amends list, and I pray to my Higher Power to make me willing.

Today I work on solutions rather than problems. I continue to do Al-Anon service. I have a sponsor who is a Godsend, and those I sponsor are an even greater Godsend. I have heard that serenity is not life without problems, but rather the ability to live in spite of problems. Today I have tools for living and, for the most part, my attitude is positive. When I slip into negativity and hopelessness, I rush my body to a meeting where I listen carefully to the voices of healthy fellow Al-Anon members and soon I can join them again in health.

I turned down the heat.

As is often the case, a brief conversation with my wife has given me new insight into my experience of growing up with alcoholism. She noted that, when I cook, which is a fairly rare event, I tend to turn up the flame on our gas stove to its highest setting. She suggested I might burn food less often if I turned the heat down, and she asked me why I had such a stubborn tendency to cook with a high flame.

I explained a bit defensively that my mother always cooked with really high heat and that it worked fine for her. As I spoke, a picture of my mother rose in my mind and I realized that the demanding, frenetic atmosphere of cooking with high heat pretty much represented the overall feeling of my childhood. It never occurred to me, as I grew up, that I might benefit from turning down the flame both literally and metaphorically.

Much of my Al-Anon experience involves the slow discovery of practices and attitudes that encourage me to do the equivalent of turning down the flame when I cook. This concept was especially helpful in practicing Step Nine. In dealing with my family, the amends that I have made amounted to turning down the flame under these relationships. I have succeeded in forcing less and accepting more. Often making amends simply meant lowering my expectations.

Lowered expectations brought me a more balanced acceptance of family members. I began to admit with a good deal of sadness that all of us were affected by living with alcoholism and that we do not necessarily function with a high degree of

sanity together or even separately. Because of my awareness
of the effects of the disease, I am less surprised by odd or difficult behavior. I realize more often today the truth of my
wife's recent observation, "You know, your family is not very
relaxed." Again she has captured it in a nutshell. Living with
alcoholism made it difficult, to say the least, for my family to
relax!

By lowering my own standards and expectations, I have
found not only that I can be more comfortable with expecting
the unexpected, but also that I have increased my willingness
to appreciate the occasional level of communication and
enjoyment that I do find with relatives. Because I spend less
energy hoping and waiting for a degree of consistent support
and care that is unrealistic, I have more energy to enjoy
pleasant moments however fleeting.

Another gift is a lowered flame of expectations of myself. I
no longer bill my visits as "Mr. Hero in Recovery executes the
perfect family encounter." I try to remind myself that I am
likely to have slips when I'm in slippery situations and that
being around my family, which still suffers the effects of alcoholism, is a very slippery situation for me. I do the best I can;
when I lose my balance, I do the best I can to recover it. When
a flame is too hot, I try to turn it down, but if dinner gets
ruined now and then, I accept the problem as part of my learning and as an opportunity for growth rather than as proof positive that I am incompetent. I, too, have been deeply affected
by family alcoholism, and not even the help of Al-Anon, the
Twelve Steps, my sponsor, and my Higher Power guarantees
avoidance of all the pitfalls of being with my family.

Nevertheless, I am now more able to treat my family with
courtesy and respect and to spend less time minding their
business. In this way I make amends by treating others with

the same care I wish to receive myself. As a human being, I win some and I lose some, but when I turn down the flame a little, I'm more likely to produce a meal without smoking up the house.

Amends freed me from bondage.

I came to Al-Anon on the advice of someone I didn't even like! She said, "I know someone who was a bad drunk and he quit. Maybe he can tell you how to get your husband to quit." That was all I needed to hear. I called him, and he spoke with me for a few minutes about Alcoholics Anonymous and then directed me to Al-Anon. This moment came after thirty-four years of trying to stop the alcoholics I knew from drinking and of trying to run other people's lives. My dad was the alcoholic I started with. I knew what was wrong with Dad but not what was wrong with Mom. She taught me a lot, but I failed to learn the most important thing—that attempts to stop the alcoholic's drinking didn't work for her any better than for me. We were both powerless and unwilling to admit it.

I met a young man in school—my first close encounter with an alcoholic who was not a relative. (I had oodles of alcoholic relatives!) I became crazy about him in the true sense of the word. I would get throwing up sick when I knew he was coming or when I saw him arrive unexpectedly. I was already so insane that this seemed a good enough reason to marry him! In our eleven-year marriage we had three children and innumerable fights. He was often out drinking. Desperately frightened and out of control, I imagined every woman in the vicinity was after him. When he walked into the house I harangued him with my jealousy until he'd leave again. Then I started "getting even" by doing what I thought he did. My secret life began with drinking, running around with married men, and taking drugs. I'd show him!

What I actually did was neglect our three children, who got in the way of all the time I needed for revenge. It took a lot of time to find out what he was doing and do worse. One Saturday night, I wrecked the car. He came home drunk and determined to kill me for doing it. I was so insane at the time, I told him if he'd shoot the gun, I would be a willing target. He did pull the trigger! When nothing happened, he threw the gun at me and stormed out to take off in his wrecked car. I hid and later ran away to my mother, but I came back the next day. He tried several more times to kill me. Finally, I managed to leave him physically, although he still had mental control over me for years and years until I worked Step Nine in Al-Anon.

I married alcoholic Number Two to keep my first husband away from me. What a price I paid for protection. We drank and partied, and he liked all the things about me that my ex-husband hated. He liked my party attitude, my make-up, and the way I lived. I had a good job while we dated, so I would go out and party, take him home, go to bed, and the next morning I would go to work. After we married, I still needed my job but I couldn't always take him home from partying, as he usually didn't want to quit, so my rest had to go. Exhausted, I finally decided we would quit this drinking and partying and settle down. Wrong! Only half of "we" quit, and the fight was on. Trying to get control, I even gave my children to their father, a bad decision which was followed by many trips to court and essentially the loss of my two oldest children. I have many amends to make to my children for my insanity. They are now adults and also children of alcoholics, just as I am, who are likely to suffer as much pain as I did.

When I tried to make my second husband do things he didn't want to do, he became violent. His behavior embarrassed me now that I was sober, and I left him often, which meant sleeping in my car in the mountains, in hospital parking lots, or anywhere I could find. Until I found Al-Anon, nothing changed but the name of the man who was my husband.

In Al-Anon things did begin to change, though doing what I needed to do came very hard for me. I learned to leave him to his own devices and accept the results of my own actions. He had always called me, after the bars closed, to come get him. I'd get up out of bed, drive to wherever he was, and follow him home, since he wouldn't leave his car. I never wanted to do this, but I also didn't want to pay the price of not doing it. I heard a lot in Al-Anon about God as I understood Him, accepting things I couldn't change, turning things over, being willing, and asking myself, "What is the worst that could happen?" With my imagination, the last could be pretty dire! I decided to try the stuff I learned on the late night rescues. The next time he called, I said, "No!" and heard all the threats of what he would do. I didn't go for him, but I did go back to the bedroom, get down on my knees, and ask this God that I really didn't understand to help me accept the consequences of what I'd done. I went to sleep; my husband came home, and there was no price to pay at all. He never called again. It works, I thought!

Three years into Al-Anon I concluded that I didn't have to live the way I was living, and I decided to leave him. I told him that if he wanted help with his drinking I would help, but I would no longer live with it. He did call me for help and joined Alcoholics Anonymous. We got back together, but sobriety didn't fix things the way I thought it would. He left me for my best Al-Anon friend. That shock shook my program to its roots, but I managed to stay in Al-Anon with the help of others and my Higher Power.

Even after many years, I was not entirely free from my first husband, who was the father of my children. He is still drinking and has no plans to stop. Year after year, he continued to control and manipulate me mentally, sometimes using the children. Step Nine finally freed me from that bondage. Today I can love him because he's the father of my children and a child of God like the rest of us. Detachment came when I forgave him and amended my part. He didn't have to change at all for my freedom to manifest itself. This is a priceless Al-Anon gift that I earned the hard way. Al-Anon has given me a new life—and freedom to live it richly in the present. Al-Anon has taught me that the truth will set me free, but I notice it always infuriates me first!

Once the major wounds that we sustained while growing up with the disease of alcoholism have healed, we stand on the threshold of a glorious new life. We may be standing straight and relatively pain-free for the first time in our lives. Shame has been faced and banished, and we have learned to connect with our fellow human beings in honesty and trust. Having accepted our own part in forging healthy, loving attitudes out of the fire of disease, we recognize the need to monitor those attitudes and begin to notice when we take on responsibilities that rightfully belong to others. Wouldn't it be lovely if this serene state remained constant throughout the rest of our lives? It doesn't.

Two things prevent us from living in bliss and innocence— the stealthy return of our old patterns, and the fact that we are human beings living in a world where all living things are born, grow, diminish, and die. Change is the order of the day. Even if we could manage to catch any lurking remnant of the family disease of alcoholism every time it tried to sneak back into our thinking, we would still find ourselves confronted by the annoying reality that human beings just aren't perfect and life is never without challenges. "Oh, well," we say, with teeth just slightly clenched, "if there were no challenges, it would be boring, and we hate boredom even worse than we hate challenges." Perhaps that is why life has moments, but only moments, of absolute, joyous perfection and the rest of the time we must cope with change. The last three Steps provide us with a critical and much needed road map for sustaining the triumphs and humbler successes we have achieved by working the first nine Steps.

Some of us recognize that the Twelve Steps are an excellent path to spirituality that we might never have found, had we not had to cope with a family fractured by alcoholism. Some of us feel intense gratitude by this stage in our commitment to Al-Anon, for we realize that the gifts we received along the way were better than those we might have found on our own in a family healthier than ours. Some of us still grumble about having to practice the Steps to stay sane, even though we recognize—perhaps by trying for a while to do without it—that this is an essential part of maintaining our spiritual health, just as good food and regular exercise are necessary for physical health. Grumbling or grateful, we arrive at Step Ten, "Continued to take personal inventory and when we were wrong promptly admitted it," ready to learn how to enjoy life more every day and to meet its challenges with humor, the loving support of people like us, and the guidance of our Higher Power.

We have had enough experience to understand that messes are much more easily cleaned up if done promptly. Having staggered around long enough with huge grudges on our backs, weighed down and depressed with bitter anger, and burdened with enough guilt to sink an ocean liner, we know better—when we remember to think about it—than to let our mistakes and resentments pile up again. Members have found that spending a few minutes each evening, assessing the day and amending or planning to amend any behaviors that didn't make them proud, helped to maintain serenity. In Step Ten we learned that living one day at a time meant something more than not worrying or obsessing about tomorrow; it also meant clearing away regrets from yesterday so we could carry only the weight of today. The freedom we enjoy through the sustained spiritual discipline of Step Ten can transform life from an endless trudge into the grace and joy of a dance.

Sustaining a spiritual life requires discipline, diligence, and regularity. We hope to integrate God, *as we understand God,* into every aspect of living, not only because we need regular support to maintain health, but because we have come to believe that a Power greater than we are has our best interests at heart and can connect us to understanding and knowledge beyond our limited human intelligence. This is not to say that we should cease using our intelligence, but we discover that it is much more effective in bringing us peace when directed by our highest self, or highest consciousness, which some of us choose to call God. We recognize where ego has gotten us and the loneliness of trying to live life utterly on grit, brains, and self-will. There is a better way, the way of our Higher Power.

But how do we know when it is ego and when it is our Higher Power directing us, before we get ourselves in difficulty again? An Al-Anon member once commented, "When I realized how dreadful my childhood really was and all the misguided, damaging, and incorrect teachings my parents gave me, I pretty much decided they knew absolutely nothing and I'd have to start from scratch. I felt like an infant; it was terrifying. Then I recognized that I have a tendency to extremes, including extremes of thought. For example, my mother was filled with aphorisms. She said things like, 'Don't cry over spilled milk,' and 'a stitch in time saves nine.' She was quick with an aphorism when I cried or had done something wrong, and I hated them. Since alcoholism distorted much of what my parents modeled, I rejected everything, even the wise parts of them. I guess I 'threw the baby out with the bath water.' As I reclaim the positive aspects of my childhood, I remember Mother saying that if I did not listen to the experience of others, I would have to learn in the 'school of hard knocks.' It is very confusing to know what to take and what to leave behind, but listening to others' experience in Al-Anon, and to my Higher Power, has saved me many a class in the 'school of hard knocks.' "

Life is a rigorous classroom. We can learn by our own experience, by others' experiences, or we can refuse to learn and stubbornly cling to what we believe to be true. We've already tried running our lives on our own limited experiences and have discovered we don't have all the lesson plans. But who does? And how do we know which voice to follow? Spiritual mastery is no different from any other type of learning. Discernment takes skill, and skill takes practice. Learning to hear and follow the subtle guidance of a Power greater than ourselves requires lots of practice. Our job is to supply the willingness and the time. This is the purpose of Step Eleven, "Sought through prayer and meditation to improve our conscious contact with God *as we understood Him,* praying only for the knowledge of His will for us and the power to carry that out." If we don't care to follow God's will, we are free to refuse, and we may find ourselves once again in the not so subtle "school of hard knocks." As one member put it, "God whispers softly to me all the time. When I don't listen, I'm headed for trouble or pain. Then I listen, because pain has a loud voice!" A calm, solid peace inside is a good indicator we're on track.

Prayer has been described as talking to God and meditation as listening to God. There are probably as many ways to pray and meditate as there are understandings of Higher

Power, and we must each find those that work for us. Like a school, Al-Anon exposes us to people who have sought to improve their conscious contact with God, and we may practice some of the methods they have used until we find those that best suit our personal relationship with a Power greater than ourselves. It is helpful to have a whole variety of prayer techniques in case our favorite method doesn't always work in every situation. A prayer as simple as, "Help!" can be used throughout the day in any situation where we desire help from a Higher Power. If we practice a particular religion, we may use the methods it suggests. We can borrow prayers from Al-Anon literature, or repeat the popular Serenity Prayer:

> *God, grant me the serenity,*
> *to accept the things I cannot change,*
> *courage to change the things I can,*
> *and wisdom to know the difference.*

What matters is not *how* we pray, but *that* we pray, so we have found it helpful to practice Step Eleven regularly, remembering to say, "Thank You!" for the blessings as well as "Help!" for the challenges.

Meditation can be described as concentrated quiet. Taking time from the most hectic schedule to relax, breathe, focus, and listen can yield serenity and peace for any decision we face. Meditation is not necessarily mystical or complicated; rather, it allows us to still the many voices in our heads (some of us refer to them as the committee) long enough for a Higher Voice to whisper quietly to our minds. Many techniques can quiet us. We can concentrate on relaxed, long, easy breathing. We can think deeply about a slogan or an idea from the literature. We may work on relaxing each set of muscles, sit silently contemplating nature, or chant a single word or sound. The significance of quiet listening for God could be likened to the difference in impact between a stone thrown into a glassy, peaceful pond or into a tumultuous river. The stone leaves ripples on both, but only on the still surface of a pond can they be discerned. Thus, we recognize guidance only when we can still our own mental ponds enough to allow God's impact to reveal itself, and for most of us, that takes time and regular practice.

We had to learn that prayer was not lecturing God on what we expected or needed, but rather humbling ourselves to pray only for knowledge of God's will and realizing we don't always know what is best. We do ask and trust that what we receive will be for our highest good. Learning God's will for us, rather than demanding our own will, requires both humility and trust. If we falter in these—and often we do—we can go back to Step One and begin again. Each time through the Steps is a little quicker, easier, and deeper. We are learning, practicing, making mistakes, adjusting, and learning. As we become more adept at Step Eleven, we recognize again and again the tremendous advantages that accrue to us when we walk a spiritual path on earth, and learning becomes a joy in itself.

SUSTAINING HEALTHY LIVES

An artist learns the art of living.

I am an artist. My father is an alcoholic, but neither he nor Mother has ever recognized this. During my childhood we went from an elegant upper-middle-class life in a major midwestern city to a more humble existence in a small town. This was probably a result of Dad's drinking. Our neighbors felt

Dad was insane, but as far as I know they never suspected alcoholism. Our guest room was piled so high with empty bourbon cartons that you couldn't walk around. The boxes never went in the alley with the trash because people would see them. When I entered graduate school, my books were sent in bourbon boxes.

Because we viewed everything and everyone outside of us as totally against us, we lived in total isolation. I became a child of extremes. Everything was love or hate. There was no middle ground. Years later, when I first came to Al-Anon, a man told me an amazing thing. He said that of all the people I met, two per cent would like me no matter what I did, two percent would dislike me no matter what, and the rest would be largely indifferent. This cleared up a lot of my thinking, as I began to introduce the concept of balance and indifference into my wildly swinging hates and loves.

I grew up emotionally and spiritually unbalanced. Until I was twenty-two I had daily crying fits. I shook physically almost all the time. My parents, who could see no fault in themselves, felt that I, with my emotional difficulties, was their sole problem. Wouldn't any parent be upset if their daughter wasn't right?!

Though I grew up in the midst of alcoholism, I take responsibility for the sick person I became. Many people I have met came out of similar environments and did not act out their character defects to the degree I did. In high school and college I started doing bizarre things like touching my mother's nose and saying, "You're evil!" At times I brought her to tears, as you can well imagine, and I liked it!

I majored in art in college, so my off-beat behavior was accepted to some extent, and I rationalized that it proved that I was a true artist. I think that, actually, I was quite insane and art provided me a daily emotional purge that kept me out of an asylum. Often I started my day painting and dwelling on all the bad things I could think of around me. Because I excelled at color, design, and drawing, as well as research, I did well in college. At nineteen they gave me my own studio, and I soon got into graduate school with a teaching assistantship. Totally lacking in gratitude, I concentrated on how badly the school treated me and felt I should have been accepted at a more famous art institute. Even without alcohol, I had the princely alcoholic ego. I came into the school intending to shape up their art department!

My friends were people like me who didn't want to take any responsibility for their own lives. As we aged, consequences of irresponsibility showed up. To my horror, one of my friends began living on the street, and others teetered on the brink of homelessness. Immersed in a lifestyle that didn't work, I was fortunate to meet a new friend who had the same emotional difficulties I had, but who also had a solution—a strong Alcoholics Anonymous program. I wasn't a drinker, but she suggested that the Twelve Steps might still be an answer to my emotional difficulties, though neither of us recognized my family's alcoholism at the time. I am grateful that AA and Al-Anon do not require any proof that you belong. They just welcome you in and let you see if it helps. Not recognizing my father's alcoholism in the beginning actually was fortuitous because I kept the focus on myself.

What hooked me was the principle of gratitude. My friend gave me this principle to practice in times of crisis, which were daily occurrences so I got lots of practice. Whenever I thought I was undervalued and mistreated, I was to think of what I could be grateful for instead. I had so much self-pity, it consumed my life and made me very miserable. Ever since I learned to apply gratitude, self-pity has never again been a serious problem. It is a great relief to realize that, while frustrations and challenges always exist, the misery is optional, since it is a product of my attitude rather than the outside circumstances.

After using bits and pieces of the Twelve Steps for eight months, I decided I was ready for a full dose. During spring break, I began seriously working the Steps. My friend suggested I substitute emotional problems or emotionalism wherever I saw alcoholism. It worked. Where it said, "alcoholic," I read "emotional cripple." My family may have given me the disease, but it was my own actions and reactions that crippled me. I worked the first nine Steps, and my attitude, relationships with people, and my art work were all slowly transformed.

Now I live by Steps Ten, Eleven, and Twelve on a daily basis. As Step Ten suggests, when I do something that makes me feel bad or that hurts someone, I promptly say something to them. Sometimes at work, for example, I am tempted to meddle in situations that are none of my business or are beyond the scope of my responsibility. I once reproached someone for a mistake that should have been handled by a supervisor. Worse yet, I scolded someone in front of co-workers and embarrassed him. Today I find that if I admit my fault immediately and attempt not to repeat my error, I will probably be forgiven. Otherwise resentment poisons the atmosphere, and I am uncomfortable for a long time. Today I prefer short-term discomfort.

I make time for daily meditation, usually before I go to work. The work goes easier when I do, so I receive a regular reward for this small discipline. Sometimes it's just five minutes before I brush my teeth, but it is so pleasurable, I usually make it longer and look forward to it.

In order to live Step Twelve, I am willing to let anyone know I'm a member of Al-Anon if it appears it might be useful. This includes people at work, social events, and school.

Recently, I realized that practicing these principles in all my affairs really meant *all*. When I first joined Al-Anon, I didn't yet realize I had to practice principles like considera- tion, tolerance, and forgiveness outside of my relations with family, close friends, or in Al-Anon meetings. I conducted my art career as I had in the past. At work I continued to prac- tice defects such as intolerance (I am really ashamed that once I actually laughed at a student's work!), procrastination, envy, and resentment. Because I didn't bring the principles to work, the department removed my teaching assistantship. This was a blow, for my self-esteem and identity were tied to that job. I ended up in a minimum wage job, taping plastic over toilet fixtures so the paint crew could repaint the dorms—a very humbling experience. My Higher Power cer- tainly gave me what I needed and not what I wanted in this case. I did learn, and I got through it by fiercely clinging to my Al-Anon principles and performing the lowly job as well as I could. Because of my response, my assistantship was restored the next semester.

I also received a new stimulus for my art. While on the paint crew, I began making art for a different reason. One fear that had haunted me was that if I didn't have an artistic job, I would not have time to create art. Instead I found that, after I'd completed my work for the maintenance crew, I still had time to paint and draw. Since my thinking and approach were clearer and more systematic, no longer affording me my neg- ative purging, my art actually improved.

Principles have come to sustain my daily life. For example, after having a close call with my car, the value of patience struck home. It occurred because of a traffic situation where I could easily have let another car into the space in front of me, but I was too impatient. I lost a lot more time because of my impatience!

Al-Anon principles are like rules of the road. When I obey traffic lights and signs, and consider other drivers, driving is safe. If I unpredictably move to another lane or barge through red lights as if I'm the only person on the road, the situation becomes dangerous. The Twelve Steps are a good road map for life, making it safe and sane most of the time.

Sometimes I still get impatient with recovery. Initially when I began to change, it was very frustrating because few people noticed. At school, my friends and teachers continued to treat me in a manner based on my past instead of my present behavior. It has taken up to five years to establish trust with some of those people, especially those I hurt along the way. Finally, in the past year I gained respect from my family. Now, as I enter new situations, I tend to command respect in my associations with people. I've also learned to value people for what they do in the present, not what they did in the past. There has been so much growth in my life because of Al-Anon that today I regard the family alcoholism that led me to practice Twelve Step Recovery as a gift from my Higher Power.

Meditation brings grace to my days.

I receive peace and comfort each morning by working Step Eleven. If I do not do it early in the morning, I survive the day often feeling desperate.

I sit in my chair and repeat the words to Step Eleven. I sit quietly, close my eyes, and visualize a broom in my head sweeping out the past, my addiction to guilt, my negativity, and my fears. I breathe normally, inhaling and exhaling that

God loves me. Slowly, a peace creeps over me, and I can feel His presence.

Sometimes I sit with my palms turned upward to receive His gifts. Sometimes I sit with my hands folded. Sometimes I press my feet to the floor and allow all the hurt and fear to drain back into Mother Earth, where it will be transformed into new life and growth. When my mind wanders, I repeat the words to Step Eleven again, or I repeat the Serenity Prayer, or think the words to "Our Father" to bring myself back to peace and conscious contact.

I do this meditating approximately thirty minutes each day. So that I do not need to be distracted by considering how long I have been sitting there, I set my stove timer. When it buzzes (it is always too soon), I sit for a few more minutes. Then I know that my day has been turned over to my Higher Power. God is in charge and I am free to go about my day. When I do this, my days are graceful; when I forget, the rising emotional turmoil reminds me quickly enough.

I spend time with God.

In *The Forum* recently I read, "Religion is for those who fear going to hell. Spirituality is for those who have already been there." This idea grounded my sponsor's messages to me about working Step Eleven and having a spiritual awakening in Al-Anon. I didn't realize how much time I'd spent in hell until I discovered what joy life could possess.

At every Al-Anon meeting we read the phrase, "Without such spiritual help [meaning the help of the program], living with an alcoholic was too much for most of us." It certainly proved to be too much for me before my sponsor taught me about spirituality. The family disease of alcoholism affects each family member mentally, physically, emotionally, and yes, spiritually. The symptoms of spiritual sickness I displayed were resentment, self-pity, lack of faith, and a distorted way of showing love—in that I, as an adult child of an alcoholic, tend to love those I can pity and rescue. I also tend to think that if I can only do enough for people, they will see how much I care about them and will love and appreciate me in return. When they don't, watch out! There's a resentment brewing. It's not that I wish to buy their love; it's just that I always thought that was the way, perhaps the only way, to prove it to them. I have since learned differently.

I used to resent God for not rescuing me from the alcoholic home. Al-Anon taught me that God gave us life, and if He gave us alcoholic parents, He also gave us the Twelve Steps of recovery. It later occurred to me that, unlike a parent who has no faith in his child's ability to handle situations, who over-protects and rescues him constantly, God must have had enough faith in the inner strength He gave me to trust that I could follow His guidance when I asked for it and to stay back far enough to give me free will. I choose to do the footwork in my recovery myself and am thus strengthened each time I listen and then act on what I hear. To me, this is not neglect; it's a vote of confidence.

When my resentments were strong, they shut out the light of any source or possibility of spiritual help whatsoever. My Al-Anon sponsor introduced me to a concept of viewing those who wrong us as spiritually sick, just as we are, only perhaps with different symptoms. When confronted with someone who treats me badly, I find it helpful to say to myself, "This is a sick person. God, please relieve me of my anger. Show me how I can be helpful to both of us. If I can't be helpful, or the person refuses my help, then teach me tolerance and kindness, God, and grant me the willingness to use them."

I've also learned that when I pray for the person I resent

for a period of time, I'm relieved of much resentment. Since the alternative is to allow myself to be controlled by the perceived wrongs of those I resent, I try to do this, though I will admit there are some folks I am still struggling to pray for, after a long time. I keep working at it because if it is true that what goes around comes around, I do not want condemnation and judgments to "come around" to me; therefore, my conscience cannot allow me to continue to dish them out as I did when I knew no better.

In Al-Anon groups for grown children of alcoholics, I learned that this is a spiritual program coming from love. We cannot give what we don't have, so we cannot love others until we love and respect ourselves. We learn self-love by being loved by our families, but sometimes those families don't have it to give. When stress and irritability caused me to binge on self-pity, resentment, and festering anger in emotional outbursts, the amazing Al-Anon members loved me unconditionally. They told me the truth, sometimes with rigorous honesty, but love shone through in each comment. They literally loved me until I could love myself. I believe this is potent human evidence of the spirituality of the program.

To find the spirituality I so desperately needed, I had to learn about forgiveness. When I learned to forgive myself for the harm I had done myself, I became willing to forgive others for their faults. With forgiveness I found acceptance for everyone around me, and I believe this is evidence of spirit working in my life.

Spirituality is strength, not weakness. In Al-Anon, I have learned to take action in my own behalf and then allow God to do for me what I cannot do for myself. Self-reliance was O.K. as far as it went, but it never went far enough. I also suffered from my strong will. It caused me to step on others when I tried to control them or the situation. My self-will rarely brought harmony and peace to my relationships. Too often I assumed I was right and powerful, and it took me, a "super competent," a while in Al-Anon to accept that alcoholism is more powerful than I am. Today I know there is a Power greater even than alcoholism—my Higher Power—and my job is to step out of the way. When I do, things have a way of working out in solutions I hadn't even imagined. It's quite mysterious, but it works!

Daily practice is my key to progressing spiritually. I don't have to earn God's favor by doing everything right, as I tried to do with my perfectionist, harsh, critical alcoholic parent. I do need to renew my serenity every day with Step Ten. I use large doses of love and tolerance (learned from other members) to face my mistakes daily, and I remind myself I am a growing organism, not some perfect statue to stick on a shelf and leave to gather dust.

Spirituality is mystical at times, but it is not some vague, filmy concept. I believe that we are not humans having a spiritual experience, but rather we are naturally and essentially spiritual beings grappling with the feelings and frustrations of being human. The love and spirituality entered my life easily when I stopped resenting people and life for not being what I wanted them to be. I slip, of course, but acceptance grows each time I pick myself up, and it is easier today than when I determinedly ran my own show.

I practice Step Eleven one day at a time by letting go of my need to know all the answers and to know the outcome in advance of every situation. I'm glad that there's a Power greater than I, since I really don't have all the answers. I don't have to know the whole story to participate in it, even as I don't have to understand precisely how my car works in order to drive it. I do need to know my part for the day, so I seek it through daily quiet time. I once heard meditation described as spending time with God. It's the most pleasant, rewarding time I have ever spent in my life.

Grandfather left me gifts.

The first alcoholic in my life was my mother's father. Mother and I lived with my grandparents for the first eighteen months of my life while my father was overseas. As I grew up, I spent time with my grandparents every summer and loved those days. But I grew up confused and afraid. I didn't realize just how confused I was until I came into Al-Anon. Here I learned that, though I could not change the past, I could feel the pain and heal the present—and most definitely the future.

When he drank, my grandfather became verbally abusive. My grandparents fought and yelled at each other through me, and I felt they wanted me to choose between them. I loved them both and could not choose. The whole scene was very painful and confusing and had repercussions for many years to come.

A few years ago, my grandfather passed away, leaving me with many sad and painful memories. We never had a real talk about feelings, and, though I wished to very much, I could not find peace and warmth with his memory.

Al-Anon's support and the Eleventh Step finally cleared my head, allowing me to listen and to honestly experience my feelings for my grandfather. As I sought prayer and meditation, I learned to listen to God, to my heart, and eventually, even through death, to my grandfather. This was only possible because I came to feel my feelings and came to accept my spirituality and a Power greater than myself. I turned everything over to my Higher Power and asked for wisdom and strength to deal with the problem of my grandfather. My prayers were answered in the form of a dream. In the dream, my grandfather came to me and gave me a little gift. I opened the small box and inside was a spool of thread. As my grandfather was a shoemaker, I knew this gift was indeed from him.

Through Step Eleven, I was ready to hear when an Al-Anon friend told me that it is never really too late to say what is in your heart, and I can now say this to my grandfather: "I'm thinking of the many gifts you gave me through the years. The material gifts were few but always special; the non-material gifts were the most important. You gave me your presence— you held me and teased me. I liked that and would wait for your footsteps. Sometimes, however, there was alcohol in the air and things had changed. As I got older, I grew up in a home without hugs and kisses. I learned to be quiet. When you walked in the door, I didn't run to hug you; I don't believe I even thought of it. We've missed a lot of hugs, you and I, but that's the way it was.

"You gave me the gift of your sense of humor, and I saw it take many shapes. I saw you sober and laughing, and I cried at your alcohol-laced humor. I do think humor was a bond between us, and perhaps even the alcohol was a lace binding us together. When you were loud and laughing and thought you were funny, I hated and loved you at the same time, and I sat with you to keep you still. But I didn't laugh. Your alcohol-laced humor hurt, and inside I cried.

"You gave me many gifts. You let me watch you mend shoes. You took me in the car. You listened to me. You waited for my footsteps too, didn't you? Somehow your gifts to my daily life mean that I still share my days with you and I rejoice in this.

"Now you give me a spool of thread that fits in my pocket. A spool is a tool if I choose. I can choose my own pattern. What will I sew? I think I'll begin with my heart. There's a hole there. It has gotten smaller. It's not gaping wide as it was when you died, but it's still there.

"You have given me courage wrapped around a spool of thread. I can mend that hole and restore my spirit. I know, Grandpa, you have had a bit of sewing to do too. With the strength from my Higher Power, the serenity I gain in Al-Anon, and the spool of thread from you, Grandpa, I am healing today and I will be O.K. I am healing and eventually all that will be left is the love."

Chapter nine

SHARING OUR GOOD
FORTUNE

By the time we arrive at Step Twelve, "Having had a spiritual awakening as a result of these Steps, we tried to carry this message to others, and to practice these principles in all our affairs," we have experienced many changes and transformations in our lives and attitudes. Old relationships are changing and we have new relationships in the fellowship and with our Higher Power. Something has "clicked" for us, and we want to keep this vital new way of life. Long-time members tell us that to maintain our spiritual growth, we must give it away. They call upon us not only to talk the talk, but to walk the walk, for modeling is the best—perhaps the *only*—way to shine a light that others can use to see themselves.

Service is the heart of Al-Anon, for our program is dependent on each of us doing our share. Without service, Al-Anon would soon disappear. We can contribute simply by arriving early enough at a meeting to set out chairs or help make coffee, and we serve when we sponsor members, greet newcomers, chair meetings, volunteer to be a secretary for a meeting, order literature, create literature, and in many other ways, large and small. More important, we *want* to share our experience, strength, and hope because part of our awakening is the understanding that we are not alone but part of the human community, and that others still suffer as we suffered before we found Al-Anon.

Since many of us grew up taking care of people long before we should have been expected to, some aspects of serving may cause us to stumble on the roadway of recovery. Much of our recovery as adult children of alcoholics requires us to learn how to create and maintain reasonable boundaries. We are learning how not to give so much of ourselves away that there is nothing left for us, and yet, we need to give recovery away to keep it. Serving others while maintaining balance in our lives, and keeping boundaries firm yet flexible, requires more recovery. Thus, while we learn service in Al-Anon, we also improve our own program.

Extremists from childhood, now we can see life in shades of gray rather than black and white, and doing service allows us to practice these skills in a safe place. We don't have to give everything or nothing. We can give some and take some and benefit from both the giving and the receiving.

Working Step Twelve makes us more and more a part of Al-Anon as a group endeavor, and the value of the Twelve Traditions for group functioning and harmony becomes increasingly apparent. Some of us have noticed that the principles of the Traditions work in other group settings as well. We may also want to consult the Twelve Concepts, which are a guide to service on a broad scale. Whatever approach we take to service, we find that carrying the message is a privilege rather than one more task to add to our already overburdened souls. Our cups are no longer drained but overflowing, and when on occasion they do seem empty, we know where to go to fill them up again. We are learning that love, unlike

things in the material world, grows ever more abundant the
more we give it away.

STORIES OF GIVING AND RECEIVING

I didn't want a spiritual awakening.

What is a spiritual awakening, and what does it mean to
have one? I can only tell you what it means for me today.
Tomorrow, when I have grown more, my understanding may
change. My Al-Anon beginning was not promising. I was *not*
looking for a spiritual awakening when I came here; whatever it was I looked for, spirituality wasn't it. The talk about God
and Higher Power put me off, and because I didn't understand the difference between religion and spirituality, I feared
I'd gotten involved with a bunch of religious fanatics.

I hadn't actively believed in God since I was twelve, and I
saw no reason to start again. When people spoke of spending
twenty or thirty minutes in prayer each day, I couldn't imagine what they found to talk about all that time, and there was
no way I was getting down on my knees. I resisted fiercely
when people talked about spirituality—and about everything
else as well.

I went to my first meeting because my therapist suggested
it might help; I'd been in therapy for almost three years and
my life wasn't getting better. I didn't know I needed to recover, but even when I considered that I might, recovery seemed
like an impossible task. I kept coming back only because I
didn't know what else to do. At first the words I heard sounded like gibberish—none of them made sense. Besides not liking the God talk, I thought lots of the readings had nothing to

do with me. The alcoholic was my father, and he was dead! It irritated me when they said not to bring in outside material—aha! I thought, it *is* a bunch of fanatics afraid of any other opinion.

One thing I did understand right away was that everyone there had problems too. After a few meetings I saw that they were making progress with their problems, and that's the only thing that kept me coming back. After a few weeks I bought an *ODAT (One Day at a Time in Al-Anon)* because everyone else had one. I kept it on the table by my front door and stood there for a minute or so every morning to read it before I left the house. Though I didn't know it, this was a beginning. After a while, I found myself sitting down to read the page, and the Serenity Prayer sneaked into my morning thinking. Gradually, I added other books and began to say a prayer or two of my own. One day I noticed I was spending twenty or thirty minutes each day doing this, and, amazingly, I had plenty to say to God.

I was still apprehensive about spiritual awakenings, because they sounded too much like religion and reminded me of something a professor had said years earlier. He likened a spiritual experience he had had to being struck in the chest with a baseball bat. I thought "awakening" meant something like that or perhaps a thousand suns bursting on the horizon and I wasn't in the market for either.

Not up for an awakening, I nevertheless discovered my own idea of spirit. Spirit is what stands at the core of me, sustaining me and keeping me going through bad times and good. It took more than four years, but eventually I did find terms of spirituality that had meaning for me. What finally clicked for me was hearing another member say that for him *every* experience is a spiritual experience. Thinking about this, I began to see that my spiritual awakenings needn't be restricted to blinding flashes about a Higher Power. They can be anything that increases my knowledge, understanding, or acceptance of people and life. As long as it touches my spirit, it can be any size. Here are some awakenings I have had.

Four months after I entered Al-Anon meetings, I headed to another city on a beautiful spring day, mired in resentment. I remembered just enough of the program to recognize the resentment and realize it would ruin my trip if I let it. Recalling what one member suggested about making a gratitude list to cure resentment, I started making a mental list. I began with great cosmic things, and by the time I was down to giving thanks for guardrails that kept me from zooming off the road into catastrophe, the resentment had dissolved. I was amazed at the difference it made.

Another discovery was about the spiritual nature of time. One morning I overslept. Racing to get ready for work, I could see the remaining time shrinking. The faster I went, the less time I had. I decided the sky wouldn't fall if I arrived ten minutes late, so I slowed down. Suddenly, it was as if time began to expand. I had plenty of time. Since then, whenever I get frantic about deadlines, I slow myself down by telling myself I have enough time to do whatever I need to do. This also works in the broad sense—I have enough time in my life to do what I need to do and what my Higher Power wants me to do.

I've come to understand that each of us is a mirror for other people. Without mirrors, I wouldn't know what I look like. If other people didn't reflect my changes for me, I wouldn't be able to see my progress in Al-Anon. It is a paradox that everything I know about myself I have learned from others, and in sharing about themselves, others show me how I have changed. Other people's victories give me hope.

Another awakening came from hearing that humility is

being the right size. Neither excessive pride nor shame need bother me when I learn that I am no better than anyone else, no worse than anyone else, but I am as good as everyone else.

Some spiritual awakenings come in a moment of serenity. After my first intensive weekend with Al-Anon friends, I felt the most incredible peace and well-being—a feeling unlike anything I had ever experienced. I didn't want it ever to end. By morning it was gone, but I knew it was possible to have that feeling again—this was hope. Every time it happens, whether over muffins and marmalade or listening to music, I experience the same sense of being at one with the world, and the same wonder fills me with gratitude.

An awakening of the first magnitude came when I discovered the incredible power of forgiveness. I couldn't believe it when people said, "Pray for the person against whom you have a resentment," but I tried it. It worked! It works every time I do it.

I have also had awakenings that helped me define my Higher Power. For someone who resisted the God talk as I did, my views about God were remarkably rigid. I didn't want God, but I felt quite adequate to define Him. I got annoyed when someone at a meeting changed the male pronoun, referred to God as something neutral, or when someone dared to say "give us this day our daily strength" instead of "daily bread." I did manage to think about this rigidity and came to understand that each of us is free to define Higher Power and that in Al-Anon there is good reason not to bind us to any one view of God—or any view for that matter. In Al-Anon, tolerance for me and my struggles with spirituality is creating my tolerance for others.

My progress in this program, and in life, dates from the point at which spirit became spirituality. When I took time

each day to read and pray, even if I didn't believe, the practice made it easier to keep doing it.

I came to these rooms cut off from life, from love, from
understanding, from faith, and from hope. It was as though I
was completely wrapped in heavy black velvet cloth. My spiritual awakenings have been like pinpricks in the velvet, each
one admitting the tiniest ray of light. With the many pinpricks, the cloth has become the night, glittering with thousands and thousands of stars. Instead of a baseball bat in the
chest, as my former professor had described, I get the gen-
tlest of taps on the shoulder, awakenings which are for me
preferable to the more dramatic variety.

Whenever I have a spiritual awakening, my soul fills up,
my understanding of myself increases, and I have reason to
feel grateful. Any one of these by itself would be reason
enough to continue seeking a God of my understanding.

I don't know much more about God today than I did when
I started, but I have learned this much. To turn on a light I
don't need to understand the principles of electricity—all I
have to do is flip the switch. I don't need to understand who,
what, why, or where God is. To turn the God switch on, I only
need to do my best each day to practice the spiritual teachings of Al-Anon.

I feared service.

Throughout my childhood, I was obsessed with my incom-
petence. I thought I could do nothing right. Whatever the
task, I had no confidence in my ability to complete it. The
alcoholics in my family needed an incompetent bungler in
their midst to bolster their own self-esteem; I filled the role.

As an adult, I withdrew from the world to protect it from

harm. I felt savage, dangerous, and ignorant. I felt I belonged in a cage. Inside I seethed with rebellion against my role as an incompetent menace and fantasized about being loved and admired and doing things well.

At my first Al-Anon meeting the members said that everyone pitched in to serve the group. I chose a form of service that would protect them from poisonous contact with me—I cleaned the coffee pot. The coffee pot became my life preserver and the bathroom where I filled it my cage. The other members were safe from me, and I was safe from them. Nobody could see if I bungled the job. At the time I had no idea I suffered from false pride, thinking I was so powerfully dangerous. I studiously avoided the job of opening the hall because it required greeting people. I liked them. I didn't want to hurt them. I thought any greeting I mustered would be inadequate and might harm their recovery. Instead I volunteered to inventory literature, where my eyes would be on order forms and my back to other members. Pride blocked me from admitting that I had no social skills.

After eight months in a French Al-Anon group, I met some English-speaking members who asked if I'd join them in forming an English language group. With so few of us, there was nowhere to hide. We each shared a job as trusted servant and tended to weekly tasks. With unity of purpose, it wasn't too hard. Everyone was new at the job and learning together. For the first time in my life, I belonged to a body of equals. When my turn came to open the door, I didn't lose the key, forget the milk, or cause a single person to drop dead by shaking hands. By the time Public Information service rolled my way, the constant terror had diminished to an occasional bout of uneasiness. I carried the message happily, grateful to have a message to carry.

Business meetings provided a much needed part of my

recovery. Thanks to our Second Tradition, I learned to give my opinion without apologizing for it and to express my ideas without imposing them. I learned to detach my emotions from heated issues, and to trust a Higher Power to guide us, and I didn't fall apart when differences of opinion surfaced. Best of all, I discovered that making mistakes is a normal human activity, not a crime punishable by eternal caging. To serve the group as Group Representative, I didn't have to be perfect, though I admit it took the entire three-year term for that fact to really sink in.

Service in Al-Anon gave me solid principles to live by, a precious sense of belonging, and a zest for participation that has carried into many other facets of my increasingly full life. Without the requirement of service, I doubt I would have acquired the courage to speak out, to open up, to believe myself competent, and to risk letting others trust me. I don't always deliver the goods, but when I fail, I no longer retreat into a cage of pride and shame. I amend what I can and go on. If that's not a miracle, I don't know the meaning of the word!

Slogans are Band-Aids.

Just as in many other families, the disease of alcoholism had its devastating effects on ours. I didn't know alcoholism was the problem, but I did know something was very different about my mother and father, compared to other children's parents. My younger brother and I grew very close, because many times all we had to depend on was each other. Our neighborhood had few kids, and I spent much of my youth alone. I also chose solitude because I felt ashamed of my family. When Mother drank, she became verbally abusive to my father and others and embarrassed us in public. Once, in third grade, I had a doctor's appointment and she came to take me out of class to go. She stomped into the classroom drunk and demanded that I be let out of class. When my teacher asked her if she had checked with the school office, my mother told her nastily it was none of her business, grabbed me out of my seat, and pulled me to the door. Embarrassment was a close friend in my youth. Disappointment and fear were my other good friends. Time and again I asked myself, "Why did my mom have to act this way?"

Fear was another constant childhood companion. What would my parents do if I didn't get straight A's on my report card? What if they got a divorce? What if we got in a car accident? What if? What if? What if? The past haunted me, and the future looked terrifying. To deal with these fears, I hid or I joked. I think I appeared normal because I smiled and joked a lot, but inside I quaked and hurt all the time. I never truly smiled until my parents found sobriety.

When they found sobriety, they also found that alcoholism is a family illness and that I had been affected. They gave me no option but to go to Alateen. Since the word "no" was not a part of my vocabulary yet, I went. I can't put my finger on exactly what kept me coming back, but I think it was the first time in a long time that I had felt a positive emotion.

The first tools of the program I grabbed were the slogans. They helped me begin to learn how to live in the moment, stop reacting to everything around me, and open my mind enough to get a sponsor and work the Steps. Now I like to think of the slogans as Band-Aids, the Steps as the cure, and God as the doctor. When I am hurt, before I can get to the doctor to cure it, I usually need to patch it up temporarily to stop the bleeding—that's what Band-Aids are for. Then I seek out a doctor to prescribe the best remedy. Finally, I take the prescribed cure and heal. I now realize that growing up in an alcoholic home made me eligible for the best healthcare benefits around.

Discovering spirituality has been the greatest adventure of my life. Indeed, the people in the Al-Anon fellowship showed me the way to joy, love, and living. When I first came to Alateen, my understanding of God was cloudy because I had no idea who I believed in or what I believed. I was lost! Through working the Steps with a sponsor, I believe today that my Higher Power is all-encompassing love for everything that exists—and that includes me! My newfound spiritual awareness changed my perceptions, giving me new glasses that allowed me to see love where once there was only resentment and embarrassment. Wow! I can hardly begin to catalog the changes of perception I've experienced in Alateen. Clouds and cobwebs yielded to clear vision. When they return and all is lost in mist, I know I need to go to a meeting, talk to my sponsor, and work a Step. Steps give me clarity on what my Higher Power wants for me. Spiritual awakening came not as a blinding flash, but as the careful removal again and again of my blinders.

Shortly after joining the Alateen fellowship, I asked what I like to call "a hard-core Steps and Traditions" woman to sponsor me. She let me slide for a couple of months and then zoomed in, insisting I work the Steps. I resisted, but finally my walls of fear collapsed and I tried it.

When I first seriously took a minute to read the Twelve Steps, I was turned off, especially by the word God in them. How dare anyone tell me to turn my life over. To me that meant admitting I had failed or, worse, that I was a failure. Needless to say, I remained stubborn and miserable for some time. Not until I got involved with service did I find the willingness to try again. The first time I volunteered I was breathless and scared, but as I took the chance, I came to know myself, gain compassion and understanding for others, and find God. I put these in this order because that's how it happened for me.

First, I found a person inside who longed to love and be loved. Before taking the Steps, I didn't feel worthy of anyone's love and at the same time didn't think anyone deserved *my* love, because they would probably leave me or abuse my love. Finding out I deserved someone's love and that I could give my love away unselfishly was the grandest of the many spiritual awakenings that resulted from working the Steps.

Knowing the me who hid behind a wall of fear and insecurity, I could understand others who cowered too. My own feelings gave me compassion for other people's feelings, which usually happened to be similar to mine. My desire to judge others slipped away as I judged myself more kindly.

Through the process of learning about myself and other people, I began to recognize a Higher Power working in my life. The coincidences could no longer be called coincidences. The more I prayed and helped others, the more my desires materialized. Today I do service not just to please my sponsor but because I know in my bones it nourishes me.

Just when I began to feel a bit of confidence and trust, my sponsor told me that the Al-Anon meeting next door to my Alateen meeting was celebrating an anniversary and needed a speaker. She lovingly but firmly "suggested" I give back to the fellowship my experience, strength, and hope. Being the people pleaser I was, I accepted because I was too afraid to disappoint her. My first taste of the joy that comes from service came moments before I stepped up to the podium to share. My sponsor took me into an empty room, and we joined hands to say a prayer asking God to use me as an instrument of His peace and give me words to help others. The feeling of humility I experienced, I have come to recognize as serenity. I can't tell you what I said that night, but I can tell you that since then, I've never stopped serving whenever I'm asked. In service, God does for me what I can't do for myself—feeds my spirit. This is why service for me is the secret of recovery.

It's all been done before.

When I came to Al-Anon, I was not convinced that I had been affected by my mother's drinking, but I was convinced that my life was unmanageable. I was obsessed with the drinking problem of the guitarist in my punk band. Because of that discomfort, I attended regular Al-Anon meetings and got a good understanding of the program.

Eventually, I went to an Al-Anon meeting for adult children of alcoholics, just to check it out. I did know my mother had a problem, I just didn't think I was affected. Members at that meeting read the first page of the pamphlet, "Al-Anon is for Adult Children," and I identified instantly. This came as a surprise, for I had read lots of current publications on children of alcoholics but had never identified myself with the writing. Those few sentences made it clear to me that, through a process I did not understand and still don't understand, I had been affected.

Later I took the pamphlet, "Did you grow up with a problem drinker?" from the literature table to read. I answered "yes" to nineteen of the twenty questions! There was no longer an escape for me from the reality of my situation.

These experiences made me a real believer in Al-Anon literature. I had previously read an entire book by the author of the "Process of Recovery" in *Al-Anon Faces Alcoholism,* but her short article in our literature spoke to me, whereas before I'd missed the point. I don't know why it works better for me any more than I fully understand why I was affected, but I do know that it works.

I have many fears. As a child, I was very careful. In college and young adult life, I fretted and stewed about getting involved with groups of lunatics which I defined as political fringe groups, religious cults, and fad intellectual cults. Perhaps my own interior was shaky enough that at some level I feared I might get involved. I watched self-improvement fads come and go over short time spans with increasing dismay. Where could one go for help without risking joining the lunatic fringe? I found it comforting to know that the Al-Anon Family Groups started more than forty years ago and have worked for thousands of people. I liked that there was no single, monolithic bureaucracy but an ever-changing leadership. That no one was in charge became as important to me as the fact that it worked. If so many people managed to keep it going without any autocrat, there must be something in it.

Everything I needed to do for my recovery has been done by others—all kinds of others, from all walks of life, philosophies, education, and races. From the First Step to the Fifth Warranty of the Concepts, every bit of service work, every difficulty in living, every scrap has been done and experienced before—and by many people. This gave me confidence that if I allowed myself to follow the example of others, I would get similar results. I may not understand every nuance of the process, but I don't care what new psychological or physiological theory comes out. I don't need tomorrow's self-improvement bestseller. I have the classics in my hands.

Thanks to Al-Anon, I have had a spiritual awakening, and I want to carry the message to others, because those thousands of other people who worked Step Twelve and marked the path for me are one of the greatest blessings in my life. If I follow the path of all those who went before, I will probably get where they did. I may even widen the path for the next person. I don't really concern myself about why I am the way I am. What concerns me is first to learn exactly what way I am, and then what I need to do to become the way I want to be.

Authorities frightened me.

My mother used to stand in front of me screaming. It usually happened in a bedroom upstairs, not in the main part of the house where other people might see or hear. I know that sometimes all four of us children were there, sitting on the floor, being screamed at. I'm not sure if we were always all there or if sometimes it was just me, but I know I often felt alone there.

Eyes glaring, she would rant and rave in my face. Sometimes she paused, just glaring, and then screamed some more. I hated those silent, fuming pauses as much as the screaming. I have no idea what she raved about. I remember only the experience and my intense fear of her anger.

I tried to stay away from her as much as possible. I hid alone, staying lost and unnoticeable whenever I could. The interesting thing is, my mother wasn't even an alcoholic, but I think she was an adult grandchild. In our house, no drinking, smoking, swearing, or even playing cards on Sunday was allowed, but I believe my mother's grandfather was a drinker. The reactions to alcoholic emotional patterns go generations deep.

I became so determined to hide that I tried to get B's and C's in school so I wouldn't be noticed. That was my goal—not to do well in school, but to go unnoticed. I wanted neither too much praise nor criticism, for fear of yelling. I couldn't talk to people and still go unnoticed, so I had few friends.

I married a man who became an alcoholic. He yelled cruel

words at me until I feared him just like my mother and sought to give him nothing to yell about. Terrified of angry people, personal criticism, or judgments, I cowered through life.

Authority figures frightened me. Once, when I had to get a building permit to put an addition on our house, I couldn't do it because I couldn't give any authority figure the opportunity to judge or control me. I expected to be yelled at in city planning. I still have a great deal of trouble talking to people on the telephone because I fear their judgments. All of these fears made my life lonely and miserable.

Now in recovery, I talk to my sponsor and others. I dare to tell them things about me because I trust it is safe. They love me just the way I am, and they never yell. Their love and acceptance heals me. I still fear non-program people and authority figures, but not as much as I used to. Slowly, I am beginning to feel safe enough to try speaking to other people. As I try, despite my fear of putting myself out there, I gain courage and self-confidence. I begin to take small steps toward overcoming my fear of my husband and defining unacceptable behavior.

My sponsors have been the key to my recovery. I have more than one sponsor, because authority is so dangerous to me that I need to spread it around. How grateful I am there are many acceptable ways to work the Al-Anon program. No one said, "These are the rules; only one sponsor to a customer!" Those who have sponsored me demonstrated so clearly the value of love and service that I look forward to the day I will be brave enough to sponsor someone else—perhaps a person like me who shakes like the quaking aspen tree at each judgmental blast from anyone in authority.

STEPS TO THE FUTURE

Learning to examine our attitudes, motives, behavior, and feelings in order to keep the healing going is a tall order for those of us raised in homes affected by alcohol. We learned early in life not to talk about what we saw, not to trust anyone but ourselves, and especially not to feel, because our feelings were so often devastating. Yet we have found that we must challenge all three of these early childhood decisions about the nature of life if we are to recover from the family disease of alcoholism. Feelings, once unfrozen, are our surest guide to all the nooks and crannies of our psyches.

Coming to Al-Anon provided us with the love, understanding, compassion, and security we needed to begin challenging the most deeply rooted assumptions learned in our families of origin. The program itself remains constant, stable, and secure—qualities we knew little of at home. Ways to work the program, however, are as varied as the creativity of the human race. Each of us works it in our own way and at our own pace, and we are encouraged to develop ourselves as individuals. We learn that healthy autonomy is essential to our goal of mature adulthood.

To begin to work a Step, we have only to choose from a variety of possible methods the one that best suits us at the moment. By this stage, we know perfection is not necessary, for we are not finished with the Steps once we have "worked" them. They stand forever as guideposts to recovery and can be revisited from many vantage points throughout our lives. Some options include reading about a particular Step in Al-Anon's *Twelve Steps & Twelve Traditions* and pausing to think how it might apply to us, or asking another member how he or she did it. We can attend a Step meeting, listen to speakers, decide to do something differently just for today, or ask for guidance from our Higher Power in a moment of silence and then follow the subtle nudges of our intuition. Some of us formally write out each Step, looking for resistance, fear, anger, or any other cue, such as body tensing, that tells us we need help from a Power greater than ourselves. When we encounter resistance, we can pray for willingness or for the removal of our fear. When we are willing, it is remarkable how often a teacher appears. The teacher can be a comment from a friend, the repetition of a familiar uncomfortable situation that allows us to try again with a different attitude, or an inner awareness. To see and understand the message, we need only learn how to be open and receptive.

Commitment to systematic working of the Steps is important to recovery. Some people work one Step a month, conscious that each needn't be done absolutely to be done for that moment. Others choose to move at whatever pace feels comfortable or at the tempo suggested by a sponsor with more experience. The Steps are ordered for a reason—each provides a foundation and support for the next; however, there are no "Step Police" who give us a ticket if we are out of order. We may find consistent prayer and meditation, as suggested in Step Eleven, essential from the very beginning of our program. A particular Step may lend itself to an immediate situation even if we haven't "gotten there" yet. When we have completed all Twelve Steps once, we find that we practice them daily in many circumstances of our lives, for they truly do help us in all our affairs. As we continue using the Steps, we find ourselves unfolding in ways more marvelous than we had ever imagined.

No matter how we order our journey, we still must take but one step at a time. Putting one foot in front of the other, we walk toward freedom and wholeness.

I needed all Twelve Steps.

I love alcoholics and am grateful that my love for them caused me enough pain that I found a program of recovery called Al-Anon. My father, the first alcoholic I loved, had a special charm, and people of all ages were drawn to him. Alcohol took him away from me again and again, and I suffered deep pain.

As a small child, it seemed as if we had another member in our family—whiskey bottles. Whenever I reached into the cabinet for a towel, down crashed the bottles! I didn't know what they contained, only that when Daddy turned them upside down and drank from them, he changed and became frightening. As his disease progressed, I felt happy when he was jailed or hospitalized, because then we were safe for a while and so was he. The only sure safety was when my brothers and sisters and I lived with Grandmother. I loved it there because it was a serene harbor in a chaotic sea, but we couldn't stay all the time.

I also loved the AA meeting I attended with Daddy and Mama. It was a birthday meeting, and we had fun together as a family and held hands. But Daddy didn't remain in AA, and when they divorced, I felt relief. He left my life—no phone calls, no support—we thought he was dead. Years later, my husband and I decided to file a claim for a small life insurance policy on Daddy to relieve our financial problems, as my husband's alcoholism was sapping the little money we had. That's how we found my father was alive. For a while he came to live with us—a real disaster! He left us again and I felt pain and relief again.

Alcoholism grew in my marriage, and I thought there was something wrong with me. As the disease progressed, my insanity grew right along with it. In desperation, I even tried drinking. I reasoned, "If you can't beat 'em, join 'em." Mama saw what was happening to me and called Daddy to ask him to take me to AA. He drove to my city, took me and the children to lunch, and then took me instead to an Al-Anon meeting. I told him I loved what AA was doing for him (he was back in the program for a while), but it wasn't for me. I knew something was changing my personality and it felt like a slow death of the spirit, but I just didn't stick with Al-Anon. For a long time my husband and I played cat and mouse with the program. I'd leave him; he'd go to AA for a while and say the magic words about going where Daddy went; I'd let him come home, and all would be cozy; then we'd both stop attending and start over with the craziness. When Daddy died, I lost contact with the program though not the awareness that help was available there.

Eventually, alcohol had complete control of our lives, and I had no place else to go. I felt helpless and hopeless. What I thought was the end of all hope, however, was actually a beginning. I finally listened and came to understand the paradox that somehow we can help alcoholics only by helping ourselves.

I resented alcohol's power over me and the serious financial crises it produced. My sponsor taught me that, although I was powerless over alcohol, I didn't have to let alcohol have power over me. Thus, I learned to stop reacting, stop being a victim, take care of myself, and be responsible for myself but not for the alcoholic. Filing my own separate income tax return turned up horrifying truths. I had believed my husband's lies because they were what I wanted to believe. With the Twelve Steps, I've learned to face the truth, the whole truth, no matter how painful it is.

I had felt abandoned by God, but slowly I came to believe

that Higher Power never abandons and can restore my sanity if I stop abandoning God. To do so, I had to step out of God's way, especially regarding the alcoholic. I recognized new power in becoming powerless—the power of the Twelve Steps.

I made the best decision of my life in Step Three. I couldn't take care of myself or my family when I was emotionally upset about a loved one's drinking. Putting my life in God's hands soothed me. Putting the alcoholic's life also in God's hands replaced panic and determination with peace and acceptance.

Early in recovery I called my sponsor and announced I was starting on Step Four because I needed action in my life. She told me to put it away; it would be like a baby walking before it crawls. So I crawled through Steps One, Two, and Three again and again until I could walk through Step Four.

What a great journey of self-discovery the Steps proved to be. I was so consumed with trying to control an alcoholic, I hadn't looked at myself for a very long time. When I finished Steps Four and Five, I asked my sponsor, "Do you really think God can do something about all of this?" She replied, "I know He can!" Apparently God can, for my mother noticed the sparkle return to my eyes and continues to tell me today to thank my sponsor, who helped her little girl who was dying.

I do Step Six over and over because with each new challenge, I never stay "entirely ready." Eventually, when I get sick and tired of being attached, I become willing to detach.

Without help, I just can't change myself. Step Seven encourages me to ask my Higher Power for help. Sometimes I must get very uncomfortable before I become willing to be entirely ready, and then I must humble myself enough to ask. I like to be self-sufficient and efficient, but I need the help of other people and my Higher Power. Help is never forced on me, but if I ask, the power to change arrives.

I liked Step Eight, at least the making-a-list part. I wanted others to apologize to me if I was going to apologize to them and this desire got in my way of working the Step. Eventually, I understood that I could only do something about me, and I got ready to do it.

Step Nine was quite an adventure. It was hardest to make amends to those I loved the best. The time and place eluded me until I became willing. My sponsor helped me sort out situations in which I really needed to make amends from other areas where most of the damage I did was to myself.

Though my hope was for my husband and me to be reunited in love and sobriety, my marriage ended in divorce, and he married someone else. Telling God during Step Eleven how much I had wanted my story to go a different way helped me accept the reality. One of the hardest things I've ever done was to pray for their happiness, but this, too, eased the pain and helped me accept.

Every night I reflect on the happenings of my day and work Step Ten. If I become aware of a wrong, I try to become willing to right it. I admit it to God, to myself, and, when the opportunity presents itself, to the other person involved. I trust God to present me with the opportunity when I'm willing and when it's right.

The key word for me in Step Eleven is "sought." I don't always feel like I'm making conscious contact, but I do know that when I seek it I am doing my part. Eventually I feel the contact. Praying only for knowledge of God's will for me is a wonderful freedom. Sometimes it takes a lot of courage to carry it out, when God's will isn't my will, but each attempt strengthens my courage. This is God *en*-couraging me.

I awoke spiritually when I became aware, in the midst of despair and struggle, of a Higher Presence providing me with great peace and the ability to live with joy despite outward appearances. Serenity is very attractive, and I get more every time I give it away. Carrying the message to others, as Step Twelve suggests, helps me because I figure things out for myself whenever I share my recovery with someone else, and the opportunity to help another person enlarges my self-esteem.

My sons drink now, and their drinking causes problems. Because of our life experiences, they have an awareness of solutions available to them. Both have been to the AA program and left, but I hope one day they will return as I did. I tried to get them to go to meetings, but my sponsor reminded me that recovery is their choice. Trying to control the lives of others, even if they are my children, chokes out my own life. With my boys, I return to Step One because I find, with each person, I must learn over again what I've learned before. The difference this time is that I have a program. I may not follow it exactly, but I have it. They may descend into the valley of the shadow of alcoholism and death, but today I can love them and not go with them.

part Four

HEALING BROKEN CHILDHOOD

JOY IS OUR BIRTHRIGHT

"Ambivalence" well describes the feelings we experienced as we grew up in families affected by alcoholism. We felt ambivalent toward the alcoholics, toward non-alcoholic parents, and toward life itself. In our young lives, love and fear were as intimately blended as scotch and soda. Sometimes the fear came sharp and potent as a straight shot; sometimes the love was as sparkling as soda, but often the two emotions were confusingly intertwined. Coping with emotional extremes, both within ourselves and in our families, distorted our perceptions of truth, reality, compassion, and even human decency. We learned to deny, minimize, exaggerate, and in time we came to resent and rage against life itself. We were as oblivious to the causes of our confusion as any alcoholic. It took most of us years filled with the loving, consistent support we found in Al-Anon before we could begin to untangle the strands of our lives and weave them into our own creative, individual, beautiful visions of what life can be.

But even happiness can pose problems for adult children of alcoholics. Sometimes, as we continue to peel away the layers of our past, we discover that we had purposely forgotten our unhappy childhood or have contrived the pleasant memories of our youth. Sometimes, even today's happiness seems like just another form of denial. Having long been depressed and despairing, overly brave, numb, or living in fantasy, even when good things happen to us there lurks within us a shadow that waits for the next disaster. Because our experiences may have been those of extreme emotions or anesthetized feelings, our challenge in recovery is to balance our lives and accept the many variations of color and texture that life presents. Instead of living forever in black and white, in recovery we seek to find the rainbow within us.

Looking within is essential to our recovering from the effects of another's alcoholism, for although we may have experienced difficulties and trauma in our formative years, it is actually our continuing reaction to these things that troubles our lives today. Although we may have left the alcoholic, we did not escape the turmoil, guilt, insecurity, rage, and fear we knew in our youth. In fact, we were suffocating in our own unhappy habits, never realizing that another way, a spiritual way, could allow us to draw lifegiving breaths of hope, friendship, and love.

Awareness does not settle everything, nor does change happen overnight. Spiritual growth takes time. Making the "new" a familiar and comfortable part of ourselves takes personal commitment and the support of others in the fellowship to help us on our way. The effort seems worthwhile, though, and we try to understand and apply to our lives the terms we hear repeated at meetings. One member describing serenity with surprise said, "At first I didn't think I wanted serenity. I equated it with a kind of sleep-walking or emotional death. I didn't realize at the time how much I depended on crisis to feel alive, because I had no idea how deeply I had repressed most of my feelings. Then recently, I felt a new, unusual sensation. I felt utterly at peace with life and at the same time filled with joy. At that moment, I realized *this* was serenity, and I laughed out loud for the sheer, glorious pleasure of it!"

Living fully requires enough trust to release our manipulative, tight-fisted control of life, for only then can we accept the guidance of a Power greater than ourselves. For adult children of alcoholics, our damaged, devastated trust has to be healed and nurtured bit by bit until we feel safe enough to truly let go and let God. Trust does not come from reading a book, however inspired, but from experiencing new relationships in which we are trusted and we can learn to trust those around us. Al-Anon provides us with fine opportunities to join with others who, like us, have been hurt and betrayed. Though we are very fragile when we come to the program, we eventually manage to share our stories, as well as our experience, strength, and hope. Miraculously, we begin to heal. Personal contacts, meetings, meditation, and prayer are all necessary, but we also find that actively working all Twelve Steps of Al-Anon is essential.

If we willingly surrender ourselves to the spiritual discipline of the Twelve Steps, our lives will be transformed. We will become mature, responsible individuals with a great capacity for joy, fulfillment, and wonder. Though we may never be perfect, continued spiritual progress will reveal to us our enormous potential. We will discover that we are both worthy of love and loving. We will love others without losing ourselves, and will learn to accept love in return. Our sight, once clouded and confused, will clear and we will be able to perceive reality and recognize truth. Courage and fellowship will replace fear. We will be able to risk failure to develop new, hidden talents. Our lives, no matter how battered and degraded, will yield hope to share with others. We will begin to feel and will come to know the vastness of our emotions, but we will not be slaves to them. Our secrets will no longer bind us in shame. As we gain the ability to forgive ourselves, our families, and the world, our choices will expand. With dignity we will stand for ourselves, but not against our fellows. Serenity and peace will have meaning for us, as we allow our lives and the lives of those we love to flow day by day with God's ease, balance, and grace. No longer terrified, we will discover we are free to delight in life's paradox, mystery, and awe. We will laugh more. Fear will be replaced by faith, and gratitude will come naturally as we realize that our Higher Power is doing for us what we cannot do for ourselves.

Can we really grow to such proportions? Only if we accept life as a continuing process of maturation and evolution toward wholeness. Then we suddenly begin to notice these gifts appearing. We see them in those who walk beside us. Sometimes slowly or haltingly, occasionally in great bursts of brilliance, those who work the Steps change and grow toward light, toward health, and toward their Higher Power. Watching others, we realize this is also possible for us.

Will we ever arrive? Feel joyful all the time? Have no cruelty, tragedy, or injustice to face? Probably not, but we will acquire growing acceptance of our human fallibility, as well as greater love and tolerance for each other. Self-pity, resentment, martyrdom, rage, and depression will fade into memory. Community rather than loneliness will define our lives. We will know that we belong, we are welcome, we have something to contribute—and that this is enough.

LIVING WITH SERENITY

Recovery is untangling confusion.

When I was five, my Daddy used to carry me on his shoulders through the crowded streets and stores. He was so tall, I thought I was on top of the world and could see forever.

When I was five, my Daddy let me help him work the very hard adult jigsaw puzzles. He never made fun of me as my

brother and sister did. He just let me take all the time I needed to make the pieces fit. He even said, "Look how her little
fingers can work this hard puzzle." He was proud of me!

When I was five, my brother and sister and I slept in the
same bed together, each with our own "weapon" to hit my
Daddy with when he came home drunk and started a fight.
My brother had a baseball bat; my sister had the iron, and I
had a heavy bottle of lotion. It was all I could fit in my small
hand. I was scared.

When I was five, my Daddy took me to the swimming pool.
He would stay in the water with me as long as I wanted. He
let me use his knees as a diving board. He taught me to swim
and to dive.

When I was five, and my Daddy got drunk, he would beat
up my Mommy. She would have bruises on her the day after
they had a loud scary fight. I cried a lot. I asked my Mommy
to leave my Daddy, but she told me she had to stay with him
so we would have food. Maybe if I hadn't needed to eat, she
would have left him.

When I was five, life was very confusing. Now I am many
years older than five, and sometimes life is still very confusing. But there are some things I know for sure: my life was
affected by the disease of alcoholism; there is a place to find
recovery from that disease, and it's called Al-Anon.

Now I am many years older than five, and I still sometimes
feel scared. I pick up the phone and share my fear with another Al-Anon member, and it shrinks until it is smaller than my
five-year-old self.

Now I am larger than when I was five, and Al-Anon acceptance helps me reclaim the good things from my father—the
ability to love a small child, just as she is, without expectations.

Now I am wiser than when I was five, and I know how the

family disease of alcoholism distorted my mother's thinking and mine. Although we are powerless over alcoholism, we can help ourselves. Now I know I deserve to live.

Now I am older than five, and I go to Al-Anon meetings, where I learn to understand how alcoholism leaves lingering pain and mistrust, confusion and fear, and that there are solutions in the Twelve Steps, companions in recovery, and solace in an ever-present Higher Power.

Now I am coming of age, and I know that the solution is greater than the disease, and that love is greater than fear.

Recovery is the freedom to live your own life.

I once heard that the Steps were numbered only for intellectuals. I'm glad that little piece of freedom penetrated my head or I would have missed an important healing in my life.

My alcoholic grandmother took me home from the hospital as an infant and adopted me because my alcoholic mother couldn't care for me. My grandmother was an angry, domineering woman, and I was an inconvenient child. No matter what I did, it wasn't good enough, big enough, or right enough to please her. No anger on my part was allowed; after all, look at all the sacrifices she was making for me. I learned about resentment when I was very young. She resented me, and I, in turn, resented her and the real family I didn't have.

I also longed desperately to be seen and appreciated. In vain I tried for many years to win her affection by dutifully coming home every holiday to do all the chores she had saved up for me. Rather than thank me, she instead reproached me and reminded me I had better appreciate her, because this would be the last holiday for her on earth.

Finally, after several years in Al-Anon, I worked up the courage to stay away and enjoy my holiday. Sure enough, she went into the hospital, and I feared she would die. She didn't. She bounced into and out of hospitals until my uncle found her an assisted living situation in another state close to him.

One day, my uncle called to say she was again in the hospital. My intuition (or perhaps my Higher Power) told me this time was different. Though I had only worked through my Fifth Step, I wasn't willing to let her go without doing my Ninth Step with her. I prayed for willingness and guidance, and they came.

Since she lived far away, a personal visit wasn't possible, so I decided that making a tape was an acceptable alternative. In my tape, I accepted responsibility for all the pain I had caused her. I acknowledged the resentments and the hurt I held because of the unfair expectations I had placed on her. I told her about the things I admired in her and all the gifts she had given me. Then I released her. I acknowledged that she had done a good job of raising me and that I could now care for myself. I spoke in the kindest and most loving way that I knew, and then I sent off the tape, expecting nothing in return.

My grandmother never acknowledged receiving my tape, but I felt a great sense of relief. About six months later she died, and because of my amends, I was able to speak honestly and lovingly at her funeral. Freed of resentments and expectations, I didn't have to lie or embellish.

One more gift awaited me. At the family gathering after the funeral, my uncle described her final year. He told me of her failing health and loss of zest for life until one day she received a tape in the mail. She listened to it often, and she seemed to recover. For a while they even talked of her leaving the nursing home. For a few months she was alive and a pleasure to be around—an amazing transformation. Then she fell ill, and died quickly. He had never listened to the tape, because it was hers, but he thought I should have it back.

I think my grandmother spent her whole life taking care of others and waiting for permission to live her own life. It's unfortunate that she had to wait eighty-six years to get that permission, but I thank God and Al-Anon I gave it to her before she died. For a brief moment, my grandmother lived free as I live free now, thanks to God and Al-Anon, one day at a time.

Recovery is a lifetime commitment.

Carnival week in my small hometown is an exciting time for kids, especially the teens. They strut around all night looking "cool." Never mind the rides—they're there to see who they can see! During the last night of the carnival, I was one of those "cool" teens too, that is, until my dad showed up.

We were having a fantastic time flirting with the guys and chatting with the girls. I spotted my parents and brother in a cluster of people, so we strolled over to say, "Hi." A few minutes before I saw them, Mom had realized that they had left the carnival tickets at home. Dad was furious! He had that evil, stone-cold glare on his face I had witnessed a million times before. Instantly, he turned on me and demanded, "Do you have the tickets?!!" Before I could say "No," right there in the middle of the carnival he started hitting me. I stared straight ahead, pretending not to notice anyone, but actually seeing everyone. They saw me too and stared at us. My heart pounded and I felt the stings of every slap, but even more painful were the stares of the onlookers. I stuffed my feelings and hunched down against the blows, but I could not defend myself from the shame I felt from their staring eyes. No one tried to stop him.

Why did I stroll over to my parents? Why didn't I just wave

and keep strutting along? Why didn't I run? I know now I was utterly powerless—a child trapped in lifelong abuse.

Years later, alone and lonely, I married an alcoholic and something good did come my way—a precious baby boy! I adored him. Someone finally wanted and needed me. I had a purpose. He became my savior. Though I know today that it is unfair to expect a baby to save its mother, in a way he actually did. When he was about seven months old, his father came home so drunk he could barely walk. He practically crawled up the stairs. Then to my astonishment and horror, he stumbled back down with our baby in his arms. I don't know what came over me, but seeing my precious baby in this drunken man's arms suddenly opened my eyes to the devastation I had endured throughout my childhood, and I resolved that I would never put my child through such a thing. The next day I called Alcoholics Anonymous, and they gave me the telephone number of an Al-Anon member.

Al-Anon became my entire existence—I practiced it fiercely as if my life depended on it. It did!! Eventually, I left my alcoholic husband and found a man who is a wonderful father and a caring husband. He adopted my son, and we had another child together. My life filled up with joy and happiness.

We had another lesson to learn, however, and we learned it the hard way. Since my husband wasn't from an alcoholic background, he urged me to discontinue the meetings after we married. Remembering that my sponsor had told me I would need a program for the rest of my life, I resisted at first, but because he saw my meetings as a threat and my not letting go of them as evidence that I still clung to the past, I finally gave in. For a while I tried to work Al-Anon alone, but ours is not an "alone" program. My books sat on the shelf collecting dust while I slipped unconsciously back into old patterns.

No longer the person my husband had married, I tried to control everyone's life, and I worried about everything. The more I tried to control, the more passive my husband became. Still I tried to control, and our boys became passive, refusing to take responsibility for anything. Soon I resented both husband and children, and they in turn retreated into further passivity. It was a vicious cycle that fed on itself. Finally, I had a huge argument with my sister, partly over my attitude. Thank goodness, this disagreement opened my eyes and I saw exactly what I needed—Al-Anon!

It has been almost three years now since I returned to Al-Anon. The wonderful life I share with my husband and my children today has bloomed again since I came back to my program. My husband has learned to respect the fact that my past is part of me and that our past affects who we become. Everything is better for all of us when I am active in Al-Anon.

Al-Anon taught me that I am worth something and that I don't deserve to be abused by anyone, but—most of all—that I can choose how to live my life. Al-Anon gave me the courage and self-esteem to go to college. Ever since the first grade, I've wanted to teach elementary school, and soon my dream will become a reality. Al-Anon helped me release my efforts to control my husband and, in turn, I have gained his active partnership.

When I sat at the dining room table to jot down some ideas for this sharing, I re-experienced that carnival scene. This time I felt the feelings I had repressed so long ago. My entire body began to shake and I almost vomited, as I cried long overdue tears. My husband held me in his arms while the pain poured out of me. I felt as though I was again a fourteen-year-old girl and experienced her pain for the first time. I am so blessed today to have a loving man to hold me. I could never have recognized him without Al-Anon, and he knows what a treasure my program is for all of us. If I forget, he gently pushes me out the door on the night of my meeting. Grateful, and knowing my children are safe in their father's care, I go.

Recovery is never giving up hope.

Mother entered treatment for her disease of alcoholism at age eighty. Earlier in her life, she admitted that she had a problem, but she never chose to find help until she began hallucinating and alternatives to her living situation were being discussed. It was apparent to me—and confirmed by her counselor—that Mom had no earthly idea that her drinking had caused any problems for anyone else. She is now eighty-one and on Mother's Day celebrated six months of sobriety. At age forty-eight and after thirteen years in Al-Anon, I am absolutely ecstatic! What a gift my Higher Power has given me. For all the adult children who still have actively practicing alcoholic parents, never say, "Never."

Recovery is facing reality without losing the capacity to love.

Rejection was a way of life for my alcoholic father, who died eleven years ago. My mother had long rejected both him and me, blaming us for all of her problems. I grew up thinking my mother would love me if I were different, and if I could convince my father to love me.

I married an alcoholic who is now sober. With Al-Anon's help, I learned that what I had perceived as his rejection of me was actually his rejection of himself. It had nothing to do with me. This new freedom caused me to want to love and accept myself, but it was difficult. The notion of self-acceptance was utterly foreign to me. I had never experienced acceptance or love as a child, and I felt unworthy.

Someone suggested I make a list of all my good qualities. In the beginning, it was a very short list, but with the help of Al-Anon members, the list grew and grew. Now I see myself as a whole person with many good qualities. Even my questionable qualities were techniques I had used to try to get love from my husband. This work helped save my marriage, and I was thankful.

I still had one hurdle—*my mother!* She retained the old pattern of rejection. I confronted each roadblock with love, strength, and hope. I loved both me and her. Al-Anon supplied the strength, and I hoped for a happier tomorrow each time she rejected me. At length, we both had to face the bitter truth—my mother did not love or like me, and it was not my fault or my alcoholic spouse's fault. Neither of us had done her any wrong.

Life with Mother today is at a stalemate. We both know the truth and bear responsibility for ourselves. I cannot make my mother love me, and she cannot make me hate her. I can be open to the possibility that she may like me, even love me, in the future, but I do not beat my head against a brick wall, demanding what she cannot give. With great difficulty, I have come to realize that I do not like my mother but I respect her title.

Recovery is the gift of grace.

The day my Mom died, I stood in the backyard raging. Filled with anger, hate, self-pity, and disappointment, I felt that I had to get away from the nightmare life I lived, but I didn't know how. Going out into our tiny yard was as far as I could get at that point.

A few weeks earlier, during one of her rare sober days, my

Mom and I had been talking about high school yearbooks. Just the day before she died, I had rushed home with my first high-school yearbook. Excited, I couldn't wait to get home to show it to her. When I arrived home, the house was dark and silent, as if no one lived there—but then, in our family, no one really did live. We just existed, totally shut down, going through our routines like zombies. Mom was in her room, passed out on the bed as usual. It had happened a thousand times before, but this time I had had it. I believed we were better off without her; indeed for years I had told my Dad that. I couldn't understand why he wouldn't leave her and take us away from hell on earth. He just kept saying I exaggerated and it wasn't that bad. But it was!!

In the backyard, that Saturday morning in June, all my tempestuous emotions poured out. I cried and pleaded with a God I wasn't sure existed. I just couldn't go on. Within moments a wave of compassion came over me. I knew my mother hadn't chosen to be this way, that she was a helpless victim of the disease of alcoholism. I promised I would try not to sit in judgment of her. An amazing sense of peace came to me, melting all my turmoil. To seal my vow, I picked some lilies of the valley from the backyard and put them in a small glass. I took them to Mom, along with tea in one of her favorite china cups. She was still out, so I left a note on her bedside stand. I think it said simply, "I love you," or "I'm sorry." I had an impulse to hold her hand, but I didn't. Something held me back. I told her I'd hold onto the yearbook until she felt more like looking at it, and I left to go about my day.

Several hours later, my Dad called to me in a strange, choked voice. He told me Mom was dead and had been for quite some time. She had probably died during the night. For years I felt angry and betrayed that we never had the chance to talk as people and that I had been robbed of really knowing her. That anger almost led me to follow in her footsteps, but fortunately the smells and sights of that deathly silent morning never left me. Twenty years later I lifted up a glass of bourbon and saw in the ice cubes my mom lying dead. I knew I had to change. That and a loving co-worker who understood more deeply than I could have imagined, brought me to Al-Anon.

For a time I thought that being caught so long in my hatred had betrayed that early morning promise I had made to love and understand. Now I see that, without a program to help me heal myself, I was as powerless over my hatred as Mother was over alcohol. I also realize I took an important first step on the path to healing when I asked a God I didn't even understand for help, and God responded with a truly amazing grace. I like to think that, though her body was dead, my mother's spirit waited to allow me a proper goodbye. Things didn't turn out the way either of us wanted, I'm sure, but I know that that moment of grace, which planted the seed of compassion in my heart, was God doing for me what I could not do for myself.

I've come to realize I was never alone, even then, and that my parents were two imperfect people, grappling with a terrible disease, who fell in love and had hopes and dreams for themselves and their children that they couldn't realize. Few of us do. Fortunately, with the help of Al-Anon and my Higher Power, I can try.

Recovery is a do-it-yourself program.

For twenty years, I dove into self-help books, seminars, therapy, and churches—anything that might make me feel O.K., that would stop me from choosing people who seemed loving at the beginning, only to steal my money, property, and then threaten me with physical harm when I protested.

Eventually I met a man in AA who shared his program with me, took me to open meetings, and sometimes, while he attended AA, I went to Al-Anon. One night at an open AA meeting, I connected my present life with my childhood. The next night I went to Al-Anon ready to listen with both heart and ears. Someone mentioned that many AA people start with ninety meetings in ninety days. I figured if it was good enough for them, it was good enough for me. I tried everything they suggested.

Of all the things I heard, one statement stands out in my mind, though I recall hearing it only once. Someone said, "I wasn't born this way; I learned." When I heard that, I felt more hope than I had ever experienced. I *knew* that anything I had learned, I could unlearn!

The AA member I loved brought me into the program, but my mother was always my subject at the meetings. For the first time in my life, I found people who understood that, no matter how horrible the happenings of my life were, I wasn't talking about an evil person. I was describing someone I loved, and it filled me with pain and confusion. I stayed stuck in the confusion until my sponsor told me that the only Steps that didn't work were the ones I didn't use. So I worked the Steps. She suggested Al-Anon meetings with an adult child focus, and I went. Each step of the way, people reminded me that this isn't a *talk* program, it's a *do* program. So I did what they told me and it began to work.

In the safety of the intense, emotional adult child meetings, those tears I had stuffed in my childhood finally came out, and healing really began. I learned how to recognize my own boundaries and respect them myself. If others refused to respect them, I could walk away without defending myself or attacking them. Al-Anon adult child meetings were the linch-pin of my growth.

Then, even this safe haven began to trouble me. It seemed that some groups were at war with Al-Anon. Something went wrong, but I didn't know what. I just felt intense discomfort. I agreed with members who said it was unreasonable to tell us not to use anything but Al-Anon literature, when there wasn't any that really addressed us. I bridled at the limitation on our resources for growth. Soon I too felt at war with Al-Anon and spoke loudly for my point. Eventually, my sponsor helped me again by steering me to a deeper reading of the Twelve Traditions. The meaning of "unity of purpose" and our place in the program as students, members, and creators of recov-ery became clear when I worked the Traditions as I had once worked the Steps. Today when I hear the complaint about lack of Conference Approved Literature for adult children, I say, "Have you submitted your story? That's the only way we're going to get it—when we write our stories of recovery in Al-Anon."

There is joy in my life today and in our family as well. I saw it recently in my daughter's face as I played with her children. To see her so comfortable and at ease when she leaves the children with me, knowing that Grandma's house is a safe, happy place where the children want to come, is one of the greatest gifts I have received from working the Twelve Steps *and* Twelve Traditions.

I feel so blessed to write and contribute to the ongoing growth of Al-Anon, which has led me out of the insanity that had imprisoned me. After nine years in Al-Anon I feel alive and vibrant, and it keeps getting better. I once thought despair had no bottom, but now I know joy has no top. A ther-apist once asked me how long I planned to go to Al-Anon, and

I replied, "until something better comes along." I expect to be around a long time.

Recovery is a matter of choice.

Where do you start with a story that began almost sixty years ago? How do you express in words the wounds that have been disregarded for decades and only now begin to heal? Can a person ever find an outlet for the pain suffered as a result of being a child, adolescent, and adult in an alcoholic environment? The answer is "yes!" and you start today!

I came to Al-Anon because of my son's alcoholism. Though my life was totally out of control, I could see only what he did. After considerable time spent working very hard, attending many meetings, and learning all I could, I realized that my son was not ready to maintain his sobriety, but by then I knew enough to let him live his life in whatever way he chose. Then I received a bonus, one that was very painful at first but ultimately became the key to my own life!

When I finally felt comfortable with the anonymity and trusted the confidentiality that is the basis of Al-Anon, my buried past came to the surface. Only through the great love in this fellowship could I face what had been done to me in the past and what I had done to others.

For many years when I was a very young child, I was used as a sexual plaything. Starting when I was four or five and continuing into my teens, my uncles and cousins sexually abused me. Many of us who have suffered childhood sexual abuse wonder where our mothers and the family females were during this time. Why did they not protect us? In my family, the females were considered chattel. The grown women were treated no better than the girl children, and the only way any of us survived was to pretend these things did not happen, that the behavior was normal. To acknowledge child abuse would have required the women to face the truth about their own abuse. They couldn't, and sometimes they even added to the problem by taking out their own considerable frustrations on the children as well.

The result of this cruelty was that, throughout my life before Al-Anon, I feared any physical contact, even hugs. I wore many masks in order to please whomever was near me, and lost myself in the process. I was convinced I was so flawed that even my mother couldn't love me. I lived in a terrible prison, and I didn't even know I was incarcerated.

My legacy is not pretty and it is filled with sadness, but it is my legacy, and today I no longer feel sad. I don't have to pretend to be someone other than who I am. Beneath the veneer, I have uncovered a very nice lady, scars and all. I'm not perfect, but I don't have to be perfect to be lovable. Now when I look in the mirror, I see a worthwhile woman with many people who love her. I can't be all things to all people, but I can be someone special to some people.

Today, at sixty years (and counting on more), I know that life is what I make it. In partnership with my Higher Power, I can be happy or sad, but I can always be me. I feel anything I choose; I can be anyone I choose to be.

This is quite a statement and will likely start many arguments—except around Al-Anon. In Al-Anon I found people who could laugh and smile even though their loved ones were bent on self-destruction. They didn't have to choose self-destruction too, for they had learned that destroying themselves didn't help anyone. In these rooms I found acceptance from men and women seeking sanity in their own way and time. If we all experienced the pain that the disease brought into our lives, we also heard words of comfort and felt warmth and love together.

In Al-Anon I learned that I have the right to choose my life, what I will tolerate, what I want for myself, what is unacceptable to me. What freedom! It's not always easy to accept the responsibility of choice. Taking charge of my own life takes lots of practice. Sometimes I sound strong-willed and argumentative as I attempt to exercise this freedom, but gradually I am learning to express my choices with love and concern for others.

I learned about choice in Al-Anon, where I am not forced to accept anything that doesn't sit right with me. I learned that I could have any expression on my face I chose. I learned that I could speak my mind whether or not I was contradicted. Now no one can make me feel, think, or even look like anything I don't want. Society sets certain standards of acceptable behavior, certain notions of what is beautiful, but the choice remains mine as to which standards I adhere to and which aesthetic values I adopt. With freedom comes responsibility and consequences, but the choice is always mine.

Today I look at my life and see the pluses instead of the minuses. It was not my choice to have alcoholism in my life, but it is my choice to stop it from destroying any more of my years. Today I choose serenity and I'm willing to pay the price for it because I know how priceless it is.

Recovery is seeing the world with awe.

I remember the night. It was a Thursday. If I waited a second longer, I thought I'd lose my mind. I called the telephone number and asked, "Where is the closest Al-Anon meeting?"

The woman told me about three meetings in the area.

I wanted to cry when I got off the phone, but I hadn't cried in years, not since my first alcoholic husband. I'd cried over, to, for, and with him for so many years, I thought I had no tears left.

Now my brother obsessed me. He went in and out of recovery for years. I did everything in my power for him. I thought I'd die for him if I could. Instead I was just slowly losing my mind.

I am the oldest of ten children. When my (probably alcoholic) father died, my mother was left with ten children under fifteen. Her best friend became the bottle. In horror I watched every single one of my brothers and sisters follow the same path. I dragged them to counseling, treatment centers, Alateen, and I bailed them out of jail. Nothing changed, and I felt overwhelmed with guilt.

Alcohol fogged my life as completely as darkness enshrouded the car I drove that night to the nearest meeting. I had begun to think I was lost, when the church loomed out of the mist right in front of me. The crowded parking lot had a single space left for me right near the door. As I dragged myself from my car, a woman with an umbrella appeared, waiting for me. I don't remember who she was, but I bless her.

Afraid and sobbing inside, all I wanted was to get help for my brother. The woman next to me gave me her book, *One Day at a Time in Al-Anon*. She said I could use it until I could get one for myself. I was overwhelmed by all the love and understanding.

I sit here, three years later, amazed at what two Al-Anon meetings a week have done for me. I have found a peace beyond understanding. With a free mind, I walked recently, for perhaps the first time in my life, accompanied by my Higher Power whom I choose to call God.

The birds were singing, and I noticed tiny green buds pop-
ping out from every seemingly dead tree, and it filled my
heart with inexplicable joy. As I walked slowly, relishing
God's handiwork, such awe and love came over me, I cannot
adequately describe it. Stopping to enjoy it, I saw how some
dead trees had been toppled by the storm. Leaves littered the
ground between the trees. Other trees grew this way and that
in disarray. Few were the trees that grew straight and tall.

Standing there, observing closely, a thought came to me
about my life. Like the dead trees, unforgiveness and self-pity
mar my vision of myself. Strewn over the ground are my negative thoughts. My imperfections grow crooked, this way and
that. Yet when my God looks at me, He looks at the whole of
me with awe and love.

GIFTED WITH LIFE

There are times in our journey toward wholeness, perhaps
in the midst of a new family crisis or major life changes, when
frightening childhood feelings return and we find ourselves
struggling again with unwanted emotions. We may think that
Al-Anon doesn't work, and that, even with all our hard work,
we have achieved nothing. We may be tempted to blame ourselves yet again for not having worked a "good program."
After all, if we had, would we be in such pain? We may walk
into a new meeting and suddenly feel as alien and shy as we
did years before, the familiar greetings clanging like hollow,
meaningless words. Once again we may feel hopeless and
helpless. At such times it is helpful to remember that what we
have learned has not been lost; it might be temporarily mis-
placed or veiled, but it surely is not lost. Once again we start
out, one day (one hour, one minute) at a time, to apply the

principles we know and have worked before. We read a bit of literature; we go to a meeting not knowing what to expect, just desperate enough to go; we work up enough courage to pick up the telephone and share the truth about ourselves.

The fellowship waits for us to return. Though it may seem so, our Higher Power has not abandoned us; we have merely lost our trust. Al-Anon has not failed us; we have not failed Al-Anon. Sometimes life is hard. Sometimes it is beautiful. It helps to acknowledge both as facts. Acceptance does not mean we have to like all of it; it only means we have to realize that reality is reality.

Slowly we learn once again that we are not alone, that powerlessness is not helplessness, and that this, even this, will pass. There will always be dark nights and challenges greater than those we would choose for ourselves, but we still have the fellowship of Al-Anon and the Twelve Steps which have been our source of strength in the past.

We in Al-Anon are blessed with spiritually conscious, loving companionship on our human journey. We are gifted with life—all life—life with its laughter and its tears, its loneliness and its love, its wisdom and its idiocy, its justice and its cruelty, its family disease of alcoholism and its family recovery of Al-Anon. So today we say "Yes" to life, and "thank you, Al-Anon," for help with the courage and tenderness to live it.

E P I L O G U E

This book was written about, by, and for people who grew up in the shadow of alcoholism. The alcoholic may have been parent, grandparent, great-grandparent, sibling, aunt, uncle, cousin, or family friend—it matters not exactly whom—for alcoholism is a disease that leaves its imprint on all it touches, and all are welcome in Al-Anon.

We hope you have found in this book a small measure of the healing we have been privileged to enjoy. May you join us on our journey toward serenity. May you pass it along to anyone you know who still suffers the effects of another person's drinking. May you use it in a meeting or in the quiet of your own private space. May you recover and share the blessings of recovery with another human being, for this is how we help one another in Al-Anon.

THE TWELVE STEPS

Study of these Steps is essential to progress in the Al-Anon program. The principles they embody are universal, applicable to everyone, whatever his personal creed. In Al-Anon, we strive for an ever-deeper understanding of these Steps, and pray for the wisdom to apply them in our lives.

1. We admitted we were powerless over alcohol—that our lives had become unmanageable.

2. Came to believe that a Power greater than ourselves could restore us to sanity.

3. Made a decision to turn our will and our lives over to the care of God *as we understood Him.*

4. Made a searching and fearless moral inventory of ourselves.

5. Admitted to God, to ourselves and to another human being the exact nature of our wrongs.

6. Were entirely ready to have God remove all these defects of character.

7. Humbly asked Him to remove our shortcomings.

8. Made a list of all persons we had harmed, and became willing to make amends to them all.

9. Made direct amends to such people wherever possible, except when to do so would injure them or others.

10. Continued to take personal inventory and when we were wrong promptly admitted it.

11. Sought through prayer and meditation to improve our conscious contact with God *as we understood Him,* praying only for knowledge of His will for us and the power to carry that out.

12. Having had a spiritual awakening as the result of these Steps, we tried to carry this message to others, and to practice these principles in all our affairs.

THE TWELVE TRADITIONS

These guidelines are the means of promoting harmony and growth in Al-Anon groups and in the worldwide fellowship of Al-Anon as a whole. Our group experience suggests that our unity depends upon our adherence to these Traditions:

1. Our common welfare should come first; personal progress for the greatest number depends upon unity.

2. For our group purpose there is but one authority—a loving God as He may express Himself in our group conscience. Our leaders are but trusted servants; they do not govern.

3. The relatives of alcoholics, when gathered together for mutual aid, may call themselves an Al-Anon Family Group, provided that, as a group, they have no other affiliation. The only requirement for membership is that there be a problem of alcoholism in a relative or friend.

4. Each group should be autonomous, except in matters affecting another group or Al-Anon or AA as a whole.

5. Each Al-Anon Family Group has but one purpose: to help families of alcoholics. We do this by practicing the Twelve Steps of AA *ourselves*, by encouraging and understanding our alcoholic relatives, and by welcoming and giving comfort to families of alcoholics.

6. Our Al-Anon Family Groups ought never endorse, finance, or lend our name to any outside enterprise, lest

problems of money, property and prestige divert us from our primary spiritual aim. Although a separate entity, we should always cooperate with Alcoholics Anonymous.

7. Every group ought to be fully self-supporting, declining outside contributions.

8. Al-Anon Twelfth Step work should remain forever non-professional, but our service centers may employ special workers.

9. Our groups, as such, ought never be organized; but we may create service boards or committees directly responsible to those they serve.

10. The Al-Anon Family Groups have no opinion on outside issues; hence our name ought never be drawn into public controversy.

11. Our public relations policy is based on attraction rather than promotion; we need always maintain personal anonymity at the level of press, radio, TV and films. We need guard with special care the anonymity of all AA members.

12. Anonymity is the spiritual foundation of all our Traditions, ever reminding us to place principles above personalities.

THE TWELVE CONCEPTS

The Twelve Steps and Traditions are guides for personal growth and group unity. The Twelve Concepts are guides for service. They show how Twelfth Step work can be done on a broad scale and how members of a World Service Office can relate to each other and to the groups, through a World Service Conference, to spread Al-Anon's message worldwide.

1   The ultimate responsibility and authority for Al-Anon world services belongs to the Al-Anon groups.

2.   The Al-Anon Family Groups have delegated complete administrative and operational authority to their Conference and its service arms.

3.   The Right of Decision makes effective leadership possible.

4.   Participation is the key to harmony.

5.   The Rights of Appeal and Petition protect minorities and assure that they be heard.

6.   The Conference acknowledges the primary administrative responsibility of the Trustees.

7.   The Trustees have legal rights while the rights of the Conference are traditional.

8.   The Board of Trustees delegates full authority for routine management of the Al-Anon Headquarters to its Executive Committees.

9. Good personal leadership at all service levels is a necessity. In the field of world service, the Board of Trustees assumes the primary leadership.

10. Service responsibility is balanced by carefully defined service authority and double-headed management is avoided.

11. The World Service Office is composed of standing committees, executives and staff members.

12. The spiritual foundation for Al-Anon's world services is contained in the General Warranties of the Conference, Article 12 of the Charter.

General Warranties

In all its proceedings the World Service Conference of Al-Anon shall observe the spirit of the Traditions:

1. *that only sufficient operating funds, including an ample reserve, be its prudent financial principle;*
2. *that no Conference member shall be placed in unqualified authority over other members;*
3. *that all decisions be reached by discussion, vote, and whenever possible, by unanimity;*
4. *that no Conference action ever be personally punitive or an incitement to public controversy;*
5. *that though the Conference serves Al-Anon, it shall never perform any act of government, and that, like the fellowship of Al-Anon Family Groups which it serves, it shall always remain democratic in thought and action.*

INDEX